A Tragic Farce: The Fronde (1648—1653)

Elm Bank Modern Language Studies

General Editor: Keith Cameron

The Short Story: Structure and Statement, presented and edited by William F. Hunter.

As Mighty as the Sword. A Study of the Writings of Charles de Gaulle, by Alan Pedley.

Variability in Spoken French. A Socio-linguistic Study of Interrogation and Negation, by Aidan Coveney.

Translation: Here and There. Now and Then, edited by Jane Taylor, Edith McMorran & Guy Leclercq.

Multimedia CALL: Theory and Practice, edited and presented by Keith Cameron.

A Tragic Farce: The Fronde (1648—1653)

Wendy Gibson

Elm Bank Publications
Exeter
1998

First Published
in
1998
by
Elm Bank Publications
24 Velwell Road, Exeter, EX4 4LE, UK.

British Library Cataloguing in Publication Data Available

ISBN 0 9502595 8 6

Printed and bound in Great Britain by Antony Rowe Ltd, Chippenham, Wilts

Dedication

To the memory of Reg Roberts
A friend in need

CONTENTS

TO THE READER

To write about the Fronde[1] is to rush in where angels fear to tread. So says everyone best qualified to know: from actual contemporaries of this seventeenth-century French civil war, who put posterity on guard against slanted accounts of participants' contradictory and often inexplicable behaviour[2], to authoritative modern French historians, who pronounce the subject to be one which admits of neither accuracy, clarity, nor conciseness[3]. Observing that dire warnings did not seem to have deterred (quite the opposite) attempts to get to grips with such a notoriously slippery period of history, the present writer was emboldened to embark upon what must figure as the ultra-impossible task: that of narrating the Fronde in a coherent fashion for the benefit of English-speaking francophiles whose reading-time, prior knowledge of the period, and command of French are not unlimited. Theirs will be the privilege of verifying, amongst other things, whether Fortune has in this instance lived up to her reputation for always favouring the brave.

---

[1] 'Fronde' is French for 'sling' or 'catapult'. The civil war derived its name, according to accounts of the time, from a parallel jokingly drawn between, on the one hand, the behaviour of rebellious members of the Paris Parlement, held in check by the frequent appearances in their midst of the boy-king's uncle; and, on the other hand, the activities of Parisian youths, accustomed to break off their stone-slinging fights whenever the seventeenth-century equivalent of the local police superintendent arrived on the scene, but to regroup as soon as his back was turned.

[2] A minor activist, Louis Ardier, Sieur de Vineuil, opens his memoirs with the statement that:
It is well-nigh impossible to write a strictly accurate version of the past disturbances because those responsible, having acted on bad principles, have taken care to conceal knowledge of them, lest posterity accuse them of having sacrificed the felicity of their native land to their own interests. Apart from this reason, it is quite difficult for the person writing about the affairs of his day to remain so impartial as not to yield to hatred or flattery, which are the reefs on which truth is ordinarily shipwrecked.

Cardinal de Retz, who had his reasons for wanting to deter close examination of the conduct of leading orchestrators of rebellion like himself, punctuates *his* memoirs with many a scathing outburst against the 'insolence' of those 'vulgar historians' who persist in putting logical constructions on circumstances where in reality none are possible.

[3] 'One can only evoke, and not relate — one would need a thousand pages, half of them unreliable — the tangle of intrigues, disputes, battles, and riots...' (Pierre Goubert, *Mazarin*, Paris, Fayard, 1990, p.336). 'Even simplified, the Fronde cannot be narrated, so profoundly is its logic concealed behind spasmodic events, intrigues, plots, broken alliances, and dramatic twists and turns' (François Bluche, *Louis XIV*, Paris, Fayard, 1986, p.65).

Chapter 1

PRINCIPAL PERSONAGES AND DÉCOR

On 14th May 1643 there occurred an event which caused a ripple of relief in top French circles. The king of France, Louis XIII, died. Louis had possessed undeniable qualities: piety, physical and moral courage, dutifulness, and the capacity for self-sacrifice. Unfortunately he had been afflicted with a sickly body and a noticeable stutter, starved of family affection and hampered by lack of training for his kingly office, circumstances which had predisposed him to be morose, introspective, suspicious, changeable, extremely touchy about his authority, and over-reliant on others. His long deference to his widowed mother, the ponderous Marie de Médicis; the succession of favourites (predominantly male and unworthy) to whom he had turned for solace; and his outwardly unswerving support of his prime minister, Cardinal Richelieu, a fellow-invalid whose manner epitomised domination; all had contributed to create the image of a monarch who was weak and dependent. It was not surprising that when his lonely and painful existence had come to a premature end, Louis XIII had been the one to rejoice most.

Despite doubts about his virility, Louis had managed, after nearly twenty-three years of barren marriage, to leave two heirs to succeed him. The elder son now mounted the throne as Louis XIV. The younger son, Philippe, remained in the position of subordinate all his life. Louis XIV was not yet five years of age and since kings of France achieved their legal majority only at the beginning of their fourteenth year, a regent had to be appointed. Shortly before his death, Louis XIII had designated his wife, Anne d'Autriche, for the office in question. He had done so against his will, having reason to believe that Anne was incompetent in state affairs as well as over-zealous in the service of her native Spain. But the only other salient candidate for the job, his brother, Gaston d'Orléans, was not a model of prudence or probity either, so Louis had tried to make the best of a limited range of options by subjecting all Anne's decisions as regent to ratification by the majority vote of a regency council. Everyone's eyes were nevertheless focused upon Anne in the summer of 1643, and for once in his reign, Louis XIV was somewhat upstaged.

Anne d'Autriche began her regency with several useful aces up her sleeve. In an age when aptitude was still largely measured on the strength of pedigree, hers was impeccable. A member of the illustrious House of Habsburg (or House of Austria, as it is known), she was the daughter of Philip III of Spain and the great-grand-daughter of the Germanic Emperor Charles V, on whose abdication the Habsburgs had been divided into the Austrian and Spanish branches of the family. Her breeding showed in her regal air, and though no striking beauty (with the exception of her hands, over which beholders were careful to enthuse), she was elegant and fastidious about her person. She was adept at holding court, her genuine piety and virtuous reputation, and her liking for worldly pleasures and gallantry, enabling her to preserve a delicate balance between licence and constraint. She could have been a very real asset to her inhibited husband, but she had felt herself neglected by him in favour of his passion for hunting and male associates, and she had sought companionship elsewhere. Like Louis XIII she was not always sufficiently discerning in her choice of companions. One confidante in particular, the hypnotically beautiful Marie de Rohan, Duchesse de Chevreuse, beckoned Anne towards a series of dangerous intrigues designed to spite and topple prime minister Richelieu, whom both women detested. In 1637, when France was at war with Spain, Richelieu had detected the queen in what passed for the treasonable act of corresponding about French affairs with her Spanish relatives, and with the Duchesse de Chevreuse, then in exile at Tours on account of a previous conspiracy. The Duchesse had promptly disguised herself and ridden hard for the (Spanish) frontier, a customary feat in times of 'oppression'. Anne d'Autriche had faced interrogation by the Chancellor, Pierre Séguier, had sworn her innocence, then been forced on presentation of evidence to sign a confession of her misconduct. The necessary official reconciliation between the king and queen had ensued, but in private all remnants of trust had been destroyed. On his deathbed Louis XIII was heard to murmur: 'In my condition I must pardon her; but I am not obliged to believe her'. Paradoxically, the Val-de-Grâce Affair, as it is called, from the name of the Benedictine convent in which Anne took refuge on this occasion and in many other moments of stress, enhanced the queen's status in the public eye. She figured not as a betrayer of husband and adoptive country, but as a victim of persecution by Richelieu, whose lack of sentimentality in dealing with those who opposed his vision of a strong, unified France had won him countless enemies. The victim-image was merely fortified when it became known that Louis had planned not only to curb Anne's regency powers but to remove her two sons from her care and have them raised at the château of Vincennes, which served as a state prison.

Contact with court intrigues might be said to have given Anne a certain insight into state affairs, but it was manifestly inadequate preparation for running a country as large, complex, and turbulent as France. She had no bookish stock of knowledge upon which to draw. By nature she was none too keen on exertion. Time was not on her side: influential persons were pressing her to satisfy this demand and that claim. Moreover, the spectacle of a woman at the helm of state always upset the Frenchman's sense of what was fitting. Everything pointed to the necessity to find a male to lean on, particularly since, just four days after Louis XIII's death, she had had the restrictive terms of his will lifted and the 'free, absolute, and entire administration of the affairs of the realm during [Louis XIV's] minority' confided to her. Anne found what she wanted in a naturalised French cardinal, Jules Mazarin.

Mazarin was the eldest son of an Italian noblewoman and of a Sicilian estate-manager attached to a powerful Roman family, the Colonnas. Patronage had enabled Mazarin to enter the service of popes, first as a soldier in the papal army, then as diplomatic representative of the Vatican. A series of diplomatic missions in the 1630s had brought him to France, where he overcame Richelieu's initial aversion for him and cultivated members of that minister's inner circle. In 1639 he had entered the service of France, and taken French nationality. By 1641 he was sporting a cardinal's hat, without having taken priestly vows, and poised to step straight into Richelieu's shoes when the latter died in December 1642, preceding Louis XIII to the grave by five short months. Mazarin possessed the wherewithal to chase away unpleasant memories of the two ailing 'tyrants' who had blighted Anne's youth. He was a handsome man who took unusual care over details of his appearance such as the curl of his beard and the comeliness of his hands, and who delighted in perfumes ('You had to speak to him very early of a morning to notice that he stank', alleged the — jealous? — Comte de Brienne). His keen intelligence and expertise in affairs was acknowledged even by his opponents, though they sought to tone down their grudging praise by dismissing his skill in negotiation as deviousness, and his preference for delaying-tactics and velvet-glove methods as 'softness' and cowardice. His punctilious observation of religious rites was likewise made to weigh lightly in the balance against manifestations of his worldliness: an accumulation of ecclesiastical benefices, a fondness for gambling, for Italian music and drama, and for collecting books and art treasures. When the stock of accusations ran low, he was apt to be charged with the crime of having introduced the opera into France. Carping contemporaries conveniently forgot that Richelieu had been equally if less ostentatiously acquisitive, and ceased to brand him with expressive nicknames like 'Jupiter the Slayer'. By comparison with his upstart Italian successor, Richelieu, an authentic French provincial nobleman, suddenly appeared worthy of respect — 'Richelieu was esteemed even by those who feared him most; Mazarin was neither esteemed nor feared by anyone' (Comte de Brienne) — and was hailed as a genius: 'The constancy of the queen [Anne] was responsible for all Mazarin's success; Richelieu kept afloat through the power of his genius alone' (Princesse Palatine).

Anne d'Autriche compared the two cardinals also, but in her case the comparison worked to Mazarin's advantage. At the very start of her regency Anne asked a close confidant whether she could trust Mazarin and what manner of man he was. On learning that:

> ... in all things he was the very opposite of Cardinal Richelieu, this reply seemed to her such a great eulogy, on account of the hatred that she had for the memory of the dead man, that it was greatly instrumental in prompting her to employ him.

There were other reasons for sympathy between these two attractive quadragenarians. Both were foreigners in a land where 'outsiders', in any shape or form, were objects of suspicion and resentment, especially when they could be construed as interfering in the government or robbing honest French citizens in order to line their own pockets. The fate of Marie de Médicis' two rapacious Italian favourites, Concino Concini and his wife Leonora, the former assassinated (1617) with the connivance of Louis XIII and mutilated by the mob, the latter beheaded and burned, was there to serve as a grisly warning. Mazarin's foreign origin was underlined by the inability to lose his pronounced accent, yet another grievance that was held against him. Anne was probably more sensitive to his command of her own language and to his early links with the pro-Spanish Colonnas, one of whose sons Mazarin had accompanied on a period of university study in Spain. In 1630 Mazarin had prevented battle between France and Spain at Casale (north-west Italy) by interposing himself between their two armies — a *beau geste* later to be re-enacted in his negotiation of the Treaty of the Pyrenees (1659) which put Anne's Spanish niece on the throne of France at the expense of one of Mazarin's own nieces, for whom Louis XIV had suffered a violent attack of calf-love. It was the boy-king who, in effect, constituted the most important bond between the couple. Mazarin, in his replacement-father role of godfather and official tutor to Louis, showed the same devotion to his interests as did Anne, and was rewarded with a similar measure of deference until death.

The seventeenth century found this alliance between a proud Spanish princess and a supple Italian prince of the Church intriguing. The burning question was naturally whether relations extended beyond the council chamber into the bedchamber. Commentators above the level of the gutter press usually exonerated Anne from suspicion of dishonour, preferring to attribute her support of Mazarin to a fear of undermining her own authority if she sapped his by voicing complaints about him openly. The correspondence which passed between Anne and Mazarin when the latter was temporarily exiled during the Fronde suggests a closer partnership. Due allowance being made for continental exuberance and for the precariousness of Mazarin's position, there must be few prime ministers who have professed to be 'dying [of love] for' their queen; or claimed that 'you and I [code symbols are used in the original text] are united by bonds which could not be broken either by time or by any outside effort'; or, in a different vein, dared to chide her for indolence: 'You are surrounded by persons who almost all consider only their own interests; I refer to those persons who deal with [state] affairs: that is why you must take a little more trouble to apply yourself to these matters'. Lover? Husband? Lack of conclusive documentary evidence makes the enigma impossible to solve. At the time of the Fronde it scarcely needed solving. What mattered was that Anne and Mazarin should be able to present a united front in public, and to shield Louis XIV and the monarchy from those who seemed inclined to spare neither.

* * * * * * * *

Louis XIV's memoirs for the year 1661, when the king entered upon his personal rule after the death of Mazarin, sum up the current situation with stark simplicity: ' Disorder reigned everywhere'. The phrase might be applied with rather more justification to the opening years of his official reign from 1643 onwards.

   The root cause of disorder was undoubtedly war. The regency government's decision to prolong Louis XIII's and Richelieu's struggle against Habsburg domination meant that France continued to participate in the Thirty Years' War until 1648 (Peace of Westphalia) and to battle against Spain until 1659 (Treaty of the Pyrenees). Though France avoided large-scale fighting on her own soil, her frontier provinces had to withstand repeated invasion by the brutal breed of enemy generals and armies thrown up by the Thirty Years' War. The provinces of the interior were not immune from the depredations of the soldiery either. French armies, composed of needy or press-ganged nationals and of foreign mercenaries, all chronically underpaid, underfed, and ill-disciplined, spread as much havoc and terror as enemy troops on their march to and from the different war fronts, grabbing whatever commodity or female that came to hand, silencing objectors with torture or murder, propagating pestilence.

   Soldiers were not the only predators to darken the horizon in time of war. Tax-collectors in their various guises — *partisans, traitants, fermiers, receveurs...* — appeared to render themselves even more oppressive than usual during the years immediately preceding the Fronde. In the countryside they and their assistants were accused of exacting payment by force, seizing furniture and livestock from peasants who possessed any, causing the latter to desert their homes and leave land lying fallow. In the capital it was a similar story of 'a large number of persons of all social conditions' being clapped in prison, their revenues appropriated, and a squad of *archers* (police officials) garrisoned in their home until they felt inclined to fully satisfy 'the insatiable rapacity of these bloodsuckers'. What was especially intolerable to contemporaries like the indignant diarist quoted here was that the bloodsuckers were not being selective in their choice of prey. The cost of the war effort was felt on all levels of French society. In an attempt to meet that cost without raising ordinary direct taxes (*tailles*), which had been reduced by ten millions in September 1643 as a winning concession to the populace, the Italian-

derived controller-general of finances, Michel Particelli d'Emery, resorted to extra-
ordinary measures. He slashed pensions awarded by the king, one of the main arteries of
courtiers. He whittled down salaries attached to the venal posts of government officials
and created fresh posts for sale, thereby diminishing the value and prestige of existing
ones. He slapped taxes on the *aisés* ('wealthy'), on building in the Paris suburbs, on
merchandise entering Paris, upsetting rich and poor alike. He alienated royal revenues
for several years in advance in order to be able to constitute extra government bonds
(*rentes*) to sell, when holders (*rentiers*) of previous issues were clamouring for payment
of arrears of interest. The government's habit of evading its obligations to creditors spelt
financial disaster for small lenders. It shook the confidence and coffers of the big
lenders, the aristocrats, high-office holders and upper clergy accustomed to loan at
interest to the tax-collectors, who were required by their contracts with the king to
advance large sums of money to him before commencing the exercise of their functions.
Caught up in all the uncertainties of borrowing and re-lending in an unstable financial
climate, the tormentors of the people might easily become victims of bankruptcy and
economic distress in their turn.

D'Emery's policies were successful in keeping riots going in the provinces, used to
demonstrating violently against Richelieu's fiscal expedients, and in the capital, where
street mob agitation was accompanied by more orderly, if no less vehement, forms of
protest to the king. The most articulate protesters were those men, sprung mostly from
the middling classes, who had purchased important offices in the judicial and financial
spheres. The sale of offices by the crown was an old abuse (it dated from the fourteenth
century) that majority opinion condemned but that successive heads of state took care not
to abolish, for fear of cutting off a vital cash-flow and for lack of funds to reimburse those
dispossessed of their investments. The trend over the previous centuries was for the
number and price of offices to rise, notably during periods of crisis, and for office-holders
(*officiers*) to multiply. A modern French historian, Daniel Roche, has calculated that
whereas in the sixteenth century there were four to five thousand *officiers* for a
population of more than sixteen millions, by 1660 there were about fifty thousand for a
population of more than eighteen millions (*Les Républicains des Lettres*, Paris, Fayard,
1988, p.232). The great attraction of offices was their snob value. They carried the
nobleman's prerogative of exemption from the *tailles*, often combined with other tax
immunities and privileges. They were consequently viewed as stepping-stones to 'living
nobly' and sooner or later being accepted into the charmed circle of the aristocracy.
Louis XIII's father, Henri IV, had shrewdly traded on the *officiers'* vanity by offering
them an additional privilege in 1604: that of being able to insure the transmission of an
office to a male successor of their choice, in return for an annual premium (*droit annuel*
or *paulette*). The ability to pass offices from relative to relative facilitated the emergence
of veritable dynasties of *officiers* within prominent families, encouraged the formation of
a narrow corporative spirit, and fostered heady ambitions.

Nowhere were these ambitions more in evidence than amongst the cream of the
officiers who staffed the high courts, the *cours souveraines*. There were four types of
cours souveraines active in stoking the Fronde: the Grand Conseil, the Cours des Aides,
the Chambres des Comptes, and the Parlements. The Paris-based Grand Conseil
originally judged cases relating to ecclesiastical benefices, but by the seventeenth century
was taking on any cases where other tribunals were suspected of partiality. The Cours
des Aides dealt with litigation over taxes. The Chambres des Comptes occupied

themselves with the royal domain, the verification of the accounts of those handling public money, and the registration of all manner of acts bearing upon finances. Both Cours des Aides and Chambres des Comptes had a central establishment in Paris and counterparts in several big provincial towns such as Rouen and Montpellier. The Parlements, of which there were ten in 1648, were distributed along the same geographical lines, but had a much broader sphere of influence. The oldest and most powerful, the Parlement of Paris, was divided into eight main chambers (Grand'Chambre; five Chambres des Enquêtes, or Enquiries; two Chambres des Requêtes, or Petitions) and certain special ones, the members of which sat in judgement on everything from high treason to disputes in the fish industry. It was empowered to issue judicial and administrative decrees (*arrêts*) which had the force of law within the area under its jurisdiction, an area covering over a third of the country. It also gave official recognition to all royal edicts and declarations by solemnly registering them. It had assumed the right to examine such acts and, when they were deemed contrary to the public interest, to make 'remonstrances' to the king (*droit de remontrances*), in other words, to pronounce a veto. In the first half of the seventeenth century Parlement made full use of its right to be obstructive. To break deadlocks, the monarch alternately exiled or imprisoned opposition leaders; wrote letters of coercion to Parlement; descended personally on its headquarters at the Palais de Justice to impose his will from a specially draped throne (*lit de justice*); had his royal council quash *arrêts* and evoke cases from Parlement jurisdiction. His 'beloved and faithful', as protocol dictated that the king address his Parlementarians, responded by registering edicts but with amendments of their own invention; by dragging their feet over the implementation of royal legislation; or by ceasing to perform their duties. Strike action of any duration could starve the king of finances by halting the passage of fiscal edicts, and ruin private individuals in a society where a shortage of precise definitions of people's rights and functions made for frequent recourse to lengthy and costly lawsuits.

The men who afforded this astonishing spectacle of a group of magistrates engaged in a kind of running battle with the king, from whom all their professional status and power derived, had reasons for believing that the fight was not totally unequal, or unjustified, on their part. Several factors contributed to give the Parlementarians an elevated idea of their own importance. They were accounted as noblemen by virtue of their office, if they were not originally of noble stock, and shared many of the useful privileges accorded to the old, blue-blooded warrior nobility. They cultivated their aristocratic image attentively, using their wealth to buy estates and fiefs of which they could grandly style themselves overlord, and taking advantage of every opportunity to establish relations with grandees by birth. Princes of the blood royal and peers of the realm had seats in the Paris Parlement, a reminder of its origins in the thirteenth century when high-ranking nobles and ecclesiastics had assisted the monarch in the personal dispensation of his justice but been obliged by the growing dimensions and complexity of their task to hand over to subordinates with legal expertise. Venerable by reason of its antiquity and provenance, Parlement also had claims to the nation's gratitude. On three critical occasions within living memory it had figured as a saviour and buttress of the monarchy: in 1593, when it resisted pressure to oust Protestant Henri IV from the succession to the French throne, reserved for Catholics; in 1610 when its support for converted Henri's widow as regent after his sudden assassination again prevented anarchy; and last but not least, in 1643, when it had acceded to prematurely widowed Anne d'Autriche's request for full regency powers. In the eyes of the middle and lower classes who constituted the

Third of the three Estates (Clergy, Nobility, *Tiers Etat*) of which the French body politic was composed, Parlement was a spokesman and a protector, waxing eloquent on the miseries of the people whenever a new tax-edict surfaced for registration, putting its liberty, if not its continued existence, heroically at risk. In this respect it performed a function which the nominal mouthpiece of the three Estates of the nation, the Etats Généraux (States, or Estates, General), was impotent to carry out. The Etats Généraux were convoked when the monarch felt so inclined, which he never did between 1614 and 1789. Deputies elected to the Etats had no firm rules of procedure, acted in a purely advisory capacity, and were non-representatively drawn from the *officier* stratum of society upwards. Parlement, would-be supplanter of the Etats Généraux, was permanently active, structured and organised for professional purposes, able to vet and suspend royal policies, and capable of covering its aristocratic leanings beneath flourishes of oratory so palatable to the man in the street that he was liable to manifest violently if he thought that his champions were being harmed.

Despite their entrenched position, the Parlementarians had, precisely, the feeling of being threatened. The sensation was by no means new. Louis XIII and Richelieu had been united in wanting to confine the magistrates as far as possible to their basic judicial and administrative functions, and to prevent them from blocking government policies and machinery. As well as employing the blockbusting methods outlined above, king and premier had circumvented the Parlements by making use of special types of jurisdiction. The favourite means of circumvention was to commission individuals to act as judges and inspectors of judicial procedure in specific provincial localities. These commissioners, the best known of whom were styled *intendants*, received increasingly broad powers in the 1630s, becoming key figures in the supervision of fiscal and municipal affairs, in the restoration and maintenance of public order, and in the provision of quarters and supplies for troops. Though commissioners were chosen for preference from amongst the *maîtres des requêtes*, magistrates responsible for reporting to the royal council on petitions presented to the king and empowered to sit in the Paris Parlement, they were eyed askance by the sovereign courts and resented by provincial functionaries obliged to operate under their surveillance. If thwarted in the exercise of their duties, the *intendants* could appeal to the king's council, which was not at all averse to nullifying Parlement rulings. Humiliated by repeated trespassing on their territory, and disturbed in their fundamental conservatism by deviations from the judicial norm, the sovereign courts were dealt another blow by the government's fiscal offensive. The most objectionable of what the First President of the Paris Parlement, Mathieu Molé, described as 'damnable inventions' was the old expedient, revived by controller-general d'Emery, of putting new offices up for sale. New colleagues on the bench signified less business to go round, fewer fees to extract from clients, diminished status, and a proportionate loss on the considerable investment that an office represented. Office-creating edicts were therefore staunchly resisted and if the king refused to let himself be handsomely bribed into dropping them, newcomers seeking official recognition from established *officiers* could count on rebuffs and harassment. Consciences were salved by the argument that the habitual procedure of registering unpopular fiscal edicts via a *lit de justice* was illegitimate when the king had not come of age, which was the case with Louis XIV prior to September 1651.

An indubitable sign of the office-holders' growing awareness of insecurity was the way in which they banded together to defend their interests. The phenomenon is significantly observable in the ranks of finance *officiers* who, although they performed administrative and judicial duties like the personnel of the sovereign courts and claimed equal status with them, had a less prestigious reputation. They were readily confused with money-grubbing *partisans* and *traitants* who served the king on the impersonal business basis of a contract, not on the personal 'moral' basis of an office requiring an oath of allegiance from the possessor. In actual fact, finance *officiers* detested *partisans* and *traitants*, not least because the latter were given to collecting their pound of flesh with armed assistance from the *intendants*, who were themselves well on the way to taking over the essentials of financial administration in the provinces. Confronted with this unholy alliance, the *élus*, theoretically administering taxation in all but the large peripheral provinces, formed in 1641 a trade union which held sporadic general meetings in Paris. The *élus* took their cue from the *trésoriers de France*, colleagues with such diverse duties (tax supervision, provisioning of troops, conservation of the royal domain, upkeep of public highways, etc.) as to render collision with other administrators inevitable and self-protection imperative. The *trésoriers* had a syndicate operating as early as 1599, but an unprecedented flurry of activity in its Paris assemblies was noticeable at the start of the regency. *Trésoriers* and *élus* were therefore equipped to stand alongside the sovereign courts when war was declared on government policies.

* * * * * * *

The aristocracy were champing at the bit too. In retrospect it appears that they were going through a difficult phase. The distinction between noble and non-noble (*roturier*) was becoming ever more blurred as rich commoners treated themselves to noble status, lands, property, and sons-in-law. To be regarded as a fully integrated member of the Second Estate was still an ideal, yet that same Estate was widely criticised for parasitism and for hooliganism. Provincial nobles responded feebly to royal calls for military service, which was the traditional justification for aristocratic immunities, preferring instead to stay at home and make the weight of their seigneurial rights felt. Courtier nobles served in posts (e.g. provincial governor, royal envoy, diplomat) where possession of Crusader ancestors and sonorous titles suitably impressed underlings and foreigners, but effective political and administrative power was in the hands of *officiers* and of those who had risen from their ranks. Long-established nobles as a whole were keenly aware of this slur on what they called their '*honneur*' and their '*gloire*', that is to say the self-esteem and public esteem which they were encouraged by the heroic strain in contemporary literature to believe must be preserved at all costs, the lives of others and their own included. But they were powerless to reverse the trend. Their normally summary education in all but martial arts and bloodsports would have made them unfit to hold down any major office, even supposing that their pride, and above all their purse, had permitted them to buy one. Financially, the nobles were feeling the pinch of dwindling seigneurial revenues, fluctuating prices, large households to support, an opulent façade to preserve, and public prejudice against gainful employment for the blue-blooded. They agitated for the abolition of venality of offices, which they wanted 'restored' to persons of birth and merit, and they denounced the evils of royal taxation, which was hindering vassals from paying dues to overlords. By way of reinforcing their protests, some incited and abetted peasant uprisings against fiscal exactions.

For the élite of the French aristocracy, those who had royal Bourbon blood in their veins, or who moved in the orbit of royalty, revolt was a pastime undiminished in popularity despite the decapitation, exile, and imprisonment with which Richelieu had striven to quell it. Seeing that the grandees had tried so hard to foil and fell one cardinal-prime minister, they were unlikely to smooth the path of his successor and declared admirer. Mazarin had been in the hot seat for barely four months when a plot against him was uncovered. The plotters, dubbed '*Les Importants*' because of the airs they put on, were friends of the Duc de Beaufort, the younger son of a bastard of king Henri IV, the Duc de Vendôme, imprisoned by Richelieu for conspiracy. Beaufort, as handsome as he was inept, fancied his chances because Anne d'Autriche had marked him out to guard her children at the point of Louis XIII's death, but his subsequent pose as favourite of the queen and jealous rival of Mazarin rendered him importunate and therefore expendable. The duke's other blunder, one which helped to cost him five years of his freedom, was to force Mazarin to seek allies in two princely households which were rivals of the Vendômes: those of Condé and Orléans. The head of the Condé family in 1643 was Henri II de Bourbon-Condé, an arch-rebel turned toady to Richelieu, one of whose nieces he had begged as a bride for his eldest son Louis. On his father's death in 1646, Louis, an unkempt, beak-nosed, dare-devil commander, assumed the paternal title of Prince de Condé, and was not too long in following the paternal example of treachery to the crown. His younger brother Armand, Prince de Conti, his sister Anne-Geneviève, Duchesse de Longueville, and her husband, all threw in their lot with him. The Orléans family had only two active participants in the Fronde, but they were persons of stature: Louis XIII's brother, Gaston d'Orléans, having a last fling before enforced retirement from a long career of rebellion; and Gaston's eldest daughter, Anne-Marie-Louise, Duchesse de Montpensier, an amazon hunting for a husband with a throne. Flanked by the immense resources at their disposal in terms of retainers, clients, friends, and sympathisers, the great ones of the realm joined in a formidable but uneasy alliance with the sovereign courts whose interests they claimed to espouse, in the expectation of promoting their own.

* * * * * * *

And what of the First Estate, the Clergy, were they disposed to be drawn into the fray or to remain aloof? Traditionally, the French Monarchy and Clergy lent each other moral and material support, and ecclesiastics, according to the memoirs of Louis XIV, 'by instructing [a king's] subjects in religion, draw down the blessings of Heaven and preserve peace on earth'. Yet the clerical prop was apt to fail the monarchy and professional pacifists could be transformed into rabble-rousers. During the crisis surrounding the accession of Henri IV (1589) after the murder of his predecessor by a monk, Catholic priests had used the pulpit as a political platform from which to encourage another regicide, which was effectively committed twenty-one years later by a rejected aspirant to the monastic life. Given that the majority of people in sixteenth- and seventeenth-century France abided by Catholic ritual out of conviction or prudence, and that a high degree of spiritual, and often social, intimacy existed between parishioners and *curés* (parish priests), the potential of the latter for influencing the masses with what purported to be the word of God was enormous. Two reigns later they still had the ability to cause riots. In May 1645 controversy over who should succeed the popular *curé* of the Paris parish of St-Eustache led to a band of the deceased's female parishioners going to bombard the Chancellor with insults and invading the parish church where they beat up anyone who refused to declare in favour of the late *curé's* nephew. In the following June a similar uproar in the parish of St-Sulpice resulted in the populace expelling a new *curé* and firing his home, and a mob of women from the Faubourg St-Germain bearing down upon the Paris Parlement to demand the reinstatement of their former *curé*. Unlike their sixteenth-century counterparts, the *curés* involved in these incidents appear to have been law-abiding and to have played a passive role. Possibly they were 'used', along with the women, by unknown activists intent on discrediting the disliked Chancellor and/or behind him, the government. For when the Fronde commenced three years later, the *curés* on the whole showed no immediate propensity to revert to their former bellicose behaviour. It was not until the civil war was almost over that they manifested militant tendencies on the occasion of the surprise arrest in December 1652 of François-Paul de Gondi, coadjutor and successor designate to the Archbishop of Paris, his uncle.

Gondi, more famous under his titles of Coadjuteur and (from February 1652 onwards) Cardinal de Retz, was the only leading churchman apart from Mazarin to have a star part in the Fronde. The upper clergy certainly had the means of conducting successful rebellion: solid revenues, systematically collected; prestige derived from elevation of birth and calling; a vast following of dependent clerics, lessees, and vassals; and a ready-made, hierarchical organisation. They also had motives for rebellion: steady erosion of their fiscal independence, culminating, in 1641, in exile for six deputies to the Assembly General of the Clergy who resisted an increase in the regular subsidy (*don gratuit*, or 'free gift') which the First Estate supposedly 'volunteered' to pay to the king. However, archbishops and bishops dominating the Assemblies were to show few impulses to turn collectively on the monarch who nominated them to office, being distracted by doctrinal quarrels and famine relief, and checked by the loyalty to the crown of Retz's uncle. Retz himself was a maverick of Florentine ancestry, an accomplished intriguer who described himself in a monumental understatement as 'perhaps the least ecclesiastical soul in the world'. Had his accession to the archbishopric of Paris pre-dated the Fronde he could easily have provided a focus for clerical opposition, as was demonstrated by the fervour of his supporters at the time of his arrest, and doubtless also for lay opposition, in view of his connections with malcontents of many persuasions. Obligingly, Retz's uncle performed a last, supreme service for the monarchy. He lived, until such time (1654) as it was strong enough to deal with his nephew.

* * * * * * * *

The atmosphere in France in the 1640s was thus highly charged. From top to bottom of society men and women felt, or pretended to be, aggrieved over threats to their livelihood, social standing, or persons to whom they pledged allegiance. Anne d'Autriche, they groused, had changed from the Lady Bountiful who had seemed so sensitive at the outset of her regency to recompensing the martyrs of Cardinal Richelieu's policies, while humble and self-effacing Mazarin 'did so well that he was on top of everyone when everyone thought that he was still at their side' (Retz). Tension caused by the government's financial squeeze and by unfulfilled expectations was increased by news from abroad. In 1647 a people's revolt broke out in Naples, the latest in a series of uprisings against Spanish domination to worry Anne's brother, Philip IV of Spain, struggling since 1640 to regain breakaway Portugal and Catalonia. Neapolitan deputies were in Paris in February 1648, airing their dissatisfaction with the Duc de Guise, a reckless French prince whom the insurgents had called upon to lead them. Just across the Channel the English had foisted Charles I's impecunious wife Henriette-Marie, sister of Louis XIII, back on her compatriots to keep, and were preparing to crown rebellion with legalised regicide. With pressure building up internally and externally, an explosion was almost inevitable. It occurred in the summer of 1648, when the sovereign courts lit the fuse.

* * * * * * * *

Chapter 2

ACT I

The year 1648 began on an inauspicious note. On New Year's Day it was announced that the king would be personally taking a package of finance edicts to the Paris Parlement for registration. One of these edicts provided for the creation of twenty-four new *maîtres des requêtes*. The existing holders of that office took advantage of a royal council meeting on 9th January to impart to Chancellor Séguier and controller-general d'Emery their determination to 'perish to a man rather than suffer such an insult'. When the boy-king, convalescing after smallpox and forgetful of his lines, shamefacedly confronted his Parlement on 15th January the figure of twenty-four had been wisely halved. But the unplacated *maîtres des requêtes* voted on the morrow for strike action and refused to let themselves be intimidated, either by an irate Anne d'Autriche ('You're fine ones to doubt my authority; I'll show anyone who wants to question it'), or by instant suspension from their functions. Despite the fighting talk and gesture, Anne allowed Parlement to deliberate on all the edicts, which were supposed to have been officially passed at the *lit de justice* of the 15th, and to offer her verbal remonstrances (6th April), pointedly harrowing in their evocation of the suffering caused to widows, orphans, and paupers when legal fees were pushed up by the multiplication of judicial *officiers*.

The regency government had bargained for more compliance from the Parlementarians whose much-prized privilege of the *droit annuel* was fortuitously due for one of its periodic renewals. Since resistance to 'extra-ordinary' forms of taxation had proved to be their overriding concern, and since money still had to be procured at all costs, different tactics were tried. A royal declaration of 30th April duly renewed the *droit annuel*, on condition that the members of all the sovereign courts, with the exception of the Paris Parlement, should forfeit four years' wages. Instead of having the anticipated effect of dividing the sovereign courts, the declaration united them in fear of imminent repression. The Paris Cour des Aides, Chambre des Comptes and Grand Conseil drew their Parlement neighbour into a formal act of union on 13th May, at the same time procuring the revival of a ban on taking over a vacant office without the consent of the widow and heirs of the deceased *officier*. The government hit back where it hurt most, with total abolition of the *droit annuel*. This meant that henceforth any office vacated through death reverted to the crown, unless the holder had formally resigned forty days before his demise. *Officiers* were suddenly exposed to the risk either of depriving heirs of a staple part of the family fortune, or, if money was still owing for an office, of stirring creditors to demand the reimbursement of loans. Here was a pretext, with a vengeance, for stepping up the number of Parlement deliberations and taking vigorous resolutions.

Anne and her advisers strove hard to break up the coalition and to halt the meetings. But written and verbal reprimands, a scattering of letters of exile and arrests amongst members of the Grand Conseil, the Cour des Aides, and the *trésoriers*, and nullification of the 13th May decree of union, simply inflamed Parlement hot-heads. Those sitting in the five customarily turbulent Chambres des Enquêtes reached 'the point where they preferred to see Paris in turmoil and the countryside laid waste by foreign armies than to go back on what they had undertaken'. Temperatures rose higher when Anne's brother-in-law, Gaston d'Orléans, publicly mooted the possibility of all Parlement's immediate grievances being satisfied and Anne herself consented not only to the sovereign courts' union but to a further week of deliberations by their deputies on the present needs of the state. Parlement rightly scented fear and weakness in her entourage, and grew bolder.

At a series of meetings held in the St-Louis Chamber of the Palais de Justice in July 1648 the deputies elaborated a list of articles, the majority of which bore upon *the* most pressing problem confronting the state: finances. It was proposed that the contract-system for collecting taxes should be abolished and tax-reductions accorded. Henceforth no taxes should be levied except on the basis of edicts duly verified by the sovereign courts, who would also render themselves responsible for carrying out an enquiry into malpractices committed in the handling of the king's money. Stricter measures were outlined to ensure that *rentiers* received their due and that merchandise was taxed at the proper rate. It was requested that the queen should prune the growing sums disbursed on royal authority for purposes undisclosed in public. All of these proposals could be said to justify Parlement's consistent claim to be the voice of the lowly and the oppressed. But there were other propositions in which the benefit for the man in the street was less easily discernible. The very first article was a call for the removal of a thorn in the Parlements' side, that is to say, the *intendants*. Not content with reforming financial administration, they aspired to practical control of it, and blasted *traitants* and *partisans* (with whom they had many family and business ties) by stating that justice could not be honourably dispensed if such persons, and all associated with them, were not banned in future from serving in the sovereign courts. There was also a string of weighty clauses designed to restore to certain categories of office-holders functions commandeered by *intendants* and *traitants*, and to guard against iniquities such as retrenchment of sovereign-court wages, creation of offices without sovereign-court approval, removal of cases from sovereign-court jurisdiction, overruling of sovereign-court decrees, and detention without trial of sovereign-court personnel. Humanitarian concerns had clearly not submerged personal interests and animosities.

Having authorised, albeit under duress, a search for remedies for the state's ills, and having been presented with a collection that could appeal to the masses, Anne and her ministers had little option but to give concrete signs of recognition of the magistracy's zeal. They were intent, however, on not making blanket concessions. Particelli d'Emery was dismissed, but replaced by a high-handed relative of Richelieu, the Maréchal (Marshal) de la Meilleraye, who was known to be no friend of Parlements. The *intendants* were revoked, but not in six frontier provinces. Tax-remission was granted, but on the express condition that the *tailles* owing for the current year were fully and promptly paid at the beginning of the next. On the vital issue of detention without trial, a significant silence was maintained. Louis XIV merely promised, in a general summary of royal concessions read out in his presence in Parlement on 31st July, to summon as soon as possible a council of notabilities to advise him on how to eliminate disorders in finances and in the judiciary. 'A declaration filled with the finest words in the world, containing a few articles useful to the public, and many others that were very obscure and very ambiguous', commented the future Cardinal de Retz.

The Declaration was meant to prompt the sovereign courts to mind their ordinary business once more. Instead, a Parlement commission was straightaway set up to examine its terms, and deliberations recommenced. Anne's desire to obtain reparation for the repeated affronts which her authority had suffered finally overwhelmed her on learning from its indiscreet president that the Cour des Aides was about to proceed against some *traitants* deemed guilty of abetting reductions in *officiers'* salaries. Hitherto she had had to make valiant efforts to swallow her pride, lest the populace riot in favour of its tax-cutting champions, the cash-flow for the war dry up, and the Habsburg enemy triumph. Now, as alarmed *traitants* and courtiers financially interested in supporting them were lobbying for action against Parlement, which had taken over the case, Anne was suddenly presented with a tempting opportunity to strike at those who had humiliated her. On 26th August Parlement was summoned to turn out in full force for a service at Notre-Dame to give thanks for the Prince de Condé's recent victory over Archduke Leopold of Austria at Lens (Pas-de-Calais). No one realised the proper significance of the royal guards posted all along the king's route from his residence, the Palais-Royal, to the cathedral until, shortly after his return home, two of the most strident Parlementarians, Blancmesnil and Broussel, were arrested at their houses and hustled off to the châteaux of Vincennes and St-Germain-en-Laye respectively. The prize catch, Broussel, was a sickly septuagenarian who had endeared himself to the populace as much by his active charity to the poor as by his denunciation of fiscal oppression. As soon as the news of his abduction spread, there was uproar. Precisely who started the uproar, and who joined in during the three days that it lasted, is difficult to establish on the basis of testimonies from contemporaries who vaguely designate 'the people', 'the bourgeois'1, or 'vagabonds', though it appears that shopkeepers, artisans, and the citizen militia took the bit between their teeth as firmly as those of dubious social status. Anne remained adamant in the face of pleas for the release of the prisoners made by anxious guardians of law and order, preferring to despatch Maréchal de la Meilleraye and the Coadjuteur onto the streets to calm the crowds. Retz, foreseeing a break with Anne despite his obligation to her for the coadjutorship, had been busy securing support amongst the lower classes by copious distributions of alms and was therefore upset at having to appear to be in the anti-Broussel camp. He was even more upset at being ill-treated by the mob before they recognised him and paid some respect to his cloth and his rhetoric. The last straw was when Anne and Mazarin made light of his services and he heard reports of their mocking him and accusing him of stirring up the populace. At that moment, so he declares in his memoirs, he suppressed his lingering scruples of ingratitude and

---

1 *'Peuple'* and *'bourgeois'* were two very elastic terms in seventeenth-century France.

'Peuple' might mean the population of a whole country, or that of a town or village. In relation to a king, the word could refer to his subjects. In a pejorative sense, *'peuple'* was applied to the lower, ill-bred strata of a community, and normally qualified by another expression, e.g. *'menu'* or *'petit'* ('little'), or *'bas'* ('low'), or *'la lie du peuple'* ('the dregs of the populace').

The noun *'bourgeois'* denoted primarily the inhabitant of a town. It also designated those who belonged to the Tiers Etat, as opposed to the Nobility or the Clergy. The adjective *'bon'* ('good') was often attached to *'bourgeois'* in order to signify a citizen of some financial standing.

disloyalty and 'abandoned [his] destiny to all the actions of glory' — which is to say that he gave full rein to his bent for intrigue and self-glorification.

The rioters, who had dispersed overnight — Parisian insurgents were noted for their dislike of foregoing their supper — made up for lost time the following day, 27th August, when they waylaid and nearly murdered the terrified Chancellor Séguier on his way to Parlement, and stoned and fired upon his rescuer La Meilleraye. All the shops shut, citizens young and old armed themselves with a motley collection of weapons, hung up the heavy iron chains used to cut off access to the principal streets, and erected an estimated 1,260 barricades made of any large containers that could be filled with stones, earth, or manure. Thinking to use the commotion as a lever to petition for the release of their colleagues, a large Parlementary deputation headed by First President Molé marched in procession from the Palais de Justice to the Palais-Royal. Anne did not want to know. Pressed hard, she agreed to relent in return for an undertaking from Parlement to suspend discussions on matters arising out of the July sessions in the St-Louis Chamber. Despite the urgency of the situation, the deputies felt unable to give a reply without first holding one of the debates that had to precede their every move. But they had not trooped far in the direction of the Palais de Justice when they were stopped by an armed mob who laid profane hands on Molé's long patriarchal beard and forced him, under a hail of abuse, to return to the Palais-Royal to get Broussel. Molé, on everyone's admission, retained a stoic dignity worthy of the ancient Romans whose conduct and aphorisms frequently inspired the sovereign courts. A good many of his followers, however, needed retrieving from nearby houses, to which they had scattered, before they could hem and haw over the legitimacy of deliberating in the Great Gallery of the Palais-Royal instead of at headquarters. Mollified with the remains of Mazarin's lunch, the Parlementarians at length saw their way to postponing assemblies, except to sort out *rentes* and a tariff-list, until 11th November. Blancmesnil was released in the evening, and Broussel was escorted in triumph to the Palais de Justice on the next day, 28th August. After a few alarms caused by the movement of troops and gunpowder, weapons were put away on the combined injunction of the Parlement and municipal authorities. Barricades disappeared, shops re-opened, and the uproar subsided almost as swiftly as it had arisen.

Those who recorded the dramatic Days of the Barricades marvelled at this unforeseeable turn of events, many attributing it to nothing less than the intervention of God. The advocate Omer Talon, a key witness in view of his position as one of the king's official representatives in the Paris Parlement, finds a down-to-earth explanation: the concern of the 'bourgeois', as soon as their defence of Parlement's threatened authority became superfluous, to restore that public order which protected their own property and persons. It is Talon also who highlights the most clearly the unenviable position of all the chief protagonists in the drama at this point, from the despised or detested ministers and men of arms employed by the queen, to magistrates who dared not voice moderate opinions for fear of reprisals from the extremists in their ranks. The queen's name was amongst those dragged through the mire, and she put off her weekly visits to Notre-Dame rather than run the gauntlet of open abuse. The king alone could still command respect, 'because of the innocence of his age'.

The air in the Palais-Royal became unhealthy for literal as well as metaphorical reasons. Anne's younger son Philippe caught smallpox. Anne seized on the pretext to remove herself, her elder son, and Mazarin to Rueil (13th September), in what is now the western suburb of Paris and what was then the site of an estate bought by Cardinal Richelieu. The exit of the trio was marked by a purge. The Marquis de Châteauneuf, ex-Keeper of the Royal Seals (Garde des Sceaux), was exiled from Paris, and the Comte de Chavigny, a minister who had been the apple of Richelieu's eye, was imprisoned in Vincennes, of which ironically he was the governor. Both men were hostile to Mazarin and suspected of using their contacts and influence in Parlement to foment the recent disturbances. The treatment meted out to them sparked off violent accusations against Mazarin in Parlement and talk of renewing an edict of 1617 (the year of Concini's assassination) forbidding foreigners from participating in government. Some of the heat was taken out of the situation by offers from the Prince de Condé, freshly returned from the battlefront, and from Gaston d'Orléans, to hold conferences with Parlement deputies at St-Germain-en-Laye on the subject of the current disorders. The two conspicuous aspects of the conferences were Mazarin's absence, and the tenacity with which the Parlement deputies sought guarantees against arbitrary judicial procedures. On 24th October a full Parlement assembly enjoyed the satisfaction of graciously registering a declaration, drafted by its own deputies and First President, in which the king amplified and clarified the concessions already made by his earlier declaration of 31st July. As might be expected, 'show' paragraphs about tax-relief stood at the head of the document; but the real sting came in the tail-clause and in a couple of secret ones, all tending to ensure that no sovereign-court member would be apprehended and detained indefinitely at His Majesty's pleasure. In their anxiety to give Parlement no fresh excuse for prolonging its assemblies extraordinary Anne and Mazarin had overtly consented to everything it demanded.

Paris had a taste of peace, with the simultaneous return of the queen (31st October), autumn recess of Parlement, and announcement of the all-important but overshadowed signing of the treaties of Westphalia which relieved France of the necessity to combat the Habsburg Emperor. The breathing-space was short. Before November was over, the excitable elements in the Enquêtes and Requêtes Chambers of Parlement were demanding assemblies of all chambers, supposedly to regulate internal disciplinary matters. December came, and the pretext for assembling switched to infringements of the 24th October Declaration, with special emphasis on those which were said to be adding to the misery of the populace. Parlement 'zealots' meanwhile worked on colleagues in two of the other sovereign courts, the Chambre des Comptes and Cour des Aides, to persuade them to join in the quibbling.

Gaston and Condé were asked to intervene, but Condé adopted the reverse of a conciliatory tone in Parlement, treating clamorous Enquêtes president Viole and the rest of the august company very much like army recruits who had stepped out of line.

A prince of the blood royal trying to silence a cocky Parlement president is a tableau which neatly sums up the drift of events during the opening months of the Fronde. Whilst the prestige and popularity of the monarchy had sunk, the Paris Parlement had to all appearances ridden on the crest of the wave. It had seen other sovereign courts rally round it, citizens of the capital take up arms on behalf of its arrested members, downtrodden taxpayers of the realm hail it as a deliverer, and

princes come to parley with it. Under cover of urging an overhaul of France's
financial machinery, which all sides agreed was necessary, Parlement had pressed its
own claims to what amounted to functioning less like a supreme court of law and
more like the English Parliament. It had made the central government, concerned
with the hard reality of supporting large armies in the field, seem unconcerned about
the cost in terms of civilians' misery. It had forced the queen regent to officially
authorise assemblies which she felt herself powerless to prevent, and wrung from her
in the privacy of a conversation with her confidante Mme de Motteville the cry that
'she found her rank as queen utterly useless, since she was not the mistress' of
circumstances. But Parlement had difficulties with which to contend. Composed of
over two hundred persons, it did not often speak with one voice. Verbal and
sometimes physical conflicts were endemic, especially between the older, established
generation of magistrates sitting in the principal chamber, the Grand'Chambre, and
the younger, more restless and impetuous generation that occupied the Chambres des
Enquêtes. Friction between the different sovereign courts was equally longstanding.
Even after the celebrated 13th May act of union, grave matters such as which court's
deputies should speak first and who should sit above whom continued to make for
sharp exchanges and slow-moving business. Contenting supporters was another
headache. The *'peuple'* liked to see concrete results emerging speedily from
Parlement deliberations and were apt to turn violent when their wishes were thwarted.
Above all, Parlement had reason to fear drastic action on the part of the queen. Anne
had publicly vowed to inflict such an exemplary punishment on rebels that posterity
would never forget it. She had already run through the standard penalties to no avail.
What awe-inspiring retribution must she therefore be contemplating in order to avoid
losing face? Parlement did not have to wait long to find out.

* * * * * * *

Chapter 3

ACT II

Shortly before daybreak on 6th January 1649 there arose a great hue and cry in the streets of Paris. Sleepers were brusquely awakened to learn momentous news. Anne and her two sons, together with nearly all the royal family and Mazarin, had left the Palais-Royal overnight, bound for the ancient château of St-Germain-en-Laye, on the Seine to the west of the city. Rumours of the queen's imminent departure had been causing nervous speculation for some time, but on the eve of the actual event Anne had shown herself to be a consummate actress, participating in a household Epiphany celebration and publicly planning a schedule of engagements which she knew that she would not keep. Only her unusual gaiety betrayed her to a few of her closest attendants.

Despite the moral and economic gravity of the removal of the king from his capital and the camping-style conditions that had to be endured until royal baggage could travel unimpeded to St-Germain, Anne had some cause to smile. For she had at her side the two allies, Gaston and Condé, indispensable for a show of strength and family solidarity. Gaining the allegiance of the two men simultaneously had been no easy task. Apart from the perennial rivalry between the respective clans to which each belonged, the two princes had recently been at loggerheads over a cardinal's hat. Gaston wanted one for his favourite and mentor, the obscurely-born Abbé de la Rivière, while Condé insisted on it going to his own brother, the hunchbacked Prince de Conti, for whose upkeep he preferred the Church to be responsible. The dispute, which divided the courtiers into two opposing camps, was patched up at the king's expense, by abandoning ownership of several towns in Lorraine to Condé and a lucrative town-governorship in Languedoc to Gaston, and by accepting La Rivière into the royal council with the title of minister. When it came to proposing the exodus of the royal family from Paris, leaving the way clear for punishment of dissidents, Anne found Condé quite disposed to support her plans. The idea of social inferiors disobeying their betters mightily offended his sense of propriety, and his considerable pride was still smarting after contact with abrasive president Viole. Gaston at first refused point-blank to co-operate. Unlike Condé, he had no desire to antagonise the Parlementarians, with whom his popularity stood so high that some of their number had flattered him with the prospect of his replacing Anne as regent. Unlike Condé also, Gaston lacked warrior instincts and courage. He liked an easy life and was open to manipulation by stronger personalities. He was accordingly sandwiched between La Rivière, who realised that his cardinal's hat depended on his master remaining in favour with the heads of government, and Anne, who played on all the emotional chords she could think of, including the possibility of having to carry out her project with Condé's assistance alone. Unable to withstand the double barrage, Gaston gave his consent.

Anne's first move, once she had put Paris behind her, was to contact its chief municipal authorities, the *prévôt des marchands* ('provost of merchants', or mayor in modern parlance) and the *échevins* (city councillors), located in the Hôtel de Ville

(Town Hall). Acting on Mazarin's forward-looking advice she had earlier sought to cultivate their goodwill, offering to deposit in their hands the keys to all the city gates as a mark of her satisfaction with their conduct during the August 1648 Barricades. It was to these worthies that she now appealed for allegiance and condescended to offer an explanation of her own conduct, via a letter in the king's name: quitting Paris had proved necessary

> ... in order not to remain exposed to the pernicious designs of some of our Paris Parlement office-holders, who, being in collusion with the enemies of the state, after having on several different occasions attacked our authority, and long abused our kindness, have gone so far as to conspire to seize our person...

The 'pernicious designers' and their colleagues, by comparison, were sent on 7th January a brisk order to transfer south-east of Paris to Montargis. As with the *droit annuel* affair the previous April, the plan to sow dissension between the different administrative bodies misfired, since the *échevins* immediately recognised the authority of Parlement as replacing that of the absent monarch and could not be prevailed upon by him to assist in an act of forceful expulsion.

Pretexting a formality that had gone unobserved, Parlement delayed opening the king's ejection-order until after it had sent a deputation to St-Germain, where, tit for tat, Anne refused to see any deputies who did not emanate from the new seat of Parlement at Montargis. When Omer Talon reported, soberly, back to Parlement on the way in which he and his fellow-intermediaries had got no further than the Chancellor, who advised them that Paris was almost encircled by royal troops, his listeners promptly vented their spleen on Mazarin. The Cardinal was branded as a disturber of the peace and an enemy of the state, and given a week to vacate the country, at the end of which anyone was free to attack him (8th January). Mme de Motteville, though herself no admirer of Mazarin, was moved to note in her memoirs: 'This procedure was the most unjust and the most violent ever practised by men professing to possess some virtue'.

Fulminating against Mazarin left intact the outsize problem of policing and provisioning a populous, blockaded city in danger of rapidly running out of vital commodities. As always in times of emergency, the citizen militia-men were called out to mount day and night guard over the city gates and streets, a hazardous step since the chore was too often palmed off onto domestics and hired replacements unappreciative of military discipline. Injunctions were issued to military and municipal authorities in the immediate neighbourhood of Paris to facilitate the passage of supplies. A council of war and a council of finances were set up. Contributions to a fund for levying troops were imposed on all Paris city-dwellers, whose generosity the Parlementarians felt it necessary to stimulate (Paris was ordinarily exempt from *tailles*) by promising the biggest input.

Finding a suitable leader for the magistrates' army of resistance put Parlement in the awkward position of having to rely upon the 'outside' expertise of men more used to giving than to taking orders. The first to be privately solicited, and to offer himself with alacrity, was the Duc d'Elbeuf, recommendable by virtue of belonging to the ducal household of Lorraine, which was in the habit of pursuing its vast ambitions to the detriment of the kings of France. But following hot-foot from St-Germain in d'Elbeuf's wake came Condé's brother, the Prince de Conti, and his brother-in-law, the Duc de Longueville. Their abrupt defection from the king's side had been engineered by Condé's sister, the Duchesse de Longueville, a blue-eyed blond bombshell persuaded of the necessity to use all her natural assets to magnify the name of Longueville in the eyes of the world. Condé had disappointed her by not procuring the governorship of Le Havre for her husband, and by turning a deaf ear to her talk of aggrandisement, which he knew could only come about at the expense of that same crown which he himself was one of those closest in line to inherit. Her resentment over Condé's seeming apathy was fomented by her actual lover, La Rochefoucauld,[1] fishing for his own advantage in troubled waters, and by a would-be lover, Retz, in search of a princely nonentity to serve as a rallying-point for rebellion. The Duchesse easily won over the nineteen-year-old Conti, whose excessive adoration of his sister was whispered to be incestuous, and through him her irresolute husband, lukewarmly enamoured of charms so liberally bestowed on other males. Thanks to all this background manoeuvring, Parlement had to talk the grumbling d'Elbeuf into serving as second-in-command under his social superior, Conti, delighted at the chance to rival big brother on the latter's own terrain.

Conti was 'a zero who added up to something only because he was a prince of the blood [royal]', according to Retz's cynical valuation. Condé, furious at being deserted by his kith and kin, showed how he personally rated his deformed brother's promotion by mockingly saluting a pet monkey as 'the Parisians' generalissimo'. The teenage prince's gesture of detaching himself from St-Germain was nevertheless a signal and an excuse for other nobles to slip back to Paris, creating the effect of a celebrity review as they appeared one after the other before Parlement to offer their services. Like the sovereign courts the previous May, the group of aristocratic malcontents joined together in a formal act of union, swearing on the Bible to support Parlement and not to sue for peace until Mazarin was ousted. Their facile pledges put five-figure sums in the hands of Conti and his top aides: the shifty Duc d'Elbeuf, soon to switch his allegiance back to Mazarin; the gouty Duc de Bouillon, whose bovine physiognomy concealed a compulsion to elevate himself by fair means or foul to princely rank; the Maréchal de la Mothe-Houdancourt and the Duc de Beaufort, each committed to revenge for a period of imprisonment in the early years of the regency. To convince Parlement and the populace that they were getting returns for their money, the generals went through warlike motions, lightly peppering the Bastille with cannon-shots, reviewing troops in the fashionable Place Royale under the admiring eyes of ladies, and making ineffectual sallies outside the city. Condé's derision knew no bounds. In early February (8th) he reminded his opponents of how to fight by swooping down on their garrison at Charenton, which lay astride a vital supply-route to the capital, and slaying everyone who offered resistance.

Raiding and blockading were turning out to be much slower in starving Paris into submission than had been calculated. Heavily-escorted convoys and clandestine purveyors maintained a food-supply, notwithstanding the extraordinarily severe

---

[1]Known as the Prince de Marsillac prior to succeeding to his father's title of Duc de La Rochefoucauld in February 1650.

flooding of the Seine in January and a big freeze in February. By comparison with neighbouring townsfolk and villagers in the path of royalist and Frondeur troops, the inhabitants of the capital were unscathed. But life within the city walls was nerve-racking, as constant searches were made for caches of money denounced by informers, and individuals were set upon whenever some street-corner loafer took it into his or her head to point a finger and yell 'mazarins!'. It was the sort of atmosphere that made honest folk yearn for the restoration of order and the return of their legitimate ruler. The occupants of St-Germain, kept meticulously informed of events by Mazarin's ecclesiastical and lay agents in Paris, judged the time favourable to appeal openly for public support. In quick succession the Chevalier de La Valette was sent to distribute anti-rebel tracts in the capital, and a royal herald to offer Conti, Parlement, and the Hôtel de Ville pardon in return for laying down their arms and resuming their normal duties. Unfortunately, La Valette got himself arrested in mid-distribution, while the herald could do no more than trumpet at a city gate since Broussel persuaded Parlement to refuse him entrance. The mission could not be dismissed as a complete fiasco, however, because Parlement, wedded to formalities, decided to explain its refusal directly to the queen, thereby paving the way for interested parties to make personal contact and open negotiations.

A rapid peace-settlement was not what the Frondeur generals had in mind. Upheavals in the state always provided the high nobility with an opportunity, fully exploited, to tap the central authority for material and honorific gains. It made sense to them to hold out for a while and see if Mazarin, deemed more timorous and compliant than Anne, could be milked, as well as Parlement, for perquisites. With the aim, therefore, of compromising the magistrates to whom they had so recently sworn allegiance, and of damaging the latter's credibility as peace-seekers, the generals assisted in a little treasonable diversion staged by Retz. Through his dense network of relatives, friends, and clients, the Coadjuteur was in touch with enemy Spain, more precisely, with the Count of Fuensaldana, deputy-general of Archduke Leopold who commanded the Low Countries on behalf of Philip IV of Spain. Fuensaldana made no difficulty over despatching an envoy to the Paris Parlement with a proposal to negotiate, in Philip's name, the peace between France and Spain which Mazarin was accused of having jeopardised. Whereas Louis XIV's herald had been turned away, the Spaniards' envoy, well rehearsed in his part by Retz and cronies, was ushered into Parlement to present flattering offers of talks and troops. However, the uneasy consciences of some of the Parlementarians resulted in a motion to inform Anne d'Autriche of what had just transpired and to find out her wishes in the matter.

Anne's replies to the bearers of Parlement's explanations were sharp. The news, received in the capital several days previously (19th February), of the decapitation of Charles I at Whitehall had seemingly strengthened Anne's resolve not to put herself in an exposed position by abandoning Mazarin (as Charles had abandoned *his* minister Strafford to execution) and not to let royal authority be overruled (like that of Charles) by a power-group of the king's own subjects. Luckily for the prospect of negotiations between St-Germain and Paris, First President Molé, whose conduct usually denoted the fact that he was a crown appointee, suppressed the queen's official written retort at the first available opportunity, and stood out for a peace-conference in the face of threats against his life and property issued by paid mobsters.

Rueil, a halfway point between Paris and St-Germain, was chosen as the venue for the conference in March. That proved to be just about the only part of the proceedings that ran smoothly. The sovereign-court deputation, composed of vocal hard-liners like president Viole, bristled as soon as they learned that Mazarin would be amongst the regent's deputation, and could not be calmed until it was suggested that two deputies from each side did the actual conferring before reporting back to the two separate chambers into which their respective colleagues divided. Yet this cumbersome machinery and personnel produced, by 11th March 1649, a surprisingly quick settlement. It looked like a royal victory, too, with the Paris Parlement agreeing, amongst other things, to attend a *lit de justice* at St-Germain, to refrain from assembling throughout the rest of the year except on ceremonial occasions, and to allow the king to borrow in order to meet state expenditure in 1649 and 1650. Retz's view that the Parlementarians abandoned only for short intervals their fundamental pacifism appeared to be confirmed. He might have added to the list of reasons for their tractability the fact that the Parlementarians were under great pressure to relieve Paris from the effects of both the blockade and the normal decline in commerce attendant upon the courtiers' absence. They had found decidedly uncomfortable their alliance with the mob and the generals — scant respecters of properties, persons, and obligations — and had failed to secure their partisans' stated objective, the dismissal of Mazarin, which Gaston and Condé refused to countenance. And the Cardinal himself had just given rebels pause for thought by using bribes to procure the mass desertion of German troops which the Vicomte de Turenne, brother of the Duc de Bouillon, was proposing to lead to the assistance of Parlement and the Frondeur generals. Regrettably, Mazarin followed a neat feat of corruption with a blunder. He signed the Rueil peace-treaty.

The generals and their Parlement clique feigned outrage, not only over the signature but over the treaty's omission of specific reference to the generals' personal interests. A dagger-bearing mob, led by a disgraced lawyer, crowded inside the Great Hall of the Palais de Justice, howling for the Cardinal's signature to be burned by the public executioner, and for 'all the Mazarins' to be drowned. Amidst the tumult President Molé, with 'an unshakeable firmness and almost supernatural presence of mind' (Retz), endeavoured to calmly count votes in favour of sending deputies back to Anne to discuss the generals' business. To make sure that no detail of their demands was overlooked, the generals were invited to couch them in writing. The resulting enumeration, unadorned by the veil of public-spiritedness thrown over the Parlementarians' parallel claims in July 1648, showed all too clearly the prizes on which aristocratic agitators had set their sights: a place on the royal council (for Conti); sums of money running into tens, sometimes hundreds, of thousands; towns, countships, and other domains; governorships, to be automatically transferable to male relatives; dukedoms and peerages; the *tabouret* (the right to be seated in the queen's presence) for wives... Retz, having cunningly abstained from broadcasting his own pretensions, loftily condemned those of his fellow-conspirators as 'almost inconceivably ridiculous'. But it was Mme de Motteville who put the situation in a nutshell: '... they were demanding the whole of France'.

Effrontery had to be rewarded. For another army had appeared on the scene, one not susceptible of being bought off like Turenne's since it belonged to Spain and was commanded by Archduke Leopold in person. Throughout the Rueil conference the

Frondeur generals had been treating with the Archduke, and one of their number, the Marquis de Noirmoutier, escorted Spanish cavalry into Picardy in mid-March. A royalist army headed off the threat for the moment, but the regency government could obviously ill afford to be embroiled in domestic conflict while foreign enemies were weaving in and out of French frontiers. So cash and honours flowed in the direction of those who deemed rapacity abhorrent, in Mazarin. The Parlementarians had reason to feel equally exultant. Those clauses in the 11th March agreement which had demonstrated the king's desire to retain the upper hand were either allowed to lapse or restricted in a royal declaration presented to the Paris Parlement on 1st April.

The road to St-Germain was soon littered with thanksgiving deputations from the sovereign courts and the municipality, followed, after a face-saving interval, by embarrassed grandees like Conti and the Longuevilles. Mazarin was resolutely amiable towards all the visitors. Anne was cool. Her sentiments were revealed in response to exhortations to take the king back to Paris. She despatched Gaston and Condé to the still unquiet city but did not personally re-enter it with her son until four more months had passed.

Trouble in the provinces afforded her a plausible motive for continuing to snub the capital. Provincial unrest, like the proverbial poor, was always with seventeenth-century Frenchmen, and about as difficult to contain. Its chief manifestations were friction between representatives of the king (commissioners, governors) and local administrators, disputes amongst these same representatives and administrators as individuals or corps, and explosions of peasant and urban insurrection provoked by anything perceived as a threat to income or sustenance. Wars, whether foreign or civil, automatically tended to bring to a head situations of this kind, though mercifully for harassed monarchs, the festers, if they burst, usually did so in manageable numbers. Three of the big peripheral provinces faltered conspicuously in their allegiance to the crown during the Fronde: Normandy, labouring under the heaviest tax-burden; Provence, vulnerable to attack from Spain and Spanish-dominated Italy; and Guyenne, flowing with great rivers which lent themselves to rebel entrenchment. All three had distinguished records of revolt, with Normandy currently in the lead by virtue of having had Chancellor Séguier arrive in person to pacify the region after the Nu-pieds ('Barefoot') uprising of 1639. Memories of the severity of government repression on that occasion (including temporary suspension of the Rouen Parlement) help to explain why the governor of Normandy, Condé's cuckolded brother-in-law Longueville, gained support from the local populace when he went in January 1649 to win over the province for the generals, but also why support was not sufficiently sustained or widespread amongst persons in authority to enable him to inflame the whole area. The Rouen Parlement declared its solidarity with the Paris Parlement and decreed the confiscation of royal tax-money to pay for troops for Longueville, but largely disinterested itself from his cause after being permitted honourable seats and a hearing at the Rueil peace-talks. The problem in Provence was not a devious governor cajoling a hesitant *parlement* but an imperious governor cracking down on a defiant *parlement*. Like their counterparts in Rouen and elsewhere, the Parlementarians of Aix objected, at bottom, to the governmental obsession with creating offices and so-called 'semesters' (which doubled existing personnel by obliging office-holders to serve for only six months each year). The governor of

Provence, the Comte d'Alais, had about as much patience with bumptious burghers as his cousin Condé, and menacingly moved troops into Aix. In January 1649 the shooting of a Parlementarian's lackey by one of d'Alais' guards ignited the whole city and left the governor penned up in his own residence by the mutinous, Parlement-backed, populace. A cardinal-friend of Mazarin laboured for the governor's release with offers of copious concessions, a wasted effort in so far as the vengeful d'Alais was encamped outside the walls of Aix the following July, and a second mediator on his way from Paris to patch up a precarious peace. The use of intermediaries indicated that Anne and Mazarin had more pressing business elsewhere. The Spanish were bearing down from the north and the loyalty of governors of certain strategic towns in the front line for attack could not be taken for granted. An uneasy summer holiday had therefore to be spent by the royal circle in Picardy, monitoring acts of hostility which came from French as well as Spanish quarters.

With the chief upholders of royal authority at a safe distance away on the frontier, troublemakers in the capital had a field-day. Printing-presses, important war-machines employed by all parties during the Fronde to discredit enemies and whip up support, increased output, in defiance of tougher legislation against the publication and distribution of libels[2]. One Claude Morlot actually shot to fame on the strength of being rescued by fellow-printers as he was on his way to the gallows for publishing a pamphlet accusing Anne and Mazarin of gross indecency. The irreducible elements amongst the Frondeur aristocracy made their particular bid for mob favour by assisting the Duc de Beaufort to publicly manhandle the Marquis de Jarzé, a harebrained client of Condé, and by beating up a couple of royal footmen in the street. Authority in any form had, it seemed, ceased to be respected, whence several reported cases of sacrilege in churches.

Not for the first nor the last time during the civil war, acts of lawlessness worked to the advantage of the monarchy by frightening the orthodox heads of the urban community, municipal officials, prosperous merchants and master guildsmen. A deputation of these *'bons bourgeois',* as contemporaries referred to them, found Anne d'Autriche willing at last to be persuaded to grace Paris with the royal presence: the Spanish had haughtily rejected peace overtures made in the name of a king 'who dared not return to his own capital'. Appropriately, it was a selection of *'notables bourgeois'* from each quarter of the capital who followed the *prévôt des marchands* and *échevins* out along the road from Paris to St-Denis on 18th August 1649 to meet the approaching royal party. The king was begged by the *prévôt* to 'believe that he could not go to any place in his realm where he would find more devotion to his service than in the hearts of the Parisians'. Louis reciprocated by holding his eleventh birthday celebrations at the Hôtel de Ville on 5th September and dancing with the *prévôt's* wife.

The 'happily-ever-after' note was not to be prolonged. Reconciliation soon gave way to rifts as old problems of finances and personalities resurfaced. The

---

[2]The libels and pamphlets produced during the Fronde are collectively termed *'mazarinades'*, regardless of whether they are for, against, or about, Mazarin.

disturbances in Paris had caused arrears in the payment of interest to the *rentiers*, the purchasers of government bonds. The significance of this breach of good faith for all sections of society is underlined by lawyer Talon:

> ... the income from these *rentes* maintains luxury in great households, meets the everyday expenses of medium-sized families when they are properly paid, and supplies vital necessities to the poorest [households], whose entire wealth consists in some small *rente* acquired or inherited.

An undertaking from briefly reinstated Particelli d'Emery to put up interest payments did not appease the *rentiers*, who began assembling — always an ominous move during the Fronde — and electing syndics to oversee their affairs. One of the syndics, Guy Joly, in Retz's employ, arranged to get himself shot at in order to give his fellow-Frondeurs an opening to call the populace to arms. On the production of a poorly simulated bullet wound in his arm, an official investigation was set up. It coincided with a second investigation into a separate shooting incident on the very same day, 11th December 1649, the target this time being the carriage of the Prince de Condé, empty of its forewarned owner.

Whether this was another organised farce, or a genuine assassination-attempt, and in either case who the instigators were, people of the day could not make up their minds. There is no doubt, however, that in the latter half of 1649 Condé, war hero and pillar of the monarchy hitherto, indulged his youthful instinct to behave provocatively. He was influenced by reconciliation with his stop-at-nothing sister, the Duchesse de Longueville, and by mounting animosity towards Mazarin, whom he considered to have ill repaid him for shouldering the unpopularity of enforcing the Paris Blockade. Instead of employing his military talents and prestige to drive back the Spanish in the north, he allowed another general to go, and botch the job. By withholding his consent to a marriage between one of Mazarin's nieces and Beaufort's brother, the Duc de Mercoeur, he obtained an extra governorship in explosive Normandy for his own brother-in-law Longueville. Through abetting the clandestine marriage of the young governor of Le Havre, a great-nephew of Richelieu, he effectively added the strategic Norman seaport to the family possessions. He flirted with notorious enemies of Mazarin like the Comte de Chavigny and the Duc de Bouillon. His intervention for or against various contenders complicated the lengthy Tabouret Affair, a dispute over the seating of titled women in the queen's presence that triggered assemblies of the aristocracy, manifestos and calls for convocation of the Etats Généraux. He behaved insultingly towards Mazarin in public, and extorted from him a signed promise to resolve no important state issue, nor even conclude marriages for his relatives, without the prince's assent (2nd October). As a crowning piece of insolence he attempted to force his *protégé* Jarzé onto Anne d'Autriche in the capacity of gallant and replacement for Mazarin. Anne was cut to the quick, and vengeful, but she was also a woman of too delicate a conscience to stoop to political assassination, and Mazarin was the man to counsel temporisation, dissimulation, and guile, not bloodshed. Condé thus spent his Christmas unmolested, while a plot to clip his wings took shape.

Looking back over 1649, the queen and her prime minister must have been aware of the history of 1648 repeating itself, but with certain worrying developments.

Relying on Gaston d'Orléans' co-operation and Condé's army they had again launched against the apologetically rebellious Paris Parlement what turned out to be a counterproductive offensive and had had to retreat to bargaining which left their opponents in the morally stronger position. The salient difference between the two years lay in the physical and verbal escalation of the conflict, as Parlement drew willy-nilly to its side an ill-assorted collection of indocile allies — restive princes and nobles, outbreaking provincial *officiers*, meddlesome agents of Spain — and pamphlets of vindication and vituperation flew in all directions. Mazarin had been formally declared Public Enemy Number One and exposed to being hunted down like a common criminal. Anne had been taxed in print with unmentionable vices. Louis XIV had been forced to spend well over half the year outside his own capital. Now royalist Condé was acting like a man in need of restraint. It seemed that the situation could hardly deteriorate further. But the worst was yet to come.

* * * * * * *

Chapter 4

ACT III

The curtain-raiser to 1650 was an arresting act: the summary imprisonment of Condé, Conti, and Longueville (18th January). As with the royal family's exodus to St-Germain the previous January, prior preparation had been necessary in the form of securing allies, but the allies on this occasion represented a surprising reversal of regency government policy. For they were hard-bitten specimens of Frondeurs, a term to which Retz and Beaufort had given wider currency after the Peace of Rueil in order to distinguish between the loosely aligned 'party' of malcontents whom the two of them were recognised as heading, and those who had been formally reconciled with Anne and Mazarin. The leading intermediary between the queen's supporters and the Frondeurs was a woman, a marked characteristic of the later stages of the Fronde. The woman in question, the Duchesse de Chevreuse, arch-conspiratress of Louis XIII's reign, had been exiled for involvement in the Importants' plot of 1643 (see above, p.11) but returned to Paris without permission in April 1649 and worked hard to reassert her former ascendant over Anne d'Autriche. The Duchesse was linked to Retz by her taste for political and amorous intrigues, and by her daughter's attention to satisfying his considerable sexual appetites. She, the Duchesse, arranged for direct dialogue between Anne, Mazarin, and Retz, and undertook with the help of her stepmother the Duchesse de Montbazon (an obese belle who 'governed' Beaufort) to foment Gaston d'Orléans' deep-seated jealousy of Condé. The Frondeurs anticipated that once they were relieved of Condé — who suspected them of organising the December attack upon his carriage and was threatening to take justice into his own hands — they would be able to bend Gaston, Anne, and Mazarin to their will. The royalist trio had similar expectations of being able to subjugate the Frondeurs. For the moment, therefore, the detention of the prince and those males of his family in a position to avenge him suited almost everybody.

The lion, the monkey, and the fox (Gaston's definition of the three princes) were lured to the Palais-Royal on the pretext of an important meeting of the royal council and safely netted, despite the overturning of their carriage en route to Vincennes, an incident which, curiously, had also marked the forcible removal of Broussel to St-Germain in 1648. Parlement listened to the royal justification of events without a stir. The people of Paris lit bonfires of rejoicing. Retz and Beaufort joined the flock of Frondeurs mouthing compliments at the Palais-Royal as soon as they had both been acquitted of complicity in the events of the previous 11th December. So far so good. But the partisans of the princes still had to be rendered inoperative, and they were scattering fast to places where they had influence. The Duchesse de Longueville and her step-daughter Mlle de Longueville escaped to Normandy with the assistance of their friend the Princesse Palatine, whose talents as negotiator for the Princes' release were soon to emerge. The Duchesse's lover, La Rochefoucauld, retreated smartly to Poitou, of which he was governor, to assemble an army of local nobles. Another of her admirers, Turenne, occupied the fortress of Stenay on the river Meuse, with the ulterior motive of thereby hastening royal compensation for the loss of the family principality of Sedan (Ardennes), forfeited in 1642 to save the neck of his treasonable brother the Duc de Bouillon.

To counteract the effects of provincial campaigns for the assistance of the Princes and to evade their demanding new Frondeur allies, Anne and Mazarin took the winsome young Louis XIV on a tour of trouble-spots. Normandy was the first stop. The Rouen Parlementarians went out of their way to greet the royal visitors with a double-size deputation, and governors of strongholds in the region capitulated with virtually no resistance. The Duchesse de Longueville held out as long as she could in the château of Dieppe before risking a night-time escape by sea. High wind and tide overbalanced the sailor carrying her to the boat and she had to be fished from the water half-drowned. Happily, immersion stiffened only her determination, and she was soon off, on horseback, in search of more reliable transport to Holland. By this circuitous route she eventually rejoined Turenne at Stenay, where the two of them made contact with Archduke Leopold.

The royal party reappeared only briefly in Paris in late February before setting off again (5th March), this time for Burgundy, of which Condé had been governor. The cavalcade had the deceptive air of a family outing: Anne was accompanied by both of her sons, and Mazarin by three of his nieces, imported from Italy in 1647 for acclimatisation prior to usage as marriage-pawns. Taking the youngsters along was, amongst other things, a safety measure. Gaston d'Orléans was so nervous at being left in the capital that he insisted on having royal guards ring his palace. Yet his sister-in-law had taken precautions to keep the Frondeurs on his side in the event of an adverse move from the Condéens during the king's absences. Deferring to Frondeur pressure, Anne had restored the important post of Keeper of the Royal Seals to the Marquis de Châteauneuf, seventeen years after he lost it for conspiracy with the Duchesse de Chevreuse, and she had confirmed Parlement's unauthorised bestowal of the governorship of the Bastille on Broussel's son. Gaston's fears were nevertheless well founded. While Louis' charisma and Mazarin's money melted rebel hearts in the provinces, Condé's campaigners were bringing Paris to the boil again. Women, especially, got themselves mentioned in despatches for openly enlisting support for the pinioned hero. Whether they were acting spontaneously — out of genuine attachment, a passion for intrigue, or a desire for personal aggrandisement — or whether they were 'prodded' by self-serving men, these women were shown that they could not propagandise with impunity. The Comtesse de Fiesque, whose house had been transformed into a recruitment-centre for the Condé party, was commanded to leave Paris, in company with two of her imitators, Mmes de Bonnelle and de Saint-Loup. Condé's mother, Charlotte de Montmorency, slipping back from recently imposed exile in order to make an emotional petition to Parlement, was firmly instructed by Frondeur-backed Gaston to wait outside the city until the regent returned to examine her case. Turenne's sister and sister-in-law, forceful personalities accused of inspiring in their menfolk the immoderate ambitions which led them to declare for Parlement and then Condé, were shut up in the Bastille.

Two committed female propagandists remained at large: Condé's sister and his wife. The Duchesse de Longueville had rapidly disposed Turenne to conclude a treaty with Spain, and had the honour of being named ahead of himself, his brother Bouillon, and La Rochefoucauld as a superlative traitor — 'guilty of treason in the first degree' — in a royal declaration of 9th May. The Princesse de Condé, Claire-Clémence de Maillé-Brézé, had hitherto cut a pallid figure beside her flamboyant sister-in-law. Coupled too young to a man who loved elsewhere and despised her 'lowly' rank as Richelieu's niece, she had narrowly saved herself from repudiation by giving him an heir. The imprisonment of her husband catapulted her out of domestic obscurity and into the hands of agitators who calculated on exploiting her wifely devotion. 'She wished to follow him [Condé] everywhere, even at the head of an army', the princess told Pierre Lenet, Condé's right-hand man of affairs, shortly before he arranged to spirit her away from her appointed place of exile at Chantilly and embarked her on a course of action which was to place her for long years outside the pale of France.

The immediate plan was to convey the princess, via selected halts on pro-Condé territory, as far as Bordeaux, the affluent capital of the province of Guyenne. Bordeaux was a choice terrain for political activists: far enough away from the central authority in Paris but not too far away from the Spanish frontier; linked by trade to revolutionary England; home to a disgruntled Parlement and an effervescent populace, each griping about familiar evils like taxation and tax-collectors, creation of offices, and victimisation by crown representatives. The governor, the Duc d'Epernon, was favoured by Mazarin, who looked upon his son as a possible in-law. But d'Epernon had incurred hatred in the Bordeaux region for adopting an overbearing manner, and an equally overbearing local mistress. His idea was to control and fortify locations on the rivers Dordogne and Garonne which would permit him at times of sedition to cut off the city's lines of supply, trade, and communication with neighbouring provinces. The Bordelais met force with force, improvising an army in imitation of the blockaded Parisians, attacking fortresses that hemmed them in, and presenting to d'Epernon the business-end of their muskets when he ventured in July 1649 to place the Bordeaux Parlement under a royal interdiction. Mediation achieved nothing. The Paris Parlement, harangued the following October by an uncompromising deputy from the Bordeaux Parlement, insisted on settlement of the province's affairs ahead of other matters. Mazarin happened at the time to be amenable to this demand. The Cardinal needed, temporarily, to keep on the right side of Condé, whose opinion of d'Epernon was low. Instead of being punished for armed resistance to the king in the person of his governor, the Bordelais were consequently gratified with a royal pardon and tax-concessions in December 1649. For five months Bordeaux simmered down, until Bouillon and La Rochefoucauld escorted Condé's wife and son to the city gates on 31st May 1650.

Agents of the Princes did their work of subversion so well that in next to no time the Bordeaux populace forced the hesitant municipal authorities to open the gates, the Bordeaux Parlement took the weeping Princesse de Condé and her son under its protection, and the presence of the declared traitors Bouillon and La Rochefoucauld was tolerated in the city. Raising money with which to fund troops was the next item on the rebels' agenda. The Princesse pawned her jewels, and Bouillon squeezed out of Spain an envoy bearing a modest contribution. The Bordeaux Parlementarians drew, or affected to draw, the line at playing host to an enemy of the king, but their dithering infuriated the rabble who cooped them at sword-point in their own meeting-place until a posse of *'bons bourgeois'* were summoned to the rescue. Enlightened by their experience, the Parlementarians took less than a fortnight to renew their official protection of the Princesse and her followers, impute all the province's ills to Mazarin, and order arms to be taken up (21st July). They made this diplomatic decision at the precise moment when their king was advancing steadily towards them.

Louis XIV was certainly getting to know his extensive realm at first hand. After the excursions to Normandy in February, and to Burgundy in March-April, he had been whisked off to the Picardy front once more by his mother at the beginning of June in the hope of putting heart into their under-subsidised troops, thinly deployed against Spanish armies swollen with reinforcements from Turenne. Amidst the gloom of chronic cash shortages, defecting soldiers, and Spanish sieges of French garrisons, came news of the downward spiral in Guyenne. Their Majesties returned to Paris on 29th June. On 4th July they departed for Bordeaux. Gaston d'Orléans was to hold the fort again, under the watchful eye of a then trusted royalist, Secretary of State for War Michel Le Tellier. Relatives and clients of front-rank Frondeurs were given a few more baubles (headship of finances, the admiralty, and the municipality of Paris) to keep them all occupied.

The royal party's journey south-westwards was stately and unhurried, a means of sounding the loyalty of other provinces traversed as well as giving Guyenne time to reconsider. The Bordelais were not, however, minded to repent. The Bordeaux Parlement, nervous of rough handling by the king, the partisans of Condé, or the mob, requested Louis to keep his distance so long as he was accompanied by Mazarin, protector of d'Epernon. The stand which they had taken was announced via their deputies in the capital to Gaston and to the Paris Parlement, where expressions of hostility towards Mazarin and calls for the liberty of the Princes were punctuating deliberations. To disarm the Bordeaux deputies and silence the Princes' loud speakers, Gaston took it upon himself to promise in public the recall of d'Epernon, plus a generous amnesty for Bordeaux, and safe conduct home for the rebel aristocrats whom the city was harbouring. Mazarin protested that the concessions were a bitter pill which Anne could hardly be brought to swallow. But digest it she had to. Royalist troops proved shamefully inadequate to the task of softening up Bordeaux, and Mazarin was desperate for money to keep them in action. Under cover of royal clemency and removal of all excuses from the rebels, the Cardinal suspended and re-suspended hostilities, remarking indignantly that Paris and Bordeaux were negotiating as if the king was nowhere in the vicinity. The breakthrough came on 22nd September 1650 when, as Pierre Lenet sourly explains in his memoirs, peace articles were accepted so that the *'bons bourgeois'* of Bordeaux could harvest their grapes in safety.

The queen and her prime minister tarried only a short while in Guyenne after the 'pacification' of Bordeaux, just long enough to receive hollow protestations of loyalty from the departing Princesse de Condé, Bouillon, and La Rochefoucauld, and a snub from the local Parlementarians who adamantly refused to pay respects to Mazarin on the occasion of the royal entry into the city (5th October). The manifest ill-will of the Bordelais, coming on top of all the emotional stresses of the last few years and the physical strain of shuttling up and down the realm, took its toll of menopausal Anne's health. She fell ill with what developed into a fever and persisted well after her delayed return to the capital in mid-November.

Gaston hesitated to go and greet his sick and dejected sister-in-law, knowing of her discontentment over his intervention in the Bordeaux talks, and envisaging possible arrest. The timorous prince's apprehension of sharing Condé's fate was being carefully magnified by Retz and his agents. The Coadjuteur had decided, on the pressing advice of his friends, as he takes pains to emphasise in his memoirs, that the time had come for him to think again about pursuing a cardinalship. Fulfilment of this ambition, nobly shelved during the Paris Blockade when 'the blood of the people' had to be defended, was now represented to him as the only means to protect himself from being duped, or worse, by a resentful Condé and an ungrateful Mazarin. Having sagaciously concluded that 'magnanimity is most praiseworthy but least merits taking to extremes', Retz permitted his friends to put out feelers in the direction of the government and the Princes while rendering Gaston suspicious of both these parties. The response from the government side, sounded out by the Duchesse de Chevreuse, was not promising. Mazarin was free enough with his offers of service, benefices, and money, but secretly determined not to put Retz on a par with himself. Châteauneuf, Keeper of the Seals, was also inclined to block Retz's promotion because, despite links with the Frondeurs and hostility towards Mazarin, he coveted that minister's political and ecclesiastical rank for himself. From the Princes' party Retz did not receive the rebuff that might have been expected in view of his support for Condé's arrest; their first priority was the Princes' release, which the talents of a recruit with his reputation seemed admirably suited to secure. In this camp Retz was called upon to treat with the Princesse Palatine whose extra-ordinary capacities he could admire almost on a level with his own. Originally destined for the cloister, the Princesse Palatine was a self-educated woman who had kept out of the political limelight until the arrest of her friend Condé galvanised her into action. She kept him supplied with news, correspondence, even weapons, during his detention; turned her house into an assembly-room for workers in his cause; and negotiated with anyone likely to be useful to him. Finding Mazarin reticent on the subject of liberating his prisoners, the Princesse aimed to force his hand by forming a powerful coalition between Frondeurs and Condéens. In conjunction with the Duchesse de Chevreuse and with Mme de Rhodes, a frenetic conspiratress distantly related to the Duchesse and beloved by Châteauneuf, the Princesse was putting the final touches to a marriage-deal. In seventeenth-century French society, marriage was arranged primarily with an eye to the standing and influence of future in-laws, the compatibility of the actual partners being more or less immaterial. The Fronde gave rise to a number of matrimonial projects (incidentally enhancing the importance of women, as marriage-brokers or bargaining-counters) in which this outlook was glaringly apparent. The Princesse Palatine's brainwave was one such, for it involved uniting the Duchesse de Chevreuse's beautiful and skittish daughter with Condé's weakly and mis-shapen brother Conti. However, Mlle de Chevreuse looked approvingly on the rank of her proposed fiancé, Conti was avowedly more interested in a prospective bride's connections than in her person, and Retz had other fish to fry, so the Princesse Palatine was able to make headway. By the time that she and her female collaborators had finished, a second marriage of convenience — between Condé's son and (any) one of Gaston's daughters — was resolved, together with financial profits for the mercenary Duchesse de Montbazon, a cardinal's hat for Retz, and the premiership for Châteauneuf. A clutch of agreements, tending to motivate everyone best equipped to free the Princes and destroy Mazarin, were thus formally signed by prickly personages with diverse interests. It was no mean feat of feminine diplomacy.

Feverish activity behind the scenes coincided with an all-out effort to swing public sympathy round to Condé at Mazarin's expense. A fortuitous attack by a band of thieves on the Duc de Beaufort's carriage as it was going to collect him from the Duchesse de Montbazon's house served to set the necessary wheels in motion while the queen was still wending her way painfully home from the Bordeaux expedition. Though the thieves maintained under the direst judicial torture that their motive was robbery, not political assassination, it suited Beaufort and his companions to clamour that Mazarin had tried to kill him. Less than a week later (4th November), oil paintings of the prime minister, with rope knotted round the neck-part, were found tied to posts in certain well-frequented thoroughfares of Paris. Placards underneath listed the crimes for which he had been 'executed', including assassination, and warned the bourgeois of Paris to beware of suffering the fate which Beaufort had just missed. On the day of Anne's arrival in the city (15th November), the Princes were transported to their third place of imprisonment, Le Havre, to lessen the risk of liberation-attempts. Engravings depicting Condé being led in triumph like a slave by his heavily-armed royalist escort went promptly on exhibition, and poetry was written about his pastime of tending potted carnations in his original prison at Vincennes, which became a tourist attraction. Before the hoped-for indignation had time to cool, Parlement was handed on 2nd December a petition from Condé's wife (drafted at the Princesse Palatine's house by Retz and some Parlement allies), asking for her husband to be guarded royally in the Louvre palace. Parlement deliberations on this request, and on a supporting one from Longueville's daughter, gave rise to more tirades against Mazarin. Even the corpse of Condé's mother, deceased on 2nd December also, was pressed into service. Pamphlets wrung hearts softened by tear-jerking funeral services and orations in honour of the lingeringly beautiful dowager who had been brought, sorrowing over the imprisonment of loved ones, to an exile's grave.

The monster with all the dastardly deeds to his credit withdrew, once more, from Paris to launder his public image. He betook himself to the province of Champagne where Turenne and the Spanish were preparing to repeat raids of the previous August which had carried them within easy striking-distance of the frightened capital. Injections of the Cardinal's cash and affability put the French army in a mood to recapture the town of Rethel from the enemy in four days and to beat back the superior forces of Turenne bringing tardy reinforcements. The plotters in Paris were aghast at the news. Their smear-campaign nevertheless bore fruit: not only did Mazarin receive scant praise for his part in the victory of Rethel, but the will to crush him redoubled. While he held the Princes' fate in the palm of his hand he was still in a position to do the crushing. It was vital, therefore, that he be relieved of the custody of the three prisoners. Foes of Mazarin and friends of Condé worked harder on the Paris Parlement whose leader, Molé, was inclined (under the influence of an ardent Condéen son) towards procuring freedom for the Princes, but only by legal means. Retz spoke, and there was light. On 30th December Parlement came to a formal decision on the Princesse de Condé's petition, exceeding her demands by a significant margin. Remonstrances were to be made to the king for the Princes' release, and Gaston was to be asked to add his intercession to obtain what was *justly* sought, the implication being that the regency government had committed an *injustice* in confining the princely trio to prison. Not unexpectedly, Parlement's decree was hurried into print and hawked around the streets of Paris.

1650 figures as the calmest of the Fronde years, by comparison with those which preceded and followed. After the January arrest of the Princes the only French news that could be qualified as headline was the short siege of Bordeaux and the sporadic invasions by Turenne. But the sterility of spectacular events was amply compensated by the fertility of undercover (often female) activity, strikingly illustrated by the resulting realignment of the core Frondeurs with the Princes' partisans and by the whitewashing of Condé in the public eye. Anne and Mazarin, unwilling to reside on top of the smouldering volcano that was Paris, had taken to the road again, this time for nearly three-quarters of the year, not counting Mazarin's trip to Champagne, which he spun out through the whole of December. But further family journeys in the near future were rendered impractical by Anne's delicate state of health; besides which, Mazarin logically had no reason to run away. If he could overthrow the combined might of Spain and Turenne, surely he could get the better of a bunch of boudoir intriguers?

* * * * * * * *

Chapter 5

ACT IV

Mazarin was in a quandary. He needed little perspicacity to see trouble brewing. The capital was bulging with an influx of individuals from the provinces, amongst whom were noblemen assembling with their Parisian peers to agitate for deliverance of the Princes and for convocation of the Etats Généraux as the machine through which state reform could be effected. Representatives of the Clergy, gathered in the city for their regular quinquennial Assembly, insisted on the release of Conti whom they counted as one of their number since he was titular head of some large abbeys. The Parlement, in the person of First President Molé, issued such blistering remonstrances to Anne d'Autriche over the Princes' captivity that the listening Louis XIV had a strong urge to eject him. Beaufort and Retz were giving the Palais-Royal a wide berth. Gaston blew cold and lukewarm. Mazarin's problem lay in discerning who would let fall on him the sword of Damocles. His usual attempts to gain time and dissolve opposition by means of parleys and promises could not undo the good work spearheaded by the Princesse Palatine and Retz in the second half of 1650. Nor could they offset the effects of the refusal, signified to Parlement by Anne on 30th January 1651, to free the Princes before the partisans of the latter disbanded.

It was Retz who cast the first stone, from behind someone else, according to his habits. The Coadjuteur had been sweating to obtain over Gaston d'Orléans something of the influence exercised in the 1640s by that prince's favourite, Abbé de la Rivière, fallen from grace in January 1650. Gaston's weak will, inconstancy, and cowardice made him a thoroughly unreliable ally, and in middle age he was manifesting symptoms of another infirmity which Retz found exceedingly trying: scruples. But his popularity with the people had not been recently compromised, like that of Condé, and he could speak more authoritatively in public as uncle of Louis XIV and lieutenant-general of the realm during the king's minority. Using Gaston's wife, the pro-Spanish Marguerite de Lorraine, to help him put some backbone into the flaccid prince, Retz finally got Gaston to agree to notify the Parlementarians of his unequivocal support for their stand in respect of the Princes. Gaston jibbed at personally making what amounted to a binding declaration against Mazarin, and therefore against Anne and Louis. So Retz 'exposed himself for the public good' (his words), and made the announcement for him on 1st February. He subsequently added, for greater effect, an embroidered report of Gaston's abrupt abandonment of Mazarin on hearing the Cardinal compare the French Parlement to the regicidal English Parliament and individual Frondeurs to so many Thomas Fairfaxes and Oliver Cromwells. Anne's immediate justification of her prime minister and indictment of Retz's incendiarism failed to bring round either Parlement or Gaston. With seemingly the whole of well-indoctrinated Paris, from the upper crust to the dregs, baying at his heels, Mazarin was ready to listen to falsely charitable advisers like the Duchesse de Chevreuse and Châteauneuf who urged him to decamp until the storm passed.

On the night of 6th-7th February he stole out of the Palais-Royal in disguise and rode for St-Germain, leaving Anne to cover his retreat, which she did with the same aplomb as in January 1649 when she herself was on the verge of flight. Bereft now of her most visible support, she came in for persistent harassment. Parlement added to its two previous demands, for the Princes to be released and proclaimed innocent, a third, for foreigners (even naturalised) to be barred from government. Noting that Mazarin was hastening slowly to leave the neighbourhood of Paris, and that Anne was non-committal about the duration of his absence, Parlement decreed (9th February) that he should be hunted down if he did not remove himself and his dependants from the country within a fortnight. Gaston, informed via the Châteauneuf-Chevreuse network of an authentic plan by Anne to take her elder son to rejoin the fugitive, gave way to his wife's insistence that the city gates nearest the Palais-Royal be secured, and instructed the captain of his personal guard to go and view the king in bed. Beaufort and other Frondeurs tightened the security-cordon with nocturnal patrols of cavalry round the palace. The king and his mother were to remain thus, under house-arrest, for over a month. Anne put on a brave face, despite her fears of being confined to a convent and having Louis XIV taken from her, propositions with which Retz was assailing Gaston. She managed to joke over the comfort of imprisonment in her own home, and to turn certain situations to her own advantage, for example by encouraging *'bons bourgeois'* to guard the city gates instead of rabble or Frondeurs, and by permitting members of the suspicious populace access to the king's bedchamber. To only a few faithfuls did she dare reveal her heartbreak, as in the anguished confession preserved by Mme de Motteville:

> I wish that it were always night, for though I cannot sleep, the silence and the solitude please me, because in the daylight I see only people who betray me.

Isolated and politically immobilised, Anne could only bow to the dictates of those responsible for her plight. On 11th February a deputation composed of La Rochefoucauld (newly received in Parlement as duke and peer), president Viole, and other representatives of the Princes, the Frondeurs, and the government, left Paris for Le Havre with orders to terminate the imprisonment of Condé, Conti, and Longueville. Their errand turned into something of a farce. Mazarin, in what his contemporaries saw as a desperate gamble to retain some of the credit for liberating the Princes, raced ahead of the deputation and carried out their mission a few hours before they arrived (13th February). The ridicule incurred by the Cardinal's lightning dash to offer unconditional freedom to men whom he had placed under lock and key, and would have kept there, was emphasised by the tongue-in-cheek promises of friendship with which they gratified their obsequious liberator. Three days later, bonfires were lit in the capital, albeit with less gusto than in January 1650, and the Princes entered on a whirl of embraces and compliments from their supporters. Gaston threw an élite stag party in their honour, at which toasts were drunk to the health of the king, and to a future without Mazarin.

But the Cardinal could not seem to get it into his head that his presence was no longer wanted. The 9th February decree expired and still he lingered within the frontier, as much because of genuine difficulty in finding a safe haven for himself and for the nieces with whom he was encumbered as because he hoped to be recalled. Anne herself was constrained to send and tell him to move further afield, whereupon he wrote her a clever letter in which, beneath expressions of absolute obedience and loyalty, he warned his enemies not to push him too far, given his knowledge of state secrets, the number of his friends, and the likelihood of adverse foreign reaction to his expulsion. Parlement tried to focus his thoughts by ordering on 11th March seizure of his person for trial, and an investigation into his handling of the king and of public affairs, the latter stipulation being a covert way of simultaneously undermining his supporters in the government. As an extra safeguard, Parlement registered on 19th April a royal declaration excluding from the king's councils not just foreigners but all cardinals. This proposal, inadvertently made by Broussel in the rush to kick Mazarin while he was down, dealt a death-blow to the ambitions of Retz and Châteauneuf, both of whom had their sights on the cardinalship and on the ministry. Informed opinion attributed to the intrigues of the outwardly uncomplaining Coadjuteur a formal protest from the assembled representatives of the Clergy about the dishonour to the Church and disservice to king and state done by the exclusion-clause. Peeved Parlementarians refused, however, to be sidetracked by the public reprimand, administered in the name of a long-standing rival power-block, and favourable to replacement of the very man whom they were still bending over backwards to expel.

By early April, Mazarin had found a tolerable bolt-hole, at Brühl near Cologne. Since his enemies could no longer object to his physical presence they bubbled with indignation over his continued political and moral presence, making itself felt via copious correspondence between Brühl and Paris. The content of the letters in question reveals that, contrary to propagandists and popular belief of the day, the exiled Mazarin's every word was not a law unto the queen regent. He did indeed try to carry on exercising his prime-ministerial functions from afar, preparing memoranda for Anne to read, listing possible candidates for posts and gratifications, offering advice on whom to trust, how to handle others, what steps to take to preserve themselves and the monarchy. But his advice was often ignored, judging from the more or less veiled criticisms and grumbles with which his letters to Anne and other confidant(e)s are sprinkled:

> You [the letter is addressed directly to Anne] cannot imagine the extent to which Sedan [code-name for Mazarin] is resigned to the wishes of 37 [code-figure for Anne]..., despite the little account taken hitherto of the advice of 200 [code-word for Mazarin]...;

> [To Anne again]...though it hurts him [Mazarin] to see that others, who do not possess as much zeal or capacity, prevent his advice from being taken into account, nevertheless...that in no way alters his belief that H [code-letter for Anne] is his greatest friend.

In a letter of September 1651 to his factotum Jean-Baptiste Colbert, destined to fame as the Cardinal's successor at Louis XIV's side, Mazarin put his finger on the problem:

> I observe more and more that little account is taken of what I write, either concerning the choice of persons or the decisions that must be made on many matters, because the Queen thinks that if I was on the spot and saw things at close quarters I would have a completely different opinion, and that is true to the extent that not only has she said it many times to Ondedei [a faithful Italian agent of Mazarin, recompensed with the bishopric of Fréjus in 1655], who has had the honour of conversing with her, apologising almost for not

following my advice in a lot of things, but She Herself has done me the
honour of writing to me in these terms...

On the eve of Mazarin's exile Anne may have promised, as he claims elsewhere in his
correspondence, not to take any vital decisions without first consulting him; but once
they were parted, the promise proved impossible to keep. Anne was in a tight corner,
literally — the guard on the Paris gates was not lifted until the end of March 1651 —
as well as metaphorically. With the political situation in Paris fluctuating to the
rhythm of innumerable intrigues she had to react much faster to keep pace than a
correspondence-course would permit, taking counsel from those who remained beside
her in the thick of events, since she habitually mistrusted her own judgement and had
not shaken off her distaste for mental fatigue. The apparent facility with which Anne
switched to other advisers lent substance to the Duchesse de Chevreuse's prediction
that Anne's attachment to Mazarin would not long survive his absence, and confirmed
Longueville's memorialist daughter (future Duchesse de Nemours) in her opinion that
'after the cardinal's departure, he and the Queen rarely acted in harmony, and were
often dissatisfied with one another'. Enforced separation of unforeseeable duration
had clearly placed the governing couple's relationship under a tremendous strain,
causing each to feel uneasy about the other's attitude and to put that feeling into
words. Yet despite the friction, Anne did not sever links with Mazarin, when political
expediency gave her every justification for doing so. She had once said that fidelity
and reliability in persons to whom she confided power enabled her to overlook their
human failings. Mazarin's demonstration of those two qualities over the previous
eight difficult years of regency government seemingly paid dividends at the
opportune moment.

Loyalty and dependability were not outstanding virtues in the leading contenders
for Mazarin's post, and he may well have benefited, in the queen regent's eyes, from
the contrast. Before Anne was let out of her palace-prison, Gaston and Condé
converged on her, with warnings of the violence that was sure to break out in the
capital if she failed to heed the call from the nobles' assemblies for convocation of the
Etats Généraux. Anne held out for a convocation-date fixed well after Louis XIV was
due to achieve his kingly majority on 6th September 1651, at which time he would be
in a position to overrule any legislation forcibly extracted from his mother. Gaston
and Condé wore her down to agreeing to 8th September, in return for which
concession they persuaded the assembling nobles to disperse and placated the
Assembly of Clergy. This thorny affair, in which the Second Estate momentarily
drew the First Estate into a formal coalition smacking of opposition to the crown, was
still being sorted out when Gaston, with Condé's approval, put in another demand. He
wanted the regent's entourage to be weeded of certain 'mazarins' to whom she lent a
ready ear: Secretary of State Michel Le Tellier; her household secretary, Hugues de
Lionne; the latter's uncle, Abel Servien; and an active 'postmistress' of the Cardinal,
Mme de Navailles. Her princely jailors' clumsy move to clear the way for their own
creatures helped Anne (and Mazarin) to grasp the necessity, argued by the 'mazarins'
in question, for a cabinet reshuffle which would allay suspicions about the exile's
return. Back into government came Chavigny (imprisoned for over five weeks in
September 1648) and Séguier (thrust aside to make way for Châteauneuf in March
1650), both held up by Anne as proof that she had no intention of recalling the prime
minister responsible for their political eclipse. Out went the veteran exile

Châteauneuf, whose guardianship of the royal seals was transferred to President Molé. Gaston fumed at being presented with a *fait accompli*. He detested Chavigny and could not stomach the idea of Molé simultaneously directing Parlement and holding a leading government office. Retz's consternation was equally patent. Sober Molé was no friend of his either, whereas womanising Châteauneuf had served as a useful link with the Duchesse de Chevreuse and with the host of satellite plotters revolving around her. The ugly little Coadjuteur suffered another setback on discovering that his ally Beaufort, whose blond tresses and slow wits he had hitherto excused in view of the duke's pliability, was no longer disposed to follow his call to arms. Beaufort, resentful of Retz's disinclination to confide in him fully, ranged himself alongside Condé, who squashed suggestions of violence to reverse the cabinet changes with a quip about 'chamber-pot warfare'. Beaufort's 'defection' and Condé's moderation rendered Gaston, with Retz at his back, none the less able to exact from Anne the sacrifice of Molé. Ten days after accepting the Seals, the First President quietly relinquished them (13th April) in favour of Séguier, and refused substantial compensation offered to him by the mortified regent.

Restraint generally disagreed with Condé, but he made no fuss over the ministerial recalls and dismissals because they had been decided with Anne in the course of negotiations which did not long remain secret. The prince had soon tired of fraternising with Retz's group. The Princesse Palatine's handiwork — the projected Conti-Chevreuse alliance — was brusquely destroyed, whereupon the piqued matchmaker offered her redoubtable talents to Mazarin, in return for the post of superintendent of the queen's household. But a prospective sister-in-law who had passed through the hands of Retz, and others, scarcely merited preference over richer prizes which Anne's intermediaries dangled before Condé: the governorship of Guyenne and financial satisfactions. Condé took Guyenne, while retaining certain fortresses in his existing governorship of Burgundy, and then held out his hand for the governorship of Provence for Conti. He pocketed money in thousands, then complained of over two millions of debts incurred in the king's service. Seeing the impossibility of contenting the insatiable prince, Anne and her advisers made advances towards Retz and his circle, who were still digesting the rejection of Mlle de Chevreuse. Anne took the trouble to confer personally with the wily Coadjuteur because both she and Mazarin suspected that her chief negotiators leaned towards Condé. She found the 'veritable demon', as the Coadjuteur said that she archly called him to his face, willing to countenance Mazarin's recall on two conditions: nomination as a cardinal and as a government minister; and freedom to publicly malign Mazarin in order to retain influence with the populace. The co-operation of Retz's intimates was made worthwhile with glib promises: the premiership for Châteauneuf, a ducal son-in-law (i.e. a nephew of Mazarin, promoted) for the Duchesse de Chevreuse, etc. The pact-makers recognised that Condé stood in the way of their plans, and must be removed, by re-arrest at least.

News of the conferences between Anne's party and Retz's was leaked to Condé, indirectly, by Hugues de Lionne, Anne's own retainer. Since his release the apprehensive prince had kept a close look-out for signs of re-imprisonment, which, now more than ever, he was courting by his acquisitiveness and general absenteeism from the royal presence. When, therefore, he heard a misleading report about royal guardsmen marching in the direction of his Paris residence, he bolted overnight with his brother, sister, and wife to the château of St-Maur-des-Fossés near the Bois de Vincennes (6th July). In written communications to Parlement and in verbal retorts to envoys of Anne, he dictated the terms on which he would resume his duties at Their Majesties' side: definitive exile of Mazarin and removal from office of the latter's three 'valets', that is to say, Le Tellier, Lionne, and Servien. Ironically, the loyalty of all three of these men had become suspect to Mazarin, and Anne was not heartbroken to see Lionne and Servien fall victim to the intrigues of Chavigny and others who wanted to take over their functions. Their administrative capacities were, however, of a high order, and while consenting to their exile (20th July) Anne was secretly resolved not to fill their vacated posts with permanent replacements. Condé had expected more resistance from Anne, and finding none, had to cast around hurriedly for another pretext to keep his distance. Honouring Parlement with the visit that he refused to pay to the Palais-Royal, the prince delivered himself awkwardly of his umpteenth demand, for Le Tellier, Lionne, and Servien to be included in the declaration forbidding Mazarin's re-entry into office. President Molé's vigorous reply invited him to think about giving satisfaction rather than asking for it. But it was nearly a fortnight before the presidential exhortations took some effect and Condé suffered Gaston to lead him to Anne and Louis for a short interview (3rd August).

The courtesy call solved nothing and was not repeated. Condé rode around Paris with an escort fit for a king, while Anne seethed and despaired. Retz and his familiars proposed a non-violent remedy for her frustration: publication of a catalogue of Condé's offences wrapped up in the form of a royal declaration banishing Mazarin from France forever. The advice suited Anne, but Gaston, perplexed as usual over which side to support, upset the apple-cart by sending a written justification of Condé's actions to Parlement, only two days after the sovereign courts had received the king's condemnation of those same actions on 17th August. Gaston's tergiversation facilitated Condé's task of rebutting before Parlement charges meant to stick. Parlement investigations over the previous few months into Mazarin's activities and agents had afforded the presiding magistrates occasional laughs on account of the triviality of accusations made. But participants in the deliberations over Condé's comportment were tense and tight-lipped. Trouble was expected between Condé and Retz, who were at daggers drawn because of Retz's recent manoeuvres at the Palais-Royal. On 21st August the prince and the Coadjuteur each brought a large protective retinue to the Palais de Justice, filling the approach to the Grand'Chambre with armed men on battle-alert. In the confusion which followed, La Rochefoucauld, on his own admission, took it into his head to rid Condé of the troublesome priest for good. According to Retz's version of the affray, La Rochefoucauld trapped him by the neck between two flaps of a door as both of them were trying to respond to Parlementarians' pleas for evacuation of intruders, and for some terrifying moments the prelate's hind quarters were exposed to the swords and pistols of Condé's excited followers. The intervention of President Molé's son, a Condéen capable of imitating paternal magnanimity, transformed what might have been an ignominious blood-letting into an exchange of insults between the released victim and the thwarted aggressor. The very next day, a providential street-encounter between Retz in procession with his *curés*, and Condé in his carriage with La Rochefoucauld, gave the Coadjuteur a chance to demonstrate to the public at large that his spirit had not been crushed along with his surplice. Condé alighted, but only to sink piously down on bended knee, whereupon Retz obliged him with a benediction and a deep bow, 'so great was the Christian humility of the one and the pastoral charity of the other', remarked an undeceived contemporary.

As if unwilling to be outdone in play-acting, Anne gave Parlement a declaration against Mazarin to read out on 6th September. A separate declaration of Condé's innocence was reserved until the morrow, the fateful 7th on which Louis XIV, purposefully controlling his frisky horse, rode in gold-embroidered state to Parlement for the proclamation of his majority. Condé was insultingly absent from amongst the princes and dignitaries who lined up behind Anne and Gaston to pay homage. His modesty suffered, he wrote lamely to Louis, at the thought of having to sit through a public reading of the declaration in his favour. A more solid justification for absenteeism was the promotion, which accompanied the royal majority, of parties uncongenial to the prince: the elevation of Châteauneuf to presidency of royal councils; the reinstatement of Molé as Keeper of the Seals; the restoration to office of a superintendent of finances in the 1620s, the ageing Marquis de La Vieuville, whose son had sensibly captivated the string-pulling Princesse Palatine. Least palatable to Condé, perhaps, was the nomination of Retz, with Mazarin's overt approval, to the cardinalship.

Condé's withdrawal from Paris on the eve of Louis XIV's official assumption of power was not the decisive break that it appeared to be. He hovered near enough to the capital to be contacted by bearers of acceptable peace propositions, though these were delayed, either by accident, or by design on the part of Gaston, relieved at the removal of an oppressive presence. According to memorialists best placed to know the underside of events, Condé had no active desire to make war. Nor had the majority of his inner circle, with one marked exception, his own sister. The adulterous Duchesse de Longueville feared maltreatment from her husband if stable conditions forced her to rejoin him in his governorship of Normandy, and preferred to preserve her liberty at the cost of counselling rebellion. Her lover La Rochefoucauld, the prime mover and chronicler of events in Condé's camp at this stage, had no option but to support her stand, or so he affirms in memoirs composed after the end of the amorous liaison, and weaker admirers like Conti posed no obstacle. Condé's better judgement is thus represented as having succumbed to the onslaught of the principal members of his entourage, who insured themselves against any backsliding on his part by privately agreeing that in the event of his making a separate compact with the government they would unite in a 'third party' under Conti's leadership. The seventeenth-century mentality liked to shift at least partial responsibility for the crimes and errors of the great onto self-interested counsellor figures, and was steeped in classical and scriptural examples of mighty men brought to ruin by scheming women. Judgements of Condé, whose warrior-halo dazzled even his enemies, and of his sister, whose disdainful beauty irritated some as much as it fascinated others, were possibly coloured by this outlook. What is certain is that for a hero dragged by a conspiracy of lesser mortals into waging treasonable war against his will, Condé made his preparations with customary decisiveness and thoroughness. Previous allies of importance — Longueville and Turenne — were not keen to rejoin him; so La Rochefoucauld was set to work on enticing replacement nobles to lend their sword-arm. Towns which declared for the prince — Bourges (capital of his governorship of Berry) and Bordeaux in the first instance — were honoured with his personal presence. Sums of tax-money destined for the royal coffers were seized in the provinces and used by his agents to assemble troops. The faithful Lenet was directed towards Spain, with instructions to secure a treaty. Nor did Condé overlook the detail of leaving a 'back door' open to a renewal of negotiations with the government.

Deliberations in the king's camp as to where to strike at Condé in order to stem the damage that he was doing to finances and morales resulted in the decision which Louis XIV himself favoured: to dislodge the Condéens from Bourges and then to march on Bordeaux, where Condé had been rapturously received by the inhabitants. The young king's hunch proved to be correct. On 8th October he entered Bourges, hastily vacated by Conti, the Duchesse de Longueville, and a pockmarked supporter, the Duc de Nemours, who all thought it high time to pay a surprise visit to Bordeaux. Louis, Anne, and their retinue moved to winter quarters in Poitiers, nearer to the centre of military operations, while the appointed leader of the royal army in Guyenne, the barrel-shaped Comte d'Harcourt, harassed the rebel troops with a zeal whetted by Condé's publicised mockery of his figure. Victories did not come as easily as usual to the prince whom Retz qualified (in retrospect) as 'the greatest captain in the world, without exception'. He was in the, for him, novel situation of fighting with raw recruits; and against his own compatriots. Some disquieting reinforcements nevertheless arrived at Bordeaux, including a small fleet from Spain, and a crack contingent of infantry and cavalry detached from the French army in Catalonia by its pro-Condé commander. The royal riposte was to issue an indictment of the prince's treason, finally pushed through the Paris Parlement on 4th December, and reiterated orders for the recall of Mazarin.

The Cardinal, though worried about being supplanted in the queen's good graces by the experienced Châteauneuf, was equally concerned not to give his enemies any opportunity to proclaim that hopes of restoring peace to the realm had been sacrificed on his account. He edged his way back slowly towards France, collecting an army en route. News of his advance, deliberately relayed by the jittery Gaston, spread fears that some signal vengeance was about to fall upon Paris or its Parlement, fears which increased when President Molé and top finance officials obeyed a peremptory summons to rejoin the king at Poitiers. To halt the bogeyman in his tracks, Parlement improved on the ferocious decree that had marked a similar moment of panic on 8th January 1649. Whoever brought Mazarin to justice, 'dead or alive', was now assured, on 29th December 1651, of a fabulous reward, to be raised by commandeering the victim's revenues and selling his library of some forty thousand books.

'Thus ended the year 1651, in an incredible confusion on all sides, each trying to achieve his ends by any means, even by deceiving his companion.' Recent events had given *'bons bourgeois'* like the one who penned that summary just cause for bewilderment and moral indignation. The positions of leading protagonists in the conflict had seesawed dramatically: first Mazarin's flight and Condé's return, then Condé's flight and Mazarin's return; Gaston, aptly nicknamed 'L'Incompréhensible', kneeling to kiss Louis XIV's hand in homage only a few months after imprisoning him; government men promoted one minute, demoted the next; Parlement simultaneously waiting on the king and proscribing his prime minister. Cracks had appeared in seemingly cast-iron alliances, causing universal concern to secure ports against impending storms, even if that meant treating with enemies while vilifying them before friends. Mazarin could fairly claim, in circular letters distributed amongst the populace, that his absence had plunged France deeper into chaos. But would his reappearance, with an army at his back, restore any measure of harmony and order?

* * * * * * *

Chapter 6

ACT V

Considering that Mazarin had been expressly designated as an Undesirable upon whom it was not only legal but gainful to lay violent hands, he had a remarkably smooth re-entry into France. The Paris Parlement did indeed commission a few of its members to organise the demolition of bridges on his route, but one was taken prisoner and another narrowly escaped capture by the soldiers of the Maréchal d'Hocquincourt, who was waiting with several other governors of frontier fortresses to salute the Cardinal on his arrival in the province of Champagne. When Gaston d'Orléans tried to exploit this outrage to provoke Parlement into countenancing seizure of public funds to pay for troop-levies, he ran into objections, phrased in defence of the king's prerogatives, but based on fears of *rentes* and office-holders' wages going unpaid. The only man militarily capable of persuading the well-escorted exile to turn tail — Condé — was busy skirmishing in the south-west, stalked by the tenacious Harcourt. Mazarin thus marched unopposed to Poitiers where, on 28th January 1652, took place the reunion which Anne d'Autriche had given so many solemn undertakings never to permit.

The Cardinal resumed his political harness as though he had never divested himself of it. Châteauneuf, well over seventy, took early retirement. Le Tellier had already been recalled, and another efficient administrator who had suffered for his connection with the Cardinal, Servien, rejoined the royal party as it retraced its steps in the direction of Paris. The main object of what looked like a surprising decision to give the rebellious south-west a respite was to tackle urgent threats to royal authority nearer to the capital. Maréchal d'Hocquincourt's troops made fairly short work of the efforts of the governor of Anjou, the Duc de Rohan-Chabot, to secure that province for Condé. But even while they were doing so, an armed force in the pay of the king of Spain was marching behind Condé's supporter the Duc de Nemours from Flanders towards the Seine.

Representations on these matters which the king sought to make to Parlement were eluded or overruled by the natural eloquence of his uncle Gaston, who had been moved by Mazarin's progress to sign a formal treaty of union with Condé towards the end of January. By dint of evasion Gaston hoped to give the Flanders army time to get within close proximity of Paris, to reinforce it with troops of his own under the command of Beaufort, and to keep the king at a healthy distance. Everything began to go according to plan. In the first week of March, Nemours was able to cross the Seine at Mantes unchecked, owing to the connivance of the town's governor, who happened to be a son-in-law of the disgruntled ex-Keeper of the Seals, Séguier. Louis XIV, by contrast, was refused entry to Gaston's apanage of Orléans, vacillating inhabitants of which were encouraged to keep their city gates shut by a distribution of bribes and by a vigorous harangue from Gaston's eldest daughter, the Duchesse de Montpensier, newly arrived (27th March) amidst a cavalcade of noblewomen fittingly dressed as amazons. With Beaufort and Nemours in attendance, the elated Duchesse sat down to a council of war. At that point the rebel princes' plans suffered a setback.

Though Nemours was married to Beaufort's sister, the two men were jealous and contemptuous of one another. Tempers flared and blows were almost exchanged. The Duchesse calmed the two belligerents, temporarily; within a few months Nemours would die by Beaufort's hand. The quarrel showed up the fragility of the princely coalition and emphasised the need for a strong, authoritative presence to maintain some degree of unity amongst headstrong aristocrats. The Duchesse de Montpensier, a wilful and imperious female, mistrusted by her father, could not hope to keep order in the rebel camp for long. Only with Condé's eagle eye around the place was there a chance of preventing further fatal dissensions and possible defections. The prince was therefore persuaded to abandon the relative safety of his provincial strongholds and to make for Paris, around which the struggle for supremacy was converging.

Not that he was particularly sorry to leave. The war of attrition being waged against him by Harcourt was denying him opportunities to repeat the feats of arms which had nurtured his reputation in the past. The extension of hostilities into provinces bordering on Guyenne brought him more military humiliations than successes, and he was losing his hold on Bordeaux, where open friction between his brother and sister fostered the development of factions within the local Parlement and amongst the populace. Gaston and Retz could not be trusted to resist any royal peace overtures made at his expense, another good reason for Condé to show his face in the capital. So the pamphleteers in his employ prepared for the master's coming, straining to rouse the masses to decisive action:

Let us not pretend any longer; the grandees make sport of our patience; and because we put up with everything, they think they have the right to make us suffer everything. Let us take off the mask; the present situation demands it. Let us see that the grandees are only grand because we carry them on our shoulders. We have only to shake them off to strew the ground with them, and to strike a concerted blow that will be forever on men's lips. After noting which party [i.e. Condé's or Mazarin's] we plan to reinforce by a general uprising, let us massacre the other without respecting great or small, young or old, males or females, so that not even a single one remains to bear its name. Let us spread the alarm in all quarters, hang chains across the streets, rebuild the barricades, unsheathe swords; let us kill, pillage, destroy, and sacrifice to our revenge everyone who will not join in the crusade to signal the freedom party.

These, and other incendiary devices of the same kind, were successful in amassing on the Pont-Neuf, over which Condé was expected to pass on his April arrival in Paris, a rowdy welcoming party of five to six thousand persons, mostly vagabonds and craftsmen taking an Easter holiday, but with a hard core of armed men under instructions from agents of the rebel princes to cause mayhem. They proceeded to do precisely that when the hero did not materialise. Passers-by were molested and forced to shout anti-Mazarin slogans, while a pro-Mazarin secretary of state had his town house vandalised with axes and hammers. After the consecrated night's rest, the rioters were disposed to recommence, but were deterred by troops wearing Gaston's liveries. The hanging of one of the ringleaders, a mason, comforted persons of quality with the thought that a semblance of law and order was being maintained.

Condé did not manifest himself, grimy and long unshaven, to his Paris fans until 11th April, just over a week after the riots in his honour. Following a hazardous dash across France he had gone straight to join the Nemours-Beaufort army, with whose assistance he had quickly struck terror into the hearts of what were labelled Mazarin's, not the king's, troops. In a series of combats around Bléneau (Burgundy) he had fought for the first time against his military equal Turenne, whose skill in strategy saved heavy loss of life, though not of baggage, on the part of the fleeing royalist army. It was on a wave of victory, therefore, that the prince swept back into the capital, albeit that the victory had stained his hands with French blood, a fact which was pointed out to his face when he and Gaston touted for support in the sovereign courts. Forced to lend colour to his pamphleteers' portrayal of him as the saviour of the city from imminent blockade by Mazarin, the ex-blockader of Paris bit his lip and affirmed that he would lay aside his arms as soon as Mazarin and all the latter's 'adherents' departed from the realm. His once-bitten listeners were still not satisfied, until the prince consented to drop the loaded word 'adherents', applicable in effect to the queen herself or any members of her entourage, and to repeat his declaration before a Town Hall assembly of representatives drawn from all quarters of the city. With the benefit of hindsight, Retz criticised Condé's meekness before the sovereign courts as being a dangerous incitement to lack of respect and to resistance. He also blamed Condé for paying insufficient attention to curbing the rise in street violence, which burst out again at the end of the month when 'an infinite number of rogues' assailed with fists, stones, and staves no less a personage than the *prévôt des marchands* and an escort of *échevins*. Acting in the name of Condé, even when his agents were not spurring them on, the mobsters spread fear of the prince in the *'bons bourgeois'* circles which he needed to conciliate, obliged him to make embarrassing public disavowals of rowdyism, and gave Parlement a pretext to issue decrees of repression which were not in his interests.

The art of being a party-leader, with all that it implied in the way of deft manipulation of people, patient parleying, and eloquent speech-making, was not Condé's strong point. He preferred to leave diplomatic niceties to others, whose qualifications were not always instantly apparent. His (and the Duc de Nemours'...) latest passion, the beguiling Duchesse de Châtillon, thus joined the would-be peacemakers thronging around Louis XIV in the royal refuge of St-Germain. Mazarin, the canal through whom all delegates were being constrained to pass, flattered the jealous beauty's secret desire to steal the limelight from the Duchesse de Longueville, fed her with empty promises, and used her to keep Condé inactive in Paris while plans to overwhelm his army were put into operation.

Condé's forces had been encamped for several weeks at Etampes, on the route from Paris to Orléans. Manoeuvres by the royalist army had failed either to entice or drive them away from their profitable occupation of stripping the fertile locality and its inhabitants of all they possessed. In late May, Turenne presented himself, equipped for a siege, before the town. His young king made an appearance beside him, 'like a rising sun' enthused one diarist, anticipating the imagery that was to be inseparable from the name of Louis XIV. But the sun had to sink into the distance when enemy cannon-fire got too close for comfort, and a week later (7th June) the siege was raised. Turenne's withdrawal was precipitated by the intrusion of a buffoonish personage: Charles, Duc de Lorraine, brother-in-law of Gaston. Charles had been dispossessed of his dukedom by Louis XIII and Richelieu after his sister's clandestine marriage to Gaston in 1632, and had taken to living the life of a glorified bandit, roaming round central Europe with a wolfish army whose services he placed at the disposal of the highest bidder, normally a Habsburg ruler. With a little prompting from the Spanish, who continued to nibble away at French border possessions in the background, Charles bethought himself to lend assistance to Gaston and Condé in relieving Etampes. The Lorrainer army and its omnivorous camp-followers lurched across Champagne, picking the province clean as it went. The Parisian populace gave its leader a tumultuous welcome regardless, and Gaston, Condé, and Beaufort fell over themselves to do him honour. Charles excelled himself at playing the fool, but he had an eye to business. Confiding the command and the lives of his ruffians, his sole money-spinner, to Condé, who possessed some of his confiscated domain, did not appeal. His uncertainty and resentment provided an opening for the Duchesse de Chevreuse, an old flame, allied by marriage to the house of Lorraine, to make a proposition from Louis XIV to reinstate Charles in his territories and lift the siege of Etampes provided that the duke took his horde back to whence they came. Charles grasped the face-saving offer, but needed steering in the direction of the Low Countries by the menacing advance of Turenne's army.

The intervention of the Lorrainers sent the already acute level of hardship and misery soaring to a fresh peak. France seemed doomed to become a vast wasteland, after swarm upon swarm of troops of all denominations had sated their locust-appetites in strategic provinces and were now closing in on the capital. The author of a popular rhymed gazette of the day, Jean Loret, likened the soldiery to

> ... furious torrents
> Which murmuringly destroy
> Houses, fields, woods, meadows, and vines
> And don't even spare the nobility.

Loret was referring specifically to foreign mercenaries like the Lorrainers, the Flemish, and the Germans, who were the most dreaded for their brutality. But Condé's and Gaston's troops, in their efforts to control all avenues of approach to Paris, were ravaging the surrounding countryside, burning bridges, looting private houses, and holding individuals, including nobles, to ransom 'with as much impunity as if they had been in a conquered land'. As for the king's men, striving to clear a path for him between St-Germain and Paris,

> ... they did great damage everywhere, pillaging the houses of all sorts of persons; and the terror was so great that all the peasants within a ten-league radius of Paris withdrew into that city with their movable goods and domestic animals.

Though seventeenth-century testimonies such as these make it clear that members of the upper strata of society were harmed, in their properties if not in their persons, as a result of troop-movements, the suffering endured by the peasants and their urban equivalents was infinitely worse. Two days after the departure of the Lorrainers, a general assembly was held in the Paris Parlement (18th June) to work out how to continue to cope with the city's estimated 100,000 poor, whose numbers were increasing daily. There did indeed exist an abundance of charitable fervour in the capital, ably stimulated and directed by the ubiquitous priest (St) Vincent de Paul and by devout associations of which the secretive Compagnie du Saint-Sacrement was one of the most energetic. The Compagnie had branches in provincial cities, and Vincent de Paul stretched his network of male and female helpers as widely as possible in town and countryside. But tales of horror kept pouring in, of ravenous peasants trying to crop grass and tree-bark, gnawing at their own clothes, and sometimes even their own flesh.

The nightmare had no foreseeable end in the summer of 1652. Recourse was had to St Geneviève, patron saint of Paris, whose relics it was customary in dire emergencies to carry in procession to the cathedral of Notre-Dame; but the solemnity of the occasion, on 11th June, was offset by the hypocritical capers of a rosary-waving Condé and Beaufort who rushed to smother the passing reliquaries with kisses. Overt and covert negotiations between St-Germain and Paris dragged on. Illustrious persons offered their services as mediators: the exiled Charles II of England and his French mother Henriette; Queen Christina of Sweden. Louis XIV affirmed his decision not to withdraw his troops from around Paris until his enemies had done likewise. Gaston and Condé vowed to lay down their arms the instant that Mazarin departed. The king tossed the ball back into their court by agreeing to let Mazarin retire provided that the princes indicated in detail, at a conference, how they would disengage themselves from commitments made to their foreign and French allies. Gaston fell ill, a habit of his whenever he wished to postpone an awkward debate in Parlement. Beaufort contributed to disrupt talks, from which he felt that he had been insultingly omitted, by assembling a throng of roughs in the Place Royale and preaching spoliation of all the 'mazarins'. He was also under strong suspicion of provoking a wave of assaults on Parlementarians. In an ugly incident on 25th June magistrates trying to slip unobtrusively away from the Palais de Justice were mauled by an armed mob comprising local artisans exasperated by a decline in business for which Parlement's pretensions were blamed. The battered Parlementarians had just voted an affirmative response to the king's peace-conference initiative.

Very soon, the name of Condé himself stood defiled by accusations of terrorism. His position at this stage was frustrating. His agents were unable to get his peace-terms accepted by the evasive Mazarin, not surprisingly, since it was a question of satisfying a grasping prince plus clients and supporters, who included a whole province (Guyenne) and a foreign realm (Spain). Hopes of improving his bargaining-strength through (a decisive) military action receded when his army was intercepted by Turenne as it skirted Paris on a nocturnal march from St-Cloud to Charenton. In a murderous combat in the Faubourg St-Antoine (2nd July) Condé's men were saved from annihilation by the composure of their leader and by the resolution of Gaston's irrepressible daughter, the Duchesse de Montpensier, who defied the king's exhortations to keep the city gates closed, and had the Bastille cannons fired on royal troops to cover her allies' retreat. The bravery of Condé and his aristocratic lieutenants (Nemours counted thirteen blows to his body and weapons; La Rochefoucauld paraded a musket-holed face...) caused in the prowess-loving Parisians an upsurge of sympathy on which it was vital to trade. The opportunity to do so was furnished by a meeting at the Hôtel de Ville on 4th July to discuss security-measures in the capital. Several hundred lay and ecclesiastical delegates, the cream of

the Paris citizenry, were summoned. Whoever had these heads of the community
under his control could reckon on dealing his opponents some stinging blows.
Condé and Gaston exerted what influence they could over the election of the
delegates and hand-picked the soldiery set to guard the Hôtel and adjoining square,
the ill-omened Place de Grève, where public executions were carried out. A password
was issued ('Vive Roger!'), and pieces of straw, a newly-invented rallying-sign of the
princes, were pressed by the soldiers upon the arriving dignitaries. Gaston and Condé
delayed their own arrival until the late afternoon in order to curtail debating time, and
bade the company a brusque farewell when they heard talk of sending a deputation to
the king. The departing princes' expressions of discontentment brought into play the
sharpshooters and *agents provocateurs* waiting with an impatient crowd in the square
outside. Volleys of musket-shots splattered against the windows of the Hôtel de Ville,
and all the doors were set on fire. The terrified delegates inside the building paused
to make confessions of sins to the religious personnel in their midst before fleeing to
barricade themselves in inner rooms or braving the flames, the gunfire, and the loot-
hungry mob. Miraculously, some lived to tell the tale, by dint of paying hefty
ransoms and signing a document of union between Paris and the princes. Beaufort
sauntered around late at night, with the Duchesse de Montpensier in tow, to inspect the
afternoon's work and to accept the ready resignation of the near-roasted *prévôt des
marchands*. Gaston and Condé had remained impassive in the face of appeals to
intervene. Thinking people were shocked. For once, they were hard put to pass off
the massacre as one of Mazarin's deep-laid plots. On the other hand, it seemed
incredible to have to attribute responsibility to either of the two princes of the blood
royal, one renowned for his poltroonery and distaste for violence, the other vaunted
for his deeds of valour. Perhaps princely instructions to sway the delegates had been
misunderstood or taken too far? By whom? Beaufort sprang to mind; and as if to
confirm his nonchalance towards blood-shedding, he shot dead his own brother-in-
law Nemours in a duel at the end of July. Those closest to the princes erected a wall
of silence. La Rochefoucauld pretended in his memoirs that he had no idea how the
trouble started or who gave the orders. The Duchesse de Montpensier stated
categorically in hers that she was glad not to know the truth of the matter.

The Town Hall Massacre had two immediate effects. It extinguished sympathy
for Condé, who protested his innocence too much; and it illuminated the objectives of
the instigators. The civic headship of Paris, relinquished under duress by the *prévôt
des marchands*, passed directly into the hands of Broussel. The governorship of the
city, abandoned by the royalist Maréchal de l'Hôpital after a brush with death in the
Town Hall inferno, went to Beaufort. The master-stroke was saved till last. On 20th
July Parlement pretexted Louis XIV's 'detention' by Mazarin to proclaim Condé
military supremo under Gaston, to whom were restored the powers of lieutenant-
general of the realm which had officially ended at the king's majority. The new
ruling junto in the capital had now only to put into effect the immense authority
which they possessed on paper.

That task promised to be arduous. The provinces showed minimal interest in
Gaston's elevation. He remembered only one provincial governor bothering to reply
to his information circular; the large towns were reticent; and the Parlements, with the
exception of that of Bordeaux, would not give unqualified support to the July decree.
The amount of respect which he commanded in the capital was illustrated by quarrels

of precedence amongst those aristocrats whom he invited to become members of his council, and by the refusal of the citizen militia to stand guard at the hanging of two convicted Town Hall arsonists. Every enactment of the Parlement and the Hôtel de Ville which he and Condé inspired, including the declaration of his own lieutenant-generalship, was promptly annulled by the king's own council. Louis XIV had moved with his mother and godfather north-west of the capital to Pontoise in mid-July, when a Spanish army began pouring over the northern frontier. He ordered the Paris Parlement to his side. Approximately thirty magistrates obeyed. The public then witnessed a fresh round of combat, by decrees, as each half of the split Parlement nullified the other. The Parlementarians at the Pontoise end contrived to convince Mazarin privately that his withdrawal would undermine the princes, and to petition the king publicly for his removal. Louis, by prior arrangement with the Cardinal, consented. King and minister both left Pontoise on 19th August, the former to march towards invaded Picardy, the latter to enter on a second exile in the (Belgian) province of Liège.

Though plenty were sceptical about seeing the last of Mazarin, Louis XIV had ostensibly made the sacrifice for which loyal, let alone disloyal, subjects had never-endingly campaigned. He had simultaneously cut the ground from under the feet of Gaston and Condé who had made their submission conditional upon Mazarin's removal and who suddenly lost all justification for their July promotion. The lieutenant-general and his second-in-command tried stalling. They reiterated their intention to disarm, but only on the presupposition that Mazarin's exit from the realm was 'effective', and followed by an amnesty, withdrawal of royal troops to frontier areas, and safe conduct for departing Spanish allies. The publication of an amnesty on 26th August satisfied neither the Parlementarians in Paris (it emanated from the rival Pontoise Parlement) nor the princes (it required them to renounce all hostilities and subversive alliances within three days, and did not cover participants in the 25th June or 4th July riots). Now it was their turn to endeavour to draw the king to the conference-table, or at least, to embroil him in protracted correspondence.

Louis XIV was not in a position to shilly-shally. A large plundering army had Paris in its sights: the Duc de Lorraine had come ferreting round with a German ally for another fruitful pay-off. Habsburg armies were snapping back outposts which the French had fought tooth and nail to conquer and maintain in recent decades. Gravelines and nearby Dunkirk, Casale (a gateway to northern Italy), and Barcelona (capital of Catalonia, which was governed by a French viceroy), all surrendered into enemy hands between May and October 1652. Just when there was a crying need for experienced generals to reverse the demoralising trend, the Comte d'Harcourt abandoned command of the royal army in Guyenne and threw himself into Brisach, a bridgehead on the Rhine of which he fancied the governorship. A different kind of pressure was being applied to the king by well-intentioned Parisians. Around a nucleus of clerics and *'bons bourgeois'* heartily sick of the convulsions of the last four years and severely shaken by the Town Hall Massacre, there was growing a movement pledged to bring about the king's safe return to the capital and the restoration of peace. The most informative seventeenth-century historian of the movement, the Franciscan Father Berthod, tells how he and like-minded persons, liaising with Le Tellier and Servien in the king's entourage, worked to impress the peace-message upon the populace, using persuasion, money, and female activists, who could be expected to enjoy a greater measure of impunity than male counterparts if detected. Louis went so far as to sign a risky authorisation (17th September) for loyal Parisians to get together, arm and lay hands on their oppressors. Loyalists wearing paper in their hats to distinguish themselves from their straw-carrying opponents held a rally at the Palais-Royal (24th September). Attendance was sufficiently impressive to worry Gaston into banning any further rallies. But his gesture was that of a King Canute. The idea of urging the king to come back where he belonged had taken off in a big way. Ironically, Gaston had not long given the nod to his opportunist confidant Retz to renounce a spell of philosophical inaction and lead a deputation of ecclesiastics to harangue Louis...on the duties of a monarch. Then a deputation from the most prestigious of the city's trade-guilds had to be allowed to make the same trip. Then *another* deputation, of citizen-militia officers... To the returning militia-men was entrusted the escort of the dispossessed city governor and *prévôt des marchands*, symbolic forerunners of the return of legitimate authority.

Condé preferred not to wait to see what fate the king might have in mind for him. After farewell rows with Gaston and with Chavigny, he turned a, for once, smartly dressed back on Paris (13th October), leaving his guest the Duc de Lorraine to tag along behind. Chavigny, reproached for disloyalty, had a fatal seizure (11th October). Gaston, thicker-skinned, stayed put in his palace until the king's entry into Paris (21st October) and had to be dislodged by a threat of arrest. Thoughtfully, Retz glided into the breach, and stood waiting to do the honours as the royals alighted at the Louvre.

Installation at the Louvre revealed what smiles, compliments, and shouts of 'Vive le Roi' masked. The ancient royal residence-cum-fortress was more easily defensible than newer palaces like the Palais-Royal where Louis and his mother had spent some of their most agonising moments. The king could not trust his 'good city of Paris', still feverish from its recent bout of rebellion. To lower the temperature, he administered some calmatives. The breakaway Parlementarians of Paris, with the exception of certain notorious rebels like Broussel and Viole, were ordered to attend a *lit de justice* at the Louvre on 22nd October. They went in contentious mood, criticising the terms of a second royal amnesty while awaiting the sovereign's presence. Louis, significantly attended by men promoted to the rank of marshal instead of by the hereditary dukes and peers customary on such occasions, is said to have had indignation written all over his countenance as his wishes were read out. The first two royal declarations — the amnesty and the re-establishment of Parlement in Paris — were expected. But the third made everyone sit up. It exiled from Paris all known adherents of the Condé family, from dukes (Beaufort, La Rochefoucauld) down to the servants of Condéen troops; forbade the Paris Parlement to interfere in general matters of state and in finances, and to take any action against government personnel; and prohibited any royal office-holder from becoming closely involved in the affairs of princes and grandees. Louis thus denied in principle the validity of those concessions which, four years previously almost to the day, the sovereign courts had wrested from his tearful mother (see above p.19). Other masterful acts followed. A bevy of titled Frondeuses — the Duchesses de Montbazon and de Châtillon, plus confidantes of the already exiled Duchesse de Montpensier, etc. — were constrained to take the air outside Paris. Likewise the now ailing Châteauneuf, whom death shortly cured of addiction to intrigue. A *lit de justice* was arranged for 13th

November in order to lend extra solemnity to another declaration of treason against Condé. Retz was apprehended during a courtesy visit to the Louvre (19th December) and immured at Vincennes, where he had leisure to repent his rejection of Mazarin's offer to exile him honourably to ambassadorial employment at the Vatican. Thirteen fiscal edicts were registered without demur at a *lit de justice* on 31st December, undoing in detail what Parlementarians saw as the good work of October 1648, the erection of a 'barrier between the sovereign power, the exactions of the financiers, and the need and powerlessness of the people' (Denis Talon, son and successor of Omer Talon).

The royal display of vigour and assertiveness stunned troublemakers, but did not paralyse them. Banished persons tarried in Paris or close by, making a mockery of reiterated royal injunctions for their removal and generating continued unrest. Parlementarians oozed solidarity with their exiled colleagues, and obliged the embarrassed First President Molé to remonstrate at the Louvre over a measure which, in his other capacity as Keeper of the Seals, he had both advised and rendered operable. Retz's captivity brought on an itch for protest-deputations amongst the clergy in the city, grudgingly supported by the prisoner's jealous uncle, the Archbishop of Paris. The *rentiers*, activated by non-payment of their interest, took to ganging up noisily outside ministers' doors, provoking Parlement to ban all assemblies on pain of death (22nd January 1653).

Mazarin's definitive reinstallation at the king's side on 3rd February 1653 had little sedative effect at first. The *rentiers* were temporarily gagged by mellifluous reassurances of money in the offing, backed by a shake-up in the Finances Council following the death of the superintendent La Vieuville. But there was no shortage of agitators to relay them. Parlement, albeit under new management from April 1653 when Molé resigned the leadership to a supple friend of the Duchesse de Chevreuse, President Pomponne de Bellièvre, heaved with renewed indignation over further arrests and expulsions of its members for miscellaneous acts of disrespect towards the powers that be. Emissaries of Condé were intercepted, bearing letters for former aristocratic allies, and manifestos to refuel the Paris populace. Even the city's butchers, amongst whom Retz had acquaintances, showed their contempt for authority by shutting up shop over the reimposition of a tax on livestock. In the provinces, old habits of disobedience died hard. A number of nobles connected to Condé or Retz refused to hand militarily vital governorships over to the king, until the price was right. Provence, despite the replacement of controversial governor d'Alais by Mazarin's in-law the Duc de Mercoeur, still shuddered from earlier upheavals. Guyenne carried on uninterruptedly with full-scale revolt.

The struggle to subdue Bordeaux prolonged the civil war well into 1653, a monument to the strength of provincial resistance against the crown. The unhappy city was rent by increasingly violent factionalism as Conti and the Duchesse de Longueville became more preoccupied with outmatching one another than with holding out for Condé while he torched villages up and down Champagne and cultivated his tepid Spanish allies. Effective power had passed into the hands of one particular faction, that of the Ormée, so called from the elm-planted promenade where its members had first begun to assemble. The Ormée was dominated by men who had taken some steps up the social ladder — merchants, craftsmen, minor functionaries —

and who committed themselves to forcibly removing the blockage to further ascension constituted by the closed-shop policy of the Bordeaux Parlement and municipal oligarchy. Their effusive tracts spoke of reverence for God and king, loyalty to the fatherland, brotherly love, and protection for the disadvantaged. Their actions ultimately degenerated into tyranny and treason, as they terrorised opponents, sent embassies for help from Oliver Cromwell, and openly discussed the establishment of a republic. The violence of the Ormistes, together with the economic stagnation and shortages caused by the progressive royal reconquest of Guyenne from January 1653 onwards, created at Bordeaux a climate of reaction which Mazarin's enterprising agent Father Berthod finally succeeded in exploiting after some hair-raising escapes from the rebels' clutches. The Ormistes' vigilance in uncovering plots against their régime and the determination of their radical wing to fight to the bitter end deterred Bordeaux's social élite from publicly negotiating with Louis' military commanders in the province until the end of July. Pro-royalist white flags replaced the red banners of Spain in anticipation of the Bordelais' outsize demands being met, and on 3rd August the city gates were opened to royal regiments. Condé's relatives had done their own secret bargaining in advance, and went their separate ways on the 2nd. Conti ingratiated himself with Mazarin, one of whose nieces he took to wife and infected with venereal disease before lapsing into rigid piety. The Duchesse de Longueville rested from her labours in a convent prior to another round of subtler rebellion as protectress of the French adherents of Jansenism, an austere religious doctrine which the Pope had just pronounced heretical and the king was to spend a lifetime trying to obliterate. The Princesse de Condé reconfirmed her unreciprocated devotion to her spouse by sharing six more years of his self-imposed estrangement from France, until Spain made peace and shed him.

Events at Bordeaux in the summer and autumn of 1653 mirrored those which had taken place in Paris during the comparable months of 1652: a crescendo of terrorism, orchestrated by last-ditch rebels, broadened opportunities for loyal servants of the government to co-ordinate anti-terrorist manifestations and eventually to get the better of usurpers of lawful authority. In each case surrender was followed by remarkably little bloodshed. A handful of Ormistes were executed, including their aptly-named ringleader, the ex-butcher Dureteste, for whom was reserved the then fashionable malefactor's death by smashing the limbs with iron bars. Otherwise, exile or imprisonment were the punishments meted out to recalcitrants who could not be amnestied. The hard hitting came in the form of acts of legislation forced through Parlement in the two and a half months after Louis XIV resumed residence in Paris. But Parlement quickly got its second wind; and other readily roused groups behaved as if nothing had changed in the capital. Condé was still at large, raiding as far into France as the Spanish would let him. Retz broke out of captivity (August 1654) and continued his intrigues in retreat at Rome. It would be a long time before Louis XIV could write, optimistically, in his memoirs for the year 1661:

'Everything was calm, in all places'.

* * * * * * * *

Chapter 7

REVIEW OF PERFORMANCE

In his journal of the Fronde years, royal butler Jean Vallier remarked, at the date of June 1653, that despite unrelenting exposure to war on the domestic front and against foreign powers, the signs were that France had not been totally drained of resources or brought to her knees; for

> this powerful realm did not fail, at the beginning of this [year's] campaign, to muster very considerable fighting forces, six to operate on land and one at sea.

The Fronde self-evidently caused violent tremors which radiated outwards from their epicentre in the capital, but its destructive effects were contained by a combination of circumstances.

The first was the relative brevity of the upheavals. If the Fronde is compared, as it often was by its participants and pamphleteers, to the Religious Wars of the previous century, the contrast springs to the eye. The Religious Wars had alternately flared and smouldered from 1562 until 1598, time............ation on an irreparable scale. The fact that the Wars in question had set Catholics against Protestants also created an extra, incalculable, dimension of spiritual disruption which was virtually absent during the Fronde. French Protestants got themselves talked about in connection with the assemblies of nobles in 1651 and with insurrectional activity in Bordeaux, but they made no collective move against the government in the name of religion. On the contrary, their loyalty was officially acknowledged in a royal declaration of May 1652, when the military salvation of the monarchy lay in the hands of the Protestant Turenne.

Secondly, the Fronde did not affect all parts of France equally. It was unquestionably the Paris Parlementarians' intention to involve the provinces in their differences with the crown, since after the flight of the royal family in January 1649 they made haste to draft a circular inviting support from large towns under the Parlement's jurisdiction and from colleagues in the other provincial *parlements*. The entry into the conflict of princes and great nobles, with family estates, governorships, agents, and clients scattered the length and breadth of the country, widened the rebels' potential sphere of influence alarmingly, especially when Gaston and Condé abandoned the royal camp. The call for revolt came across loudest and clearest in Provence and Guyenne, where a pugnacious royalist governor was cheek by jowl with a resentful *parlement*. Elsewhere, its resonance was more muted. Normandy to all intents and purposes bowed out after the royal tour of February 1650, while Burgundy did not join in until after its governor Condé's arrest. Brittany, under the nominal governorship of Anne d'Autriche and the effective one of the Maréchal de La Meilleraye, was kept on a rein. In Languedoc, of which Gaston was governor, the Toulouse Parlement published a few anti-Mazarin decrees in the wake of its Parisian counterpart, but as with the bulk of provincial *parlements*, it was engrossed in conflicts on its own doorstep. Frontier provinces like Picardy and Champagne, although they started off with rebel governors (Elbeuf and Conti respectively), were rather too prostrate from the passage of armies to think of adding to their own miseries. Within the provinces that caught the full force of the Fronde, that is to say, those adjoining Paris and Bordeaux, the towns were the key installations. It was to the shelter of their walls that countryfolk fled with whatever movables they might have saved from the soldiery, creating supplementary foyers of beggary and unrest to which beleaguered municipal authorities were sorely tempted to react with simple expulsion orders. The towns were the centre of military operations and changed hands, amongst foreign armies, royalists, and Frondeurs, with bewildering rapidity. They were also the focus of political struggles as the places which housed the principal organs of administration and the economy, cultured élites to whom polemical literature could be addressed, and conglomerations of down-and-outs who could be persuaded to distribute, shout, or commit almost anything for money. The décor of the Fronde was predominantly urban; though here again there were major towns like Lyon, in the hands of royalist governors from the Villeroy family ever since the sixteenth century, which avoided being dragged into the hurly-burly.

A third factor which checked the spread of the Fronde was the lack of cohesion and of efficient leadership in the rebel quarter. Pledges of union appealed to the Frondeurs, but they hardly knew how to honour them. One-upmanship was rife within and between the sovereign courts, who could not present a consistently united front even at times of dire necessity like the Rueil peace-talks in 1649 when Rouen Parlementarians accused their Parisian colleagues of unilaterally suing for peace and making seating arrangements displeasing to their dignity. The aristocratic generals who took over the leadership of the revolt had even more difficulty in getting their act together. The high nobility had no corporate structure resembling that of the sovereign courts; and when provincial and middle-ranking nobles made a sustained effort to create one, in 1651, by organising democratic assemblies with rotating presidents and distinctions of rank set aside, the substantial Protestant component of the meetings begged to differ from policies geared to Catholics. Individual princes and magnates, used to hot and bloody competition with their peers for royal favours, public acclaim, and politically useful females, now sparred against their own relatives for good measure. With their allies the sovereign-court magistrates, in their eyes little more than a load of upstart pettifoggers, the great ones easily lost patience. Gaston d'Orléans disguised his contempt better than Condé, but is recorded as audibly snorting that he had no intention of becoming the 'valet' of Parlement. Support for the magistrates from the middling and lower reaches of society, deceptively warm on occasions when the regency government made miscalculations like arresting Broussel in broad daylight, cooled in the event of bread shortages, interruptions to business and commerce, the fatigues of guard duty, suspension of interest-payments, and the imposition of fresh taxes to fund parasitic troops. The Palais de Justice and its denizens became a sitting target for mobs composed of identifiable (small traders, craftsmen, apprentices, boatmen, *rentiers*, fishwives...) and unidentifiable ('rogues', 'riff-raff', 'vagabonds', *'bourgeois'*...) elements of urban disaffection. During the final stages of the Fronde the populace turned on those like Retz and Beaufort who had flattered themselves that it was theirs to command, and hailed them with the same kind of insults as they had willed upon Mazarin. How could the crowd distinguish clearly between allies and adversaries when everyone reckoned to keep open his/her options of haggling with 'the Mazarin' and changing sides? An intelligent and far-sighted leader might have drawn together antagonistic groups and individuals, but no suitable candidate succeeded in imposing himself for the duration. Old Broussel, *'le bonhomme'* (i.e. virtuous but dim) to his contemporaries, had to be fed with ideas in order to act. Beaufort's blunders caused endless mirth among his peer plotters. Gaston gave an all too convincing impersonation of a man who did not know what he was about. Condé habitually conducted himself as if he was above the necessity to make friends. Retz's best performances were notoriously subterranean: 'he was a mole who was constantly digging up and moving earth within earth without being seen' (Condé). Outshining these stars of the Fronde did not pose an insuperable problem for Louis XIV once he came to kingly and manly age and could fully capitalise on the tremendous mystique which surrounded French sovereigns as the acknowledged representatives of God on earth.

The rebels expended so much time and energy on scrapping amongst themselves and on denouncing the bad faith of the government and its supporters that they had little to spare for hard thinking about ways to remedy those disorders in the state which justified, in their own opinion, anti-Establishment activity. This was a fourth reason why revolt did not turn into revolution. The dearth of constructive suggestions for reform is striking in view of the unprecedented volume of polemical literature generated by the political crisis: over five thousand printed works and several hundred more circulating in manuscript, on the count of a modern French specialist in the field, Hubert Carrier (*La Presse de La Fronde 1648—1653. Les Mazarinades,* Geneva: Droz, 1989, p.71). The shortage is less striking if account is taken of the fact that the majority of pamphleteers were obscure individuals who put pen to paper under the influence of a patron, impecuniosity, thirst for revenge or renown. They have occasional flashes of inspiration like the one encountered in the *Catéchisme des Partisans* (1649): 'Taxes should be levied...in proportion to each individual's property and ability to pay...so that no one is exempted'. But these are smothered by an avalanche of abuse against the prime minister, the 'mazarins', and the tax-collectors, on the one hand, and on the other, by unoriginal prescriptions for the avoidance of tyranny and despotism, namely: observance by the king of the laws of God and nature; limited control over his subjects' life and property; personal rule as opposed to that of ministers, especially foreigners; ability to live off his royal domain, without the need for financial subsidies in the form of taxes; willingness to defer to moderating forces (e.g. male prince-regent figure, Parlement, Etats Généraux). The legitimacy of resisting a king who breaks faith with his people, reminded of their original rôle as electors of rulers for the dispensation of justice and protection, was affirmed. But polemicists shied away from specifying what form resistance should take or what course the state should embark upon after the successful removal of its crowned head. Suppressing the office and person of an imported prime minister was one thing; forcibly terminating the reign of a hereditary Catholic king of blameless years was another. A radical switch from a monarchy, where the social élites benefited from the delegation of royal authority, to a republic, where the lower orders would have irrefutable claims to power-sharing, was a dazzling prospect upon which few men of the time could gaze fixedly.

The haze and hesitancy seemed to evaporate when the Frondeurs considered their own immediate and personal needs, instead of the long-term future of French society. The Parlementarians were quite clear, in the published results of the St-Louis Chamber deliberations of July 1648, that the sovereign courts should control the lynch-pin sector of state finances, and cocoon their privileges, investments, and persons against outside interference, by the sovereign in particular. The princes and nobles in their publicly enunciated *Demandes* of March 1649, and in their secret negotiations with Mazarin, unambiguously itemised the sums of money, grants of lands and prerogatives which would revitalise their loyalty to the crown. Thinking men and women in and around the political arena were under no illusions about the sincerity of the champions of public welfare burgeoning in their midst. The Duchesse de Nemours, daughter of Longueville, says it all:

> There was no one amongst all those who declared against the [regency government], including the office-holders of the sovereign courts, who did not have, or at least think he had, his particular reasons for doing so, and who did not wish to make believe that he was committed solely to the interest of the people and the public good. It is certain, however, that their private interest played a much bigger part therein than the interest of others.

'Self-interest' (*intérêt*). The word protrudes from the pages of every eye-witness narrative of the Fronde, and the concept behind it taints the behaviour of even those public figures who, like First President Molé, gave evidence of possessing moral fibre and of being more than nominally law-abiding. La Rochefoucauld, who turned moralist in his disillusioned middle age, did not have far to seek for a foundation-principle upon which to construct his collection of *Maximes* (published in 1665): 'Virtues are absorbed in self-interest as rivers are in the sea'.

The Fronde not only offered pickings and profits for the powerful and for the customary beneficiaries of wars throughout the ages, arms manufacturers, black-marketeers, propagandists, etc. It also opened up a source of thrills and entertainments galore. Particularly in the first phase (1648—49), the civil war created some excellent street-theatre. The sight of swords dangling awkwardly from citizens unaccustomed to bearing arms was one of the 'novelties' of the 1648 Paris Barricades which avowedly 'delighted' the retrospectively apologetic Duchesse de Montpensier ('the public good was not very well known to me, any more than that of the state'). Retz smirked over the mock siege of the Bastille in January 1649:

> ... it was quite an amusing spectacle to see women taking their chairs into the Arsenal gardens where the battery [of cannons] was, as if they were attending a sermon.

Condé declared burlesque verse to be the only appropriate medium for describing the war since participants 'spent each and all day mocking one another'. Interludes of pure farce, such as Retz's benediction of Condé or the behaviour of the latter at the St Geneviève Procession, continued to divert the crowd in the more sombre days of the 1650s. The young king was forced to become a member of the audience: it was from the heights on which the famous modern Père-Lachaise cemetery is built that he had a grandstand view of the contest between Condé and Turenne for control of Paris in

July 1652. As if to emphasise the theatricality of life in the capital, people dressed up to play parts. 'Mazarins' escaping from a lynching, or plotters circulating on nocturnal assignations, had pressing reasons for transforming their exterior. Not so the Paris troops bedecked with ribbons and ladies' favours, in imitation of their stylish commander Beaufort, who paid attention to details like matching the colour of his charger with that of the profuse plumes in his hat. The adoption of *fronde*-shaped hatbands by those who refused the peace of Rueil in April 1649 caused a craze for commodities *à la fronde*: haberdashery, gloves, muffs, fans, and even swords and loaves. 'The effect of this triviality was incredible', Retz averred; 'we ourselves were in vogue even more because of this piece of folly than because of the vital things'. The Coadjuteur affected in his memoirs, written in the 1670s when overt rebellion against the government was going out of fashion in high circles, to believe that the Fronde had tinged all around him with madness. Doubtless his aim was to persuade posterity that he alone had kept his head and allowed himself to be lucidly carried along with the rest. Yet his estimate, echoed by other observers of the curious 'carnival' spirit of the time, has had a disconcerting ring of truth for post-seventeenth-century appraisers of the situation.

It is difficult to take seriously a civil war in which the prime activists behave, and candidly admit to having behaved, in an unreasonable and insincere manner. Voltaire, a connoisseur of the absurd, more than once labelled the whole historical episode as 'ridiculous'. Recent historians have but rung the changes on that damning adjective: 'four years of the most stupid rebellion...' (P.-G. Lorris, *La Fronde*, 1961, p.407); 'comic-opera intrigue' (P. Knachel, *England and the Fronde*, 1967, p.15); 'a kind of Feast of Fools' (H. Carrier, *La Presse de la Fronde*, 1989, p.7); 'this mad sequence of disorders, follies, betrayals and killings' (P. Goubert, *Mazarin*, 1990, p.335). Extreme reactions are explicable on the part of scholars in a position to measure the Fronde against the two parallel periods of French political unrest which flank it on either side — the Religious Wars of the sixteenth century and the Revolution of 1789 — when, as in Charles I's England, a tidal wave of public animosity did not stop at battering ministers and favourites, but engulfed the king in person, necessitating a fundamental reappraisal of the status quo. By comparison, the Fronde has an unmistakable air of halfheartedness and incompletion. The boy-king Louis XIV appears to have run no serious risk of assassination or judicial murder; the barbarity of the English in decapitating the Lord's Anointed was a leitmotif of the French pamphleteers. As for scapegoat Mazarin, his fire-breathing opponents privately acknowledged that he was ill cast in the rôle of sanguinary tyrant and that he was much more use to them alive than dead, for then they could scare him into negotiating over the diverse concessions which they pursued. So they were careful to execute him only in print and in pictures. A limpet-like ability to hang on, fortified by the belief which he expressed in a letter of 9th May 1651 — 'the hatred of the French [is] never of long duration' — enabled him and his royal master and mistress to ride the political storms and steady the rocking ship of state. Far from wrecking the monarchy, the Fronde provided a powerful incentive for the young monarch at the heart of the conflict to think of ways to render his vessel storm-proof in future.

The civil war of 1648—53 was waged over the head of the boy-king in whose name everyone unsheathed swords. It was Anne d'Autriche's war and Mazarin's war, hers more than his since she was in the thick of the power-struggle without interruption and fighting as only a mother, particularly one so prideful and resentful of slights, knows how to fight for her vulnerable offspring. But Louis XIV could not be oblivious to the insults heaped upon the two closest and staunchest upholders of his authority, nor to the perpetual round of intrigues and betrayals, alarms and sudden departures, which unsettled his everyday life. Outwardly solemn and composed ('very serious by nature', wrote a contemporary), Louis gave few signs of the frustration, caused by enforced inactivity, which were later revealed in his memoirs. When the *'terribles agitations'* (the phrase employed in the memoirs) subsided, and as he progressively gained greater freedom of action, firstly by the attainment of his majority (1651) and secondly by the death of Mazarin (1661), Louis proceeded to a settlement of accounts. His mother, who had the good sense to step aside after saving his throne for him, was rewarded with almost unwavering affection and respect until her death in 1666. Mazarin — 'who loved me and whom I loved, who had rendered me great services, but whose thoughts and ways were naturally very different from my own' — was allowed to become a multi-millionaire, to marry seven nieces into the French and Italian aristocracy, and to continue his functions of minister and political tutor at the side of his godson, albeit that the adolescent was impatient for the yoke to be removed and resolved never to appoint an official prime minister in future.

In dealing with former opponents, Louis, according to his memoirs, disdained all thoughts of revenge as being unworthy and impractical. Yet his actions during his personal reign did not entirely tally with his words. The sovereign courts, 'which regarded themselves as so many separate and independent sovereignties', and above all the Parlements, 'whose excessive elevation had been dangerous to the whole realm during my minority', had to be 'abased, less because of the harm that they had done, than because of that which they could do in future'. They were forbidden to issue decrees contrary to those of the royal council (1661), demoted in title from *'cours souveraines'* to *'cours supérieures'* (1665), required to destroy their records spanning the Fronde years (1668), and ordered to register royal legislation prior to making any remonstrances (1673). Finance *officiers*, initially threatened with suspension in 1653 for banning co-operation with royal delegates engaged in tax-collecting missions, were warned of the ultimate fate of dissidents in 1664 when the superintendent of finances, Nicholas Fouquet, was sentenced to life imprisonment for imprudently advertising his ambition in the shape of a large clientèle and a fortified island off the coast of Brittany. The king promoted himself to superintendent, a clear hint that Parlement's reforming ardour in the financial sphere would be regarded as superfluous.

The nobles, less easily muzzled because of their diversity, dispersal, and independent assets, were shown the lines which they were expected to toe. Enquiries were set up into the authenticity of titles of nobility, with the idea that proven usurpers would redescend to their original commoner status and recommence paying taxes. Fresh impetus was given to ambulatory assizes designed for despatch to the provinces to punish overlords guilty of tyrannising vassals and neighbours. The law against duelling, an aristocratic mania, was reissued in stronger language. Provincial governors, 'who so often abused their power', had their funds trimmed, their client-garrisons replaced by troops loyal to the king, their term of office subjected to periodic review, and their actions kept under surveillance by royalist aides. The great magnates and lesser fry with regular access to the king were conditioned to look upon him as Dispenser of all pleasures and gratifications worth enjoying — not so much the material kind (Louis' coffers emptied rapidly like theirs) as the immaterial favours, which might begin with a royal salutation and end with an invitation to a royal retreat. Posts in the households of the members of the royal family were multiplied to keep sedentary nobles occupied and in view. Active ones were directed to ambassadorships or commands in the armed forces, occupations apt to increase dependence on royal bounty, and, in the case of the forces, to thin ranks. The Church still served as a dumping-ground for well-bred 'misfits', but ceased between Mazarin's death and that of Louis (1715) to be a supplier of government ministers. With one or two exceptions the old military aristocracy was similarly bypassed in favour of tried and tested members of the newer aristocracy which had risen to prominence through several generations of successful office-holding.

It was not in my interests to take on subjects of more eminent status,

reads a noteworthy passage in Louis' memoirs;

> ... it was necessary above all things to establish my own reputation, and to make known to the public...that my intention was not to share my authority with them. It was important to me that they should not themselves conceive higher hopes than those which I was pleased to give them, something which is difficult for persons of high birth.

Louis' policy logically ruled out ministerial rôles for his blood relatives, whose recent conduct had underlined the wisdom of not putting faith in princes. Exiled Gaston in any case succumbed to devoutness and to death in 1660, politically rehabilitated Condé henceforth confined to the battlefield demonstrations of his recovered loyalty, and Louis' younger brother Philippe rarely shook himself out of the pleasure-loving inertia which his upbringing had been calculated to foster.

Fermentation in the towns and countryside was rigorously and ostentatiously punished. Louis was to be dogged by the bogey of provincial insurrections, on which he cracked down with troops detachable from a large standing army primed to overwhelm any rival armed force within or outside of the kingdom. By way of a preventive measure, *intendants*, without that provocative title, were gradually redeployed in the provinces from 1653 onwards, supplementing those local notables who enjoyed royal and ministerial patronage in return for performing equivalent watchdog services. Paris, habitual nerve-centre of revolts, had superimposed upon its incoherent tangle of policing forces a new magistrate (1667 onwards) called the Lieutenant Général de Police, with extensive powers to ensure public order, safety, and decency. Within the newcomer's purview came censorship of the press, which had blasted so many reputations during the Fronde. Ultra-sensitive to his own renown, Louis had relentless war waged against fabricators and distributors of libels, and cut back the number of printers to achieve tighter control. The occasional imprisonment, exile, or burning at the stake of an imprudent author encouraged intellectuals at large to acquire the habit of drawing inspiration from the manifold virtues of the king, who granted pensions to selected eulogists and extended membership of prestigious academies of arts and science to promising propagators of royal glory.

But Paris, even when relatively cleansed and chastened, offered no attraction as a permanent kingly abode. The death of Louis' mother there revived memories which rendered the capital, in his own words, insufferable. He withdrew instantly to his father's former hunting-lodge at Versailles, 'the place where I could be more private'. Sixteen years and many grandiose refurbishments later, Louis removed definitively to the paternal château, shaking the famed mud of Paris off his feet with an air of finality.

* * * * * * *

THE FRONDE
AS
CONTEMPORARIES
VIEWED
AND
LIVED
IT

THE FRONDE
AS
CONTEMPORARIES VIEWED
AND
LIVED IT

I   CAUSES

i)   *Cardinal de Retz's analysis*

(Restraints on the authority of the French monarch have weakened over the centuries, largely due to ambitious ministers and favourites epitomised by Richelieu and his faithful imitator Mazarin, whose tyranny has flourished on the lethargy of the population.)

What causes lethargy in suffering states is the duration of the affliction, which takes hold of men's imagination and makes them believe that it will never end. As soon as they can find a way out of it, which always happens when it has reached a certain point, they are so surprised, so relieved, and so carried away, that they suddenly pass to the other extreme, and far from considering revolutions impossible, they believe them easy: and this disposition by itself is sometimes capable of causing revolutions. We have known and experienced all these truths in our recent revolution. Whoever had said, three months before the first hint of trouble, that any could arise in a state where the royal household was perfectly united, where the court was enslaved to the minister, where the provinces and the capital were in subjection to him, where the armies were victorious, where the companies[1] seemed totally impotent; whoever had said it would have been considered mad [...]. Consciousness flickers, a glimmer, or rather a spark of life; and this sign of life, almost imperceptible at the outset, is not given by Monsieur [Gaston d'Orléans] or by M. le Prince [Condé], it is not given by the grandees of the realm, it is not given by the provinces; it is given by Parlement, which, prior to our century, had never started a revolution, and which would certainly have condemned with brutal decrees the one it was personally engineering if anyone else had begun it. It grumbled over the tariff edict[2] and as soon as it had just made a murmur, everyone woke up. On awakening, they groped around, as it were, for the laws; they no longer found them; they got frightened, they shouted, they asked each other for them; and in this uproar, the questions to which their explanations gave rise, after being obscure and venerable in obscurity, became problematical; and subsequently, for half the population, odious. The populace entered the sanctuary: they lifted up the veil which must always cover everything said, everything believed

---

[1] *'compagnies'* is a term often used in the seventeenth century to refer to the sovereign courts, though here it could have a more general application.

[2] The tariff was a tax established by a decree of the royal finances council in 1646 on all merchandise entering Paris. The Parlementarians objected to it on two grounds: produce from their own estates was not exempted from the tax, and the decree had been registered in the rival Cour des Aides.

about the rights of the people and those of kings, which never agree so well as in silence.

[*Mémoires*, in *Nouvelle Collection des Mémoires pour servir à l'histoire de France depuis le XIIIe siècle jusqu'à la fin du XVIIIe* (eds J.F. Michaud and J.J. Poujoulat), Paris, 1836—9, 32 Vols., 3me Sér., Vol. I, pp.53-4. This collection of memoirs will henceforth be abbreviated to MP.]

ii) *Omer Talon's analysis*

(Cardinal Richelieu's tyrannical ministry (1624—42) gave rise to all manner of tax increases, but the populace was still capable of shouldering them, buoyed up by hopes of tax relief when the war with Spain ended, and a release of spoils from the clutches of his relatives and supporters once the cardinal died. Hopes were dashed when Mazarin overtly protected all that this predecessor and benefactor left behind.)

But it happened in the regency that the Queen had to reward all those who had been ill-treated by Cardinal Richelieu, and who on that account had had some sort of connection with her in her misfortunes during the lifetime of her husband the King; apart from the fact that she did not want to dissatisfy the others, for fear of rousing jealousy. Besides, the Queen's disposition is naturally kindly, charitable, and devoid of malice; and although she does not readily suffer an affront, she does not readily affront others unless forced to do so by some sort of outrage that pushes her to extremes.

Thus the Queen found herself obliged to make large and immense gratifications which exhausted the treasury, and which in the first year of her regency encumbered the King's finances with twelve millions in borrowing and deferred payments.

M. d'Emery, who was appointed controller-general and then superintendent [of finances] was infinitely lavish with gratifications to those who could help him make his fortune or whose authority he feared, chiefly Parlement, whose wrath and justice caused him apprehension; he had despised any kind of order in finances, both as regards receipts and expenditure; because to have hard cash he had given the collecting of all the *tailles* to contractors, and paid 15% interest to those who advanced cash to him. He did the same with the indirect taxes, and thus in the year 1648 he was consuming in advance the years 1650 and 1651, and he had gone so far that, having pledged more than a hundred millions of the King's finances to the *partisans* and financiers, he was keeping the state going only by means of cutbacks on office-holders and *rentes*. The sovereign companies had suffered a cut of a quarter of their wages; judges in the presidial courts[3] were receiving none; the *trésoriers*, the *élus*, the salt-tax judges, and all the finance office-holders accountable for the handling of public money were paid nothing at all, because what funds were left to them were drained by new and imaginary impositions, by taxes, and by charges to ensure heredity of office; and M. d'Emery negotiated with the *partisans* to take over the collection of all these cuts and taxes which emanated from the [royal]

---

[3]Tribunals established in the mid-sixteenth century to offload the judgement of minor offences from the Parlements.

council; and on that condition they advanced their money, subject to huge rebates[4].
Apart from that, the fighting men were not paid; the French and Swiss guards were a
dozen payments in arrears, and the Swiss [mercenaries] on the point of quitting.

This procedure caused a public outcry; not only the people in the countryside, at
village level, were maltreated, but even persons of middling status: only craftsmen and
day labourers maintained themselves in the villages; since having no movable goods
which could be seized, they lived off the money derived from their work. In Paris
most of the luxury was funded by these high interest rates which the King paid; the
merchants had largely abandoned their current trade to put their money into this kind
of infamous transaction.

The people who remained shielded to some extent were the office-holders in the
sovereign companies in Paris and in all the other provinces of the realm, who were
subsisting on three-quarters of their wages; when M. d'Emery tried to take these away
from them via the institution of the *droit annuel*, imagining that he could do so by
compensating the Paris Parlement, the only one that he feared, he made a
miscalculation; because the *maîtres des requêtes* and office-holders of the other
sovereign companies having assembled and realised their strength, and having drawn
the Parlement of Paris to their side, ostensibly abandoned their own interests to work
for those of the public, and in public concerns they found what they desired.
[*Mémoires*, MP, 3me Sér., Vol. VI, pp.299-300]

iii) *Marquis de Montglat's analysis*

François de Paule de Clermont, Marquis de Montglat, came from a family
distinguished for providing governesses for children of the blood royal. A courtier
and a soldier, he appears to have been remarkably self-effacing, especially in his
memoirs, while being fully alert to what was going on and able to express himself
incisively.

* * * * * * * *

(France seemed to have reached a high point of prosperity, but was suddenly cast
down by inconstant Fortune.)

The Queen, having become regent on the death of the King, was totally lacking in
experience of affairs, like her new ministers; and since she was kindly and charitable
she granted everything that was asked of her, not realising the consequences; so that
in a short while she entirely emptied the treasury. Cardinal Mazarin, having remained
in sole charge of the Cabinet, was highly critical of these great liberalities, and having
as controller-general of finances d'Emery, he confided to him the whole direction of
them, to the detriment of Président Le Bailleul, superintendent [of finances], who
acted only as a shadow. D'Emery sought all possible means of finding money to
sustain the war [against the Habsburgs] and to satisfy the avarice of the cardinal, who
was insatiable. As he was hard and ruthless, he did not bother about ruining

---

[4]The French term is a *'remise'*: a sum of money allocated to a tax-contractor in lieu of wages.

everyone in order to humour his benefactor. He started off by no longer paying out money for the royal household, not even to those who supplied provisions for the royal tables which were every day on the point of collapse. He struck off all the pensions, and cut the Town Hall *rentes*[5] and those in the provinces; he had taxes imposed on holders of the [royal] domains[6], and on the *aisés*[7]; he handed over to contractors the collection of the *tailles*, and arranged solidarity of payment for the latter[8]; in such a way that the *partisans* exacted payment so rigorously that furniture and livestock were seized from the *laboureurs*[9] who were forced to leave everything and let the land lie fallow. This wretchedness of the peasants and the opulence of the financiers, to whom were given such huge interest rates on their advance loans that they became rich in a trice, made everyone grumble: so that Parlement wanted to make remonstrances which were not well received [...]. Although Parlement pretexted the public good, it acted principally out of self-interest, because d'Emery had taken away the wages of all the office-holders of the sovereign courts, and refused them the renewal of the *paulette*, which had expired.

[*Mémoires*, MP, 3me Sér., Vol. V, p.195]

iv) *Cardinal Mazarin's testimony*

Mazarin confirms, with a strikingly appropriate image of voracity, the financial chaos which lay at the heart of the crisis and which was only exacerbated on the day — 31st July 1648 — when this (studiedly?) euphoric letter was composed for France's representative in Sweden, immediately after a *lit de justice* committing the regency government to implementing unrealistic measures such as restoring payment of *rentes* and office-holders' wages.

* * * * * * * *

His Majesty, with the consent of the *traitants* who have assisted him hitherto, and with their entire satisfaction, since they feared worse, has deferred their *assignations*[10] and their reimbursement and ensured a secure fund for the continuation of the war for just as long as the stubbornness of the Spanish compels us to wage it. The whole of the present year had been eaten up, and the following two, and a way has been found

---

[5]The *rentes* were commonly known as *'rentes sur l'Hôtel de Ville'* because the municipal heads of Paris in theory stood surety for the payment of interest to purchasers.

[6]By an edict registered in 1645 but not enforced until 1647, owners of property within the royal domain had to pay one year's rent, which would release them in future from paying seigneurial dues to the king.

[7]It was a question of forcing the richest inhabitants of the capital to buy *rentes* in 1644. The sovereign courts managed to exempt themselves, at the expense of the protesting financiers.

[8]If a taxpayer could not or would not pay, the other members of the community to which he belonged would be obliged to make up the shortfall.

[9]The mention of furniture and livestock suggests that the word *'laboureur'* here denotes not the humble tiller of the soil but the wealthier peasant supervising the tilling on behalf of an overlord.

[10]An *assignation* was a means of repaying a debt by stipulating that the money should come out of a particular fund, e.g. the receipts from a specific tax.

to eat them up a second time, His Majesty recovering all his revenues and giving to his creditors only interest on their money at 6%.

Thus the revenue of His Majesty totalling over sixty millions, more than fifty-four millions net will have been preserved, which will suffice, if used economically, for all the expenses of the war, without the need to make use of yearly revenues in advance of collecting them. The other six millions, or thereabouts, will be [paying] the interest of a hundred or more millions that the King owes. I was forgetting to draw your attention to another very considerable advantage in this: through the King's resolution to dock the 15% interest that he was giving, he has instantly gained fifty millions, for which, as for the capital owed to them, the *traitants* had solid *assignations*.
[*Lettres du Cardinal Mazarin pendant son ministère*, eds A. Chéruel and Vicomte G. d'Avenel, Paris, Imprimerie Nationale, 1872—1906, 9 Vols., Vol. III, p.159]

II   PERSONALITIES AND MENTALITIES

A. *The mentality of the Parlementarians*

i)   The following glimpses of *'Messieurs'* the Paris Parlementarians going about their regulation business in the 1640s illustrate two of their primary preoccupations, with formalities and with precedents, and help to explain why seventeenth-century judicial procedure was notoriously long-winded.

* * * * * * *

On Thursday 21st February [1641], the King [Louis XIII] came to Parlement very early, so early that the Chancellor [Pierre Séguier] got there before the presidents had put on their red robes; so that after his arrival, having gone one after the other to fetch their red robes and their cloaks, when they returned to their places the Chancellor did not rise from his seat as they entered, which irritated them.[...]

[The Chancellor receives instructions from Louis XIII to arrange the trial, by Parlement, of some rebel grandees sheltering at the time in Sedan.]

The Chancellor having appointed Wednesday 3rd July [1641] for this purpose, two or three difficulties arose, firstly, how the *maîtres des requêtes* accompanying him should be dressed, whether in ordinary robes or silk ones; secondly, whether the Chancellor, when taking the opinions of the presidents, should not remove his hat; thirdly, if he should not rise to his feet when the presidents entered to take their places.[...]

On Friday 5th July [1641] the Chancellor returned to Parlement. The question arose as to whether two members of Parlement should be sent ahead to meet him, some affirming that that should only happen the first time he takes his seat, and that in the year 1584, when the Chancellor had come to Parlement, it had been decreed that a deputation be sent to him 'for this once', which terms were restrictive and limiting; that at the trial of Marshal Biron[11], at which Chancellor Bellièvre had been present for seven or eight consecutive sessions, the register did not contain anything about a deputation being sent to him. The others, on the contrary, argued that this mark of respect was owed to his person and his rank; that whenever he came to Parlement with the King this honour was paid to him, and that therefore it could not be denied him. And in fact the latter opinion prevailed.
[Omer Talon, *Mémoires*, MP, 3me Sér., Vol. VI, pp.73, 76, 77]

ii)   Despite their conservatism and adherence to form, the Parlementarians were capable of eruption on a grand scale, for reasons suggested by an insider, Pierre Lenet, a Dijon Parlementarian and active client of the Condé family.

* * * * * * *

---

[11]The Maréchal de Biron was executed for treason in 1602.

The sovereign companies keep within the rules of their formalities when hope of increasing their authority or fear of seeing it entirely overthrown does not cause them to cross the boundaries prescribed by those rules; but when through one or other of these principles they have started to veer off their usual course, they easily go to great extremes, because the most prudent are not usually in the majority and are considered suspect when they seek to oppose over-bold discussions, which, degenerating for the most part into a kind of attack on the authority of the sovereign, lead their instigators to undertake everything, in the belief that it is the only way to avoid the punishments threatening them.

[*Mémoires*, MP, 3me Sér., Vol. II, p.325)

iii) A sample of the Parlementarians' objectives, as formulated by sovereign-court deputies who began assembling in the Chambre Saint-Louis on 30th June 1648, shows them to have been intent above all on self-protection.

* * * * * * * *

Articles of the propositions made by the deputies of the companies assembled in the Saint-Louis Chamber, following the decree of 13th May 1648:

• That the *intendants de justice*, and all other extraordinary commissions, not verified in the sovereign courts, shall be revoked immediately.

• The contracts for the *tailles, taillons, subsistances*12, and others, shall be immediately revoked, and the said *tailles* imposed, assessed, and levied in the old way and as before, the said contracts with a 25% reduction for the benefit of the populace [...].

• That there shall be established a chamber of justice, composed of office-holders from the four sovereign courts, and nominated by the latter, to take cognisance of and judge the abuses and malpractices committed in the administration and handling of the King's affairs, and the exactions made on his subjects [...].

• No impositions and taxes will be created except by virtue of edicts and declarations well and duly verified by the sovereign courts, to whom cognisance thereof appertains, and implementation of the said edicts and declarations will be reserved to the said courts [...].

• That in the future there shall be no creation of office, whether in the judiciary or in finances, except via edicts verified by the sovereign courts, with entire freedom of votes [...] and that the foundation of these sovereign companies shall not be subjected to change or alteration, whether by increasing offices per chamber, establishing a *semestre*, or dividing the areas under the companies' jurisdiction, in order to create and establish new companies [...].

12*Taillons* and *subsistances* were supplements of the *tailles*.

•   That the office-holders of the four sovereign courts of Paris, paymasters, clerks, and other office-holders belonging to these bodies shall be paid each year the wages attributed to them, and the increment[13] thereof, without any deduction [...].

•   That the decrees given in the sovereign courts shall not be liable to annulment, revocation, or suspension, except by legal proceedings permitted by the ordinances [...].

•   That no subjects of the King, whatever their rank and condition, shall be held prisoner for more than twenty-four hours without being interrogated, according to the ordinances, and handed over to their natural judges [...] and that those currently detained without any form or semblance of trial shall be set free, and restored to the exercise of their function and the possession of their property; and office-holders will not be obliged to defer to any *lettres de cachet*[14] forbidding them to carry out the functions appertaining to their offices or ordering them to absent themselves, unless legal proceedings have been taken against them in the usual ways [...].
[Omer Talon, *Mémoires*, MP, 3me Sér., Vol. VI, pp.241-44]

iv) The Parlementarians realised that strength lay in unity but could never achieve it for very long due to internal feuds which grew heated at the slightest provocation. Here, the perennial enmity between the Enquêtes and the Grand'Chambre of the Paris Parlement bursts forth in an interlude of violence and anarchy characteristic of the final throes of the Fronde.

The Paris Parlement having begun to implement its solemn decision of 29th December 1651 to fund the reward payable for the capture of Mazarin by selling his library, the Grand'Chambre agreed to suspend the sale less than a fortnight later in response to an offer from a finance-officer named Vialet to buy the entire collection outright. This unilateral action on the part of the Grand'Chambre upset their colleagues in the Chambers of Enquêtes who refused, at a stormy session in the Palais de Justice, to recognise the validity of the suspension on the grounds that the whole Parlement had not been assembled to deliberate on the matter.

* * * * * * * *

... with indignation bursting out against the Grand'Chambre, said to have issued this decree to preserve the library for Cardinal Mazarin, the hubbub of voices and the disputes were considerable until 10 a.m.[15] when M. Le Bailleul[16] and the other presidents [of the Grand'Chambre] rose to their feet, which caused the Enquêtes members to say very loudly that a deliberation would go ahead in the absence of

---

[13]The original French term *'augmentation de gages'* is misleading in that it did not refer to a salary increase in the modern sense but to a system whereby the king exacted a sum of money from an office-holder in return for granting him supplementary wages.

[14]Sealed letters from the monarch, usually ordering detention or exile of indefinite duration.

[15]Parlement was accustomed to suspend its morning sessions at this hour.

[16]Nicolas Le Bailleul, acting First President in the absence of Mathieu Molé.

those who withdrew; but despite that, the presidents having moved forward, the Enquêtes members barred their way and halted them for some minutes, until M. Sevin[17], preparing to do violence and lifting his hand to strike one of the Enquêtes members, received several blows under his robe and found himself surrounded by Enquêtes personnel who had crossed the barriers from all sides; so that there was great confusion, and M. Sevin went pale and white, and was indescribably taken aback; whereupon the presidents having been forced to return to their places in order to avoid worse confusion at a time when union is so necessary, M. Vedeau[18] proposed nominating commissioners for the sale of the library alongside those already nominated, deciding that evening whether it was more expedient to sell the library wholesale or piecemeal, and then proceeding with the sale accordingly: which was approved by the whole company.

[*Un Journal Inédit du Parlement de Paris pendant la Fronde*, ed. H. Courteault, in *Annuaire — Bulletin de la Société de l'Histoire de France*, 4me fascicule, Paris, 1916, p.221.]

B. *The outlook of the nobles and princes*

i)   A long letter of justification for the arrest of Condé, issued in the King's name on the day after the *coup* (19th January 1650) and subsequently read out in the Paris Parlement and at the Hôtel de Ville, highlights the power wielded by a seventeenth-century French grandee through the possession of governorships of strategic provinces and fortresses with which the monarchy was obliged to buy support.

* * * * * * * *

It has happened that all our faithful servants in our council, and outside it, have represented to us simultaneously that continued patience would soon render the malady incurable, and that the only way of protecting our State, and our person, was to arrest our said cousins[19] [Condé, Conti, and Longueville] who, holding daily family discussions on the establishment of this power that they wanted to oppose to our own, were not ashamed to count among the ways of achieving it, apart from the high offices and provincial governorships[20] belonging to or dependent upon them, the fact that they were already masters of all the great rivers of the realm, on account of the different fortresses that they have in their hands or believed loyal to their cause on the rivers Seine, Meuse, Saône, Rhone, Loire, Garonne, and Dordogne.

[*Registres de l'Hôtel de Ville de Paris pendant la Fronde*, eds Le Roux de Lincy and Douët-D'arcq, Paris, Société de l'Histoire de France, 1846—48, 3 vols., Vol. II, p.109]

---

[17]Jean Sevin, a member of the Grand'Chambre.

[18]François Vedeau de Grandmont, Enquêtes member.

[19]In his letters the French monarch styled as 'cousins' not merely princes of royal blood but dukes, peers, marshals of France, and other dignitaries whom he wished to honour. It will be noted that shifting responsibility for unpopular or dangerous measures onto adviser figures was habitual in royalist as well as frondeur pronouncements.

[20]The same document mentions that on the death of Condé's father, in 1646, the governorships of Burgundy, Bresse, and Berry were given to the household, apart from that of Champagne which it already held.

ii) Governorships, especially of or in provinces where a grandee had family estates, were ideal centres around which to weave dense webs of clients and dependants pledged, in return for protection and favours, to assist their patron in time of need. La Rochefoucauld, governor of Poitou, recalls in his memoirs the impressive number of provincials whom he was able to rally in 1650, ostensibly to mourn his deceased father, but in reality to march against royalist-held Saumur on the Loire.

* * * * * * *

He [La Rochefoucauld writes of himself in the third person] resolved to assemble for this purpose his friends, on a pretext that revealed nothing of his intention [...]. He thought that he could not find a more specious one than that of his father's burial, the ceremony of which was to take place at Verteuil, one of his residences. To that end he summoned all the nobility of the neighbouring provinces, and sent for everyone on his estates who could carry weapons to attend; so that in a very short while he assembled more than two thousand cavalry and eight hundred infantry [...].

... the Duc de La Rochefoucauld held a meeting of all the nobles who had come for his father's funeral, and told them that having avoided being taken prisoner in Paris with Monsieur le Prince [Condé], he would not be very safe on his estates, which were surrounded by troops ostensibly deployed all around on the pretext of winter quarters but effectively so as to be able to take him by surprise in his house; that he was offered a sure refuge in a neighbouring fortress, and that he asked his true friends to accompany him there and left the others free to do what they liked. Some appeared embarrassed by this proposition, and found various pretexts to withdraw [...]; but seven hundred noblemen promised to follow him. With this number of cavalry and infantry that he had drawn from his estates, he headed for Saumur [...].
[*Mémoires* in *Oeuvres Complètes*, eds D.L. Gilbert and J. Gourdault, Paris, Hachette, 1868—1883, 3 vols., Vol. II, pp.179-82]

iii) Contemporary literature offered the nobles other than purely material causes for self-congratulation by promoting the image of the aristocratic hero and heroine, brave, fearless, passionately energetic in the pursuit of *gloire* based upon self-esteem and social acclaim, and supremely conscious of living on a different plane from that of ordinary mortals. The dramatist Pierre Corneille (1606—1684) enchanted audiences with his ability to translate into quotable verses the ideals of the social group into which his father had been elevated by royal letters of ennoblement in 1637.

* * * * * * *

He who fears not death, fears not threats.
My valour rises above the direst straits
And I can be reduced to living without happiness
But not persuaded to live without honour.
[*Le Cid*, II, 1]

My glory [*gloire*] is at stake, I *must* take revenge;
And however beguiling amorous desire may be
Every excuse is shameful to magnanimous souls.

[Ibid., III, 3]

Fate which opens for us the gateway to honour
Offers an illustrious opportunity to our fortitude,
Striving its utmost to create a misfortune
More commensurate with our valour.
And since it sees in us uncommon souls,
It forges for us uncommon destinies.

[*Horace*, II, 3]

... do not believe that the stupid populace
Makes or mars a solid reputation [...]
It is the part of kings, grandees, and right-thinking minds
To observe all that there is of virtue in its slightest manifestations.
It is they alone who dispense true glory [*gloire*]
They alone perpetuate the memory of true heroes.

[Ibid., V, 3]

The greater the danger, the sweeter the reward thereof.
Virtue plunges us into it, and glory [*gloire*] follows in its wake.

[*Cinna*, I, 2]

How difficult it is for a magnanimous soul to falter!

[Ibid., III, 3]

iv) Instances of courage and wit could be cited in certain individual members of the frondeur nobility, but their collective irresolution, unreliability, and self-seeking made a greater impact on a public obliged to suffer the consequences. Jean Vallier, a royal butler who represents the royalist but anti-mazarinist outlook of many a *'bon bourgeois'* of the day, does not trouble in his journal to hide his scorn at the news of the Duc de Beaufort's escape from prison to join his peer-rebels in Paris during the 1649 blockade.

* * * * * * * *

The Duc de Beaufort arrived there [Paris, 13th January]...strongly resolved to unite with so many illustrious knights errant who had undertaken its defence, some out of pure compassion and justice (so they said), and others out of hatred of Cardinal Mazarin, and of the violence (not to say, tyranny) of the Supreme [royal] Council; but who did not know that only consideration of their private interests had summoned, or kept, them there?

[*Journal*, eds H. Courteault and P. de Vaissière, Paris, Société de l'Histoire de France, 1902—18, 4 vols., Vol. I, p.163]

v)   The great ones could not have better substantiated public doubts about their good faith than by publishing in March 1649 their *Demandes*, which invite comparison with the relatively more subtle reclamations of the sovereign-court deputies in July 1648 (see above, pp.75-6).

* * * * * * *

Demands of the Princes and Lords who have taken up arms with the Parlement and People of Paris.

- M. le Prince de Conti demands entry into, and a seat on, the Royal Council; a fortress in his governorship of Champagne; the return of Mme de Chevreuse[21]; that the Marquis de Noirmoustier be made Duke and Peer; that 42,000 *livres*[22] be given to him; that the *tabouret* be granted to the wife of the Prince de Marsillac[23]; that the latter Prince be paid 18,000 *livres* per annum that used to be levied for [his company of] Fusiliers in Poitou, though the said Fusiliers no longer subsist; that the generalship of Galleys be given to the Duc de Retz[24] [...].

- M. le Duc de Longueville demands a Crown office, a Governorship of repute in Normandy, and the right to pass on all his governorships and offices to whichever of his children outlives him; that he be paid in *assignations* on the Province all the money owing to him in pensions and loans; that M. de Matignon[25] be made Duke and Peer, and have the right to pass on his office to his son; that the Marquis de Beuvron[26] also be made Duke and Peer, and have the right to pass on his offices to his son [...].

- M. le Duc de Beaufort demands the Governorship of Brittany for M. de Vendôme, his father[27]; that the latter receive damages for his houses and châteaux razed to the ground in Brittany during the late king's [Louis XIII's] lifetime, and payment of all his pension arrears [...].

---

[21]Shortly before his death, Louis XIII had stipulated that the arch-conspiratress should never be allowed to return from exile.

[22]The *livre* was used for accounting and allied purposes, but was not an actual coin.

[23]The title by which La Rochefoucauld was known before his father's death.

[24]Two men bore the title of Duc de Retz at the time: Henri de Gondi, cousin of the Coadjuteur, and Pierre de Gondi, the Coadjuteur's elder brother, who had married one of Henri's daughters. It is a question in the passage of the younger duke, Pierre, from whom Cardinal Richelieu had forcibly purchased the generalship of galleys in 1635.

[25]*Lieutenant-général du Roi* in Lower Normandy, lampooned for poor command of his aitches.

[26]*Lieutenant-général du Roi* in Upper Normandy, and flexible in his loyalties.

[27]The Duc de Vendôme had signed away his governorship of Brittany on 1st January 1631, two days after being released from four and a half years' captivity for intrigues against Cardinal Richelieu, who succeeded him as governor on 16th September 1631.

- M. le Duc d'Elbeuf demands Montreuil[28]; payment of everything owing to his wife; 100,000 francs for the Comte de Rieux, his second son; and a reward for the services of the Comte de Lillebonne, his youngest son.

- M. le Duc de Bouillon demands Sedan or prompt compensation for its value; that the Governorship of Auvergne be removed from the Duc de Chaulnes and given to him; that he and all those of his household should be acknowledged as princes of France[29]; that the command of the army in Germany should be restored to M. le maréchal de Turenne; that the governorship of Upper and Lower Alsace should be given to the said Marshal [Turenne]; that the latter should also be given sole ownership of the domains of Thann and Haguenau, and all the others which the King [Louis XIV] possesses in Alsace; and that he [Turenne] should be given the governorship of Philippsburg.

- M. le Maréchal de la Mothe [-Houdancourt] demands compensation for the governorship of Bellegarde and six years' back-dated income from it; 100,000 *livres* for the ransom of the Marquis de Povar; 500,000 *livres* for four years' non-possession of the Duchy of Cardona which he claims belongs to him[30]; 100,000 *livres* for an unpaid gift made to him by the late king [Louis XIII]; all his pensions, offices, and wages during his imprisonment; and that he be given back his cavalry regiment.

- M. le Duc de la Trimouille[31] demands sole ownership of the Countship of Roussillon on account of the rights of his great-great-grandmother; demands Amboise, Montrichard, and Bléré which he says belong to him as sole heir of the house of Amboise; the Countship of Guines as belonging to the ancient domain of the House of la Trimouille; letters of separation of the Countship of Laval from the *présidial* of Château-Gontier; and that the sale contract which he made with the late Cardinal Richelieu for the barony of L'Ile Bouchard be annulled [...][32].
  [*Choix de Mazarinades*, ed. C. Moreau, Paris, Renouard, 1853, 2 vols., Vol. I, pp.431-36]

---

[28]In Picardy, of which Elbeuf was governor. He wanted his eldest son to have the governorship of Montreuil.

[29]The princes in question enjoyed coveted prerogatives such as the right to keep their hat on while the king gave audience to ambassadors, that of having their accommodation chalked with a 'For M. le Prince...' when the court went on a journey, and the *tabouret* for their daughters.

[30]The Marshal — Philippe, Comte de la Mothe-Houdancourt — was made viceroy of Catalonia and duke of Cardona in 1642. Rendered responsible for the French loss of Lérida in Catalonia in 1644, he was imprisoned until 1648.

[31]Henri, duc de la Trémoille (the name is variously spelt by contemporaries) had raised troops in the Poitou area on behalf of Parlement in the aftermath of the royal family's escape to Saint-Germain in January 1649.

[32]The names of nine other persons making demands on behalf of themselves and/or relatives figure on the original list.

C. *The stars of the Fronde*

i) *Anne d'Autriche*

No appraisal of Anne d'Autriche could fail to take into account the memoirs of Mme
de Motteville who, from the outset of the regency in 1643 until Anne's death in 1666,
was in almost continuous but unofficial attendance at the queen regent's side,
privileged to observe and question her at first hand, and to be the recipient of 'some
of her secrets' (Preface to the *Mémoires*). From out of the written record of this
unusual attachment both the portraitist and the sitter emerge as women of piety and
principles, but reassuringly human in their prejudices and foibles.

* * * * * * * *

The Queen, who had not gratified Parlement with a good heart[33], said, in speaking of
this affair, that she fully believed Parlement would repent of what it had done, and that
she was not sorry to have been forced to revoke the favour that she had unwillingly
accorded it, in treating it more favourably than it deserved. Since Charles V's blood
in her veins[34] made her haughty, she did not believe that any creature could or
should dare to resist the King's will; with the result that in all affairs concerning
Parlement, whose procedure and chicanery she could not understand, she always
wanted to subdue it and make it carry out everything ordered in the royal council.
But since the Parlementarians felt within them the first stirrings of revolt, they
defended themselves methodically and skilfully used manifestations of the Queen's
high-handedness and of the baseness of her counsellor [i.e. Mazarin] to cause him to
make mistakes which he afterwards had a lot of trouble putting right. This was why
this princess has often appeared more irascible than she was, and more severe than
gentle, though in actual fact, in matters about which she knew, she was the most
reasonable and restrained of women.
[*Mémoires*, MP, 2me Sér., Vol. X, p.157]

Retz's rhetorical verve is given full rein in this thumbnail sketch of Anne, who, for all
her alleged incapacity, had found the wherewithal to thwart him.

* * * * * * * *

The queen possessed, more than anyone I have ever seen, that kind of intelligence
which was necessary for her not to appear stupid to those who did not know her. She
had more snappishness than haughtiness, more haughtiness than greatness, more
façade than substance, more heedlessness about money than liberality, more liberality
than self-interest, more self-interest than disinterestedness, more attachment than
passion, more hardness than pride, more recollection of affronts than of kindnesses,
more piety in the way of intention than action, more stubbornness than firmness, and
more incapacity than all of the above [traits].
[*Mémoires*, op. cit., pp.94-5]

---

[33]The reference is to Anne's sentiments concerning her order of 18th May 1648 for the revocation of the
paulette, which had been renewed for Parlement in preferential circumstances.
[34]See above, p.3.

ii) *Mazarin*

Did Mme de Motteville have to wrestle with the dictates of Christian charity and the obligations of an '*honnête femme* ' as she penned this summary of Mazarin's character and position, and recollected what she spells out elsewhere in her memoirs: his suspicions of her, the absence of tangible marks of his appreciation for her services, and the greater degree of intimacy that he enjoyed with their royal mistress?

* * * * * * *

Cardinal Mazarin had as much intelligence as a man who had been the architect of his own grandeur could have. He had great ability, and above all, a wonderful delicacy and ingenuity in leading men on and beguiling them by means of umpteen dubious and deceptive hopes. He did harm only out of necessity to those who displeased him. Ordinarily he just complained about them, and his complaints always resulted in explanations which enabled him to regain painlessly the friendship of those who were disloyal to him or who claimed grounds for complaint against him. He had the gift of pleasing and it was impossible not to be charmed by his sweet talk; but this same sweetness, when unaccompanied by the gratifications which he led men to expect, caused them to tire of waiting and then to become fed up and disgruntled. Hitherto[35], complaints from private individuals had not made much impression on the public; they were based on aversion for his favoured position rather than on hatred for his person. The respect which the halo of royal power, shining gloriously around him, necessarily engraves on the hearts of the king's subjects, silenced that which human malice sought to blame in him; and the tranquillity of the court, combined with successes in the war, had up to that point done more to enhance his reputation than the lowliest courtier could to cast shame upon him; but gradually several faults were found in him, some attributable to all favourites, others more personal. It was said that he was ignorant of our customs, and that he did not take sufficient care to have them observed; that he was not concerned, as he should have been, with governing the state according to the laws formerly established, and that he did not protect justice as he was obliged to do in his capacity of prime minister, and was lacking in the attention that he owed to the public good. These sins of omission, although substantial, could not rightly dishonour him, because at the time he might have had good intentions which, if they were known, ought perhaps to have justified him in the public eye. One can nevertheless say that, given his temperament, the accusations were not all that ill-founded; for it was in his nature to be unduly neglectful of doing good. He seemed to esteem no virtue and to hate no vice. He appeared to have no vice; he was supposed to be a man accustomed to the employment of Christian virtues and did not show that he wanted them to be practised. He made no profession of piety, and none of his actions gave any signs of the opposite: except that he sometimes let slip mocking remarks at variance with the respect that a Christian must have for everything appertaining to religion. Despite his avarice, he had not yet appeared avaricious; and, under his administration, finances had been squandered by the *partisans* to a greater extent than in any other century. He has likewise [...] accorded Church dignities to many persons who have aspired to them out of profane motives and has not always nominated as bishops men who could

---

[35]The passage figures amongst events of the year 1647.

do credit to his choice by their virtue and piety. Religion has been too much
forsaken by him, and he has always had too much indifference for this sacred trust
which God had confided to him. He was naturally mistrustful, and one of his greatest
concerns was to study men in order to get to know them, and to protect himself from
their attacks and from the intrigues formed against him. He professed to fear
nothing, and to scorn even the warnings that he was given concerning his person,
although in fact his greatest effort was principally aimed at self-preservation.
[*Mémoires*, op. cit., p.122]

Critical contemporaries of Mazarin evidence a certain malaise at not being able to
expose in him the rugged traits which commonly facilitate typecasting in the rôle of
Tyrant, and excuse rebellion on the part of the oppressed. The cardinal was
exasperatingly 'smooth', an Eminence without eminences, so to speak. His epistolary
instructions to some of his confidential agents reinforce this image, with their talk of
non-violence, of keeping up harmonious appearances, of allowing time, bargaining,
and human nature to accomplish desired ends.

* * * * * * * *

30th July 1650, to Le Tellier [Anne is anxious for the arrest of two of Condé's men
busy trying to stir revolt in Normandy and give a coastal fortress to the Spanish].
There is no reward that cannot be promised to those who serve to have them arrested,
in order to punish them in exemplary fashion, myself being increasingly convinced
that, without that, we shall be forever starting afresh. You must believe that, when I
write to you so often on this subject, the force of reason necessarily obliges me to do
so, not being by nature very much inclined towards severity.
[*Lettres*, op. cit., Vol. III, p.648]

5th March 1651, to De Lionne: To serve the Queen well one must be on the alert
for information about everything that is happening and profit from circumstances;
because if the rosary beads once start to become unthreaded [i.e. if there is a split
between the supporters of Retz and those of the Princes] and the Queen can take
advantage of it, everything will go the way that Her Majesty wants, but one must act
and carry on negotiations everywhere, by different secret channels.
[*Lettres*, Vol. IV, p.52]

23rd May 1651, to Le Tellier [Mazarin has trouble getting money out of the
financiers]. M. Colbert must, however, dissimulate, pretending to be assured of their
goodwill; for time can arrange a lot of things.
[*Lettres*, Vol. IV, p.202]

13th June 1651, to De Lionne: I am sure that the Queen will have received Mme
de Longueville very well and tried to satisfy her, as far as possible; because, as things
and people's dispositions stand at the moment, one must treat well and cajole
everybody, for it is eminently possible that interests and passions will prove capable of
dividing the best of friends and the closest of relatives, and I see that with a little
deftness, the conduct of M. le Prince [Condé] will cause a visible diminution in the

number of his friends and alienate the majority of those who, through kinship, were united with him.
[*Lettres*, Vol. IV, p.266]

iii) *Gaston d'Orléans*

By the mid-1640s Gaston had gone some way towards toning down the brash, anti-Establishment behaviour of his youth which had earned Mme de Motteville's pungent observation: 'He resembled the son of a king, but one badly brought up' [*Mémoires*, op. cit., p.118]. It was now possible to believe that he was well-intentioned and alert to his responsibilities as uncle of the boy king. But his underlying weakness, pliability, and irresolution were also common knowledge and publicly satirised, as in this extract from Jean Loret's popular weekly rhymed gazette, *La Muse Historique*, nominally addressed to the Duc de Longueville's daughter.

* * * * * * * *

Gaston doesn't know which side to take
So scared is he of making a mistake.
Madame La Fronde and the Court[36]
In turn attract his heart.
Today the one possesses him,
An hour later the other engrosses him.
He's suspended between the two,
And, being neither won nor lost,
He says to the one: 'Be off';
Then he says as much to the other.
To the one he says: 'I'm yours',
To the other he says: 'Let's unite'.
He's harangued: he listens,
He disputes, hesitates, doubts,
He sees the bad, he sees the good,
But in the end he's unresolved [...].
How will he extricate himself
From such a complicated maze,
And what must he reply?
Will it be Court, will it be Fronde?
Take a Norman's[37] word for it, I haven't a clue,
And if I said otherwise
I'd be far too bold,
For he himself doesn't know.

[*La Muse Historique*, eds J. Ravenel and V. de la Pelouze, Paris, Jannet, 1857—78, 4 vols., Vol. I, p.71, Letter of 25th December 1650]

---

[36]i.e. the royalist camp.

[37]Loret was a Norman by birth, but he is also playing on the other meaning of the word 'normand': a person who is wily and whose word is not to be trusted.

To prevent Gaston from sitting permanently on the fence, strategies had to be developed by the press of persons vying to influence him. Retz gives an amusing glimpse of one such strategy, employed to propel Gaston into formal alliance with the Frondeurs in January 1651.

* * * * * * * *

In the end Monsieur [Gaston] signed his treaty, but in a way that will show you his nature better than everything I have said on the subject. Caumartin[38] had it in his pocket, with a writing-case on the other side; he caught him in passing, put a pen in his hand, and he signed (as Mlle de Chevreuse said at the time) in the way that he would have done a promissory note at a witches' sabbath if he had been afraid of his guardian angel taking him by surprise there.
[*Mémoires*, op. cit., p.228]

iv) *Condé*

Condé's conduct off the battlefield, as well as on it, left spectators breathless, but for different reasons. Accustomed to sweep all before him by his daring and skill in combat, he found it difficult to appreciate that attempting to ride roughshod over everyone was not the ideal way to proceed in political and social life. The feelings of animosity which the man aroused tended in consequence to be as passionate as the sentiments of admiration which the conquering hero inspired.

The Comte de Coligny-Saligny began serving under Condé in 1649 and went over with him into the service of Spain, following the prevailing aristocratic code of honour, which dictated steadfast allegiance to the individual to whom one had pledged it, regardless, if need be, of loyalty to the sovereign. Condé's nonchalance in recognising this singular manifestation of fidelity enraged Coligny-Saligny to the point where he not only exposed the Prince's ingratitude in his memoirs, but he also consigned this curious indictment to the margins of the missal in his household chapel.

* * * * * * *

I never take up my pen again without my first thought being to vilify M. le Prince de Condé, about whom, in truth, I could never say enough. I have observed him carefully over the thirteen years that I have been attached to him. But I say before God, in whose presence I write, and in a book composed in His honour, [...] that I have never known a soul so mundane, so vicious, nor a heart so ungrateful as that of M. le Prince, nor so treacherous, nor so malicious. For as soon as he is under obligation to a man, the first thing that he does is to look for something with which to reproach the latter and somehow evade his obligation to show gratitude [...]. M. de La Rochefoucauld has told me umpteen times that he had never seen a man more averse to giving pleasure than M. le Prince, and that the latter was furious at having to give even things which cost him nothing, since his gifts would have given pleasure

---

[38]Louis Le Fèvre de Caumartin, a member of the Paris Parlement, was a friend and agent of Retz.

[...]. The recognised, out and out bugger[39] that he is [...] has only two good
qualities: intelligence and courage. He puts the former to very ill use, and the latter
he intended to use to take the crown off the King's head. I know what he has said to
me on the subject several times and on what he based his pernicious plans; but they
are things that I would prefer to forget, far from writing them down.
[*Mémoires*, ed. M. Monmerqué, Paris, Société de l'Histoire de France, 1841, pp.xlviii-l]

Judging from the testimony of another firsthand witness (and victim?) — the
Duchesse de Nemours, step-daughter of Condé's sister, the Duchesse de Longueville
— the Prince's arrogance and bad manners were caught from, or reinforced by, his
family circle.

* * * * * * *

In matters of consequence, they [the Condés] went out of their way to upset people,
and in the ordinary course of events they were so unsociable as to be intolerable.
They had such mocking airs and said such offensive things, that no one could stand
them. They affected such disdainful boredom when visitors called, and showed so
openly that they were being put out, that it was not hard to deduce that they were
doing their utmost to get rid of the company. Whatever one's rank, one used to wait
endlessly in M^r le Prince's [Condé's] antechamber; and very often, after one had
waited a considerable time, he would send everyone away, without anyone being able
to see him. When one incurred their displeasure, they pushed people to the furthest
extreme, and they were incapable of gratitude for the services rendered to them.
[*Mémoires*, MP, 2me Sér., Vol. IX, p.627]

v) *Retz*

Whilst acknowledging the power of Retz's intellect, the Duchesse de Nemours
reproached him, at bottom, for not possessing the moral rectitude and moderation
attributed, justly, to herself. This discerning survey by a virtuous woman of a suspect
pillar of the Church forms a piquant companion-piece to the one quoted above
(pp.83-4).

* * * * * * *

As for the Coadjutor, although he appeared so eager and so zealous to enlarge the
Parlement party, and though it preoccupied him, he had never had any reason to
complain about the court; on the contrary, he owed his coadjutorship of Paris to the
Queen. But he had boundless ambition, and wanted to be cardinal at any price, as had

---

[39]Meaning 'homosexual'. Condé lent credence to such accusations by surrounding himself with a circle
of male favourites, the so-called 'petits-maîtres'. His triumph at the battle of Lens in August 1648 was
offset by the rumour, which his harshness incited his own troops to spread, about a captured Condéen
officer being released because Archduke Leopold wished to imply that the man 'was too necessary to his
[Condé's] pleasures for him to be detained any longer' (*Mémoires de Nicolas Goulas*, ed. C. Constant,
Paris, Société de l'Histoire de France, 1879—82, 3 vols., Vol. II, p.348).

two Paris bishops of his name. A man of common sense, integrity, and orderly
conduct, ought to have believed that the surest, shortest, most honourable and fairest
way to obtain what he wanted from the king was his loyalty; he would have made of
that his principal means, he would have sought to establish his grandeur and
reputation only on the performance of his duties; and in the end those duties and
loyalty to his king would have sufficed for him. But since the Coadjutor could only
find in extraordinary adventures the wherewithal to fulfil his vast ideas, and fully
satisfy his ample imagination, he thought that on the contrary he would do much
better out of factions and upheavals. Apart from the fact that these were much more
congenial to his natural bent, he was so inclined towards extraordinary things that he
would have preferred one such which would have been mediocre or bad, to one which
would have been good and solid, if he could have attained the latter only by ordinary
means. His mind, though penetrating and quite far-reaching, was yet subject to such
great contradictions that he prided himself generally on everything unbecoming to
him, even gallantry[40], though he was not very well built, and valour[41], despite his
being a priest.
[*Mémoires*, op. cit., p.620]

Several of Retz's essential traits, as he himself underlines them, figure in this excerpt
from his memoirs: his liking for stage-managing events, manipulating people, and
swaying the opinion of the populace; his preference for working from behind a
human shield; his impatience at being impeded by his clerical profession; his sense of
humour and irony. The picture of Beaufort which he paints — bold, blond, and
brainless — betrays the contempt of a superior intellect, but also the envy of a rival
who could not indulge with equal openness in martial and gallant pursuits.

* * * * * * * *

... I did not find that imprisonment[42] had given him any more sense. However, it is
true that it had given him more reputation. He had withstood captivity with firmness,
and emerged from it with courage. It was even to his credit not to have departed from
the banks of the Loire at a time when it truly needed skill and firmness to remain
there. At the beginning of a civil war it is not difficult to exploit the merit of all those
out of favour at court. It is a great merit not to be in favour there. Since he had
assured me some time previously via Montrésor[43] that he would be delighted to form

---

[40]Retz's affairs with women, and their repercussions on his health, are complacently detailed in his
memoirs.

[41]Retz had engaged in a series of duels in his youth, avowedly in the hope that the resulting scandal
would eject him from an ecclesiastical career. In January 1649 he set up a cavalry regiment known as the
'Corinthians' because he was titular archbishop of Corinth. The regiment fared badly in a sortie against
royalist troops, giving rise, so Guy Joly reports [*Mémoires*, MP, 3me Sér., Vol. II, p.19], to public
mockery over this 'First [Epistle] to the Corinthians'.

[42]Imprisoned at Vincennes in September 1643, Beaufort escaped in May 1648, and arrived in Paris in
January 1649.

[43]Claude de Bourdeille, Comte de Montrésor, was a veteran conspirator and exile, attached to Gaston
d'Orléans' circle, who had been imprisoned for fourteen months in 1646 on a charge of rendering
assistance to the exiled Duchesse de Chevreuse.

a liaison with me, and since I could well foresee the use to which I could put him, I had casually broadcast complimentary rumours about him from time to time amongst the populace [...]. Montrésor, who kept him closely informed of his obligations to me, had made all the necessary arrangements for a grand union between us. You will readily believe that this was not disadvantageous to him, given my standing in the party; and union was almost a necessity for me, because my profession could hamper me in umpteen situations, and I needed a man whom I could put in front of me at important conjunctures [...]. I needed a figurehead, but I needed only a figurehead; and luckily for me, it turned out that this figurehead was a grandson of Henri-the-Great[44]; that he spoke the language of the markets[45], which is not usual for the offspring of Henri-the-Great, and that he had an abundance of very long and very blond hair. You cannot imagine the weight of this circumstance; you cannot conceive of the effect that the hair had on the populace.

We left Prudhomme's establishment[46] to go and see M[r] le Prince de Conti. We placed ourselves at the same carriage-window. We stopped in the Rue Saint-Denis and in the Rue Saint-Martin. I introduced, I displayed, and I praised Mr de Beaufort. The fire flared in less than an instant. All the men cried: 'Long live Beaufort!'; all the women kissed him; and, without exaggeration, we had difficulty in getting through to the Town Hall because of the crowd[47].
[*Mémoires*, op. cit., pp.98-9]

vi) *Broussel*

Pierre Broussel's popularity with the crowds rested on rather different foundations from that of Beaufort — venerable old age, a frugal lifestyle, and forensic eloquence — but he too served as a front for persons of more nimble wit, according to this testimony, amongst others, from a Condé sympathiser, Louis Ardier, sieur de Vineuil.

* * * * * * * *

---

[44]Beaufort's father — César, Duc de Vendôme — was one of king Henri IV's numerous bastards.

[45]Beaufort's linguistic ineptitude outside the confines of the Halles was the other stick, along with his irresistibility to the lower orders, regularly used to beat him. '... if he knew how to speak, he would say fine things', was Mazarin's verdict [*Lettres*, op. cit., Vol. IV, p.309]

[46]Prudhomme ran a bathing-house which was used as a kind of hotel by noblemen.

[47]For once, Retz is not exaggerating. Cf. Dr Guy Patin, frondeur Dean of the Paris Faculty of Medicine in 1650, describing to a friend in a letter of 14th May 1649 how Beaufort, out playing tennis, was mobbed by Market tradeswomen offering to replace any money that he lost at the game: '"Mr de Beaufort, play on boldly, you won't lack money; my companion there and I have brought two hundred *écus*, and if you need more, I'm ready to go and get as much again". All the other women began to shout as well that they had some to put at his disposal, for which he thanked them. That day he was visited by more than two thousand women' [*Lettres*, ed. J.-H. Reveillé-Parise, Paris, Baillière, 1846, 3 vols., Vol. II, pp.513-14]. What is perhaps more striking than Beaufort's literal star quality is the fact that those of his party derided him for, but cynically 'used', it.

... a member of the Grand'Chambre, a personage of longstanding probity, and mediocre intellect, and who had a lifelong hatred of [royal] favourites. The good man, inspired by his own sentiments and by the persuasion of Longueil[48] and others whom he had come to believe, took the lead in voicing the most vigorous opinions, which were followed by the Frondeur cabal; so that his name caused a stir in the assemblies of the Chambers, and he had made himself head of this party in Parlement, one who was all the more influential in that his age and poverty put him beyond the reach of envy. So, since the populace, installed in the Palais de Justice, were informed that he was keenly interested in bringing them relief, they took him to their heart and gave him the fine name of 'father'.

[*Mémoires*, in *Oeuvres Complètes* of La Rochefoucauld op. cit., Vol. II, pp.508-9]

---

[48]Pierre Longueil, a fellow-member of the Grand'Chambre. He and his brother René, Président de Maisons, another Grand'Chambre judge, had the reputation of being amongst the first, most frequently consulted and most dangerous of the Frondeurs up to the point where René was fastened to the royalist camp by being made superintendent of finances in May 1650.

III INCIDENTS

i) *8th January 1648. The magistrates begin to flex their muscles*

Nettled by news of the regency government's aim to plant extra colleagues in their ranks, fifty-eight of the existing seventy-two Paris *maîtres des requêtes* met for seven hours at the Palais de Justice on 8th January to discuss contingency plans to ward off the evil. Their uncompromising mood, as reported by one of their number, Olivier Lefèvre d'Ormesson, in his *Journal*, was reflected in their unanimous decision to 'persecute by every means those who made a bid for the new offices' and in their readiness to make embarrassing revelations if coercion was attempted.

* * * * * * *

In addition it was said to be imprudent to attack us and oblige us to set an example of disobedience to the other companies at the present time, we who served to make others obey, and that we knew too well the intimate details of affairs and of finance ministers to be forced to reveal them, as we would certainly do.
[*Journal*, ed. A. Chéruel, Paris, Imprimerie Impériale, 1860—61, 2 vols., Vol. I, p.406]

ii) *15th January 1648. The king and queen regent hear some home truths*

Omer Talon's 'very humble remonstrances' (his term) at the *lit de justice* of 15th January had his listeners on the edges of their seats, for diverse reasons. Amidst flights of eloquence on the Medes and Persians, heavenly bodies, and Homer, the 'king's man'[49] represents the plight of the French people in strong language, and hints at their impatience with a war that Mazarin was accused of prolonging.

* * * * * * *

You are, Sire, our sovereign lord; the power of Your Majesty comes from on high, and you owe an account of your actions only to your conscience, after God; but it is important to your glory that we should be free men, not slaves; the grandeur of your State and the dignity of your crown are gauged by the status of those who obey you [...]. For ten years, Sire, the countryside has been ruined, the peasants reduced to sleeping on straw, their furniture sold to pay taxes which they cannot provide; and, to keep Paris in luxury, millions of innocent souls are obliged to live on bread made of bran and oats, and to hope for no other protection than that of their helplessness. These wretches own no property but their souls, because the latter could not be auctioned; the town-dwellers, after finding the 'subsistence-'[50], 'winter quarter-'[51],

---

[49]The three representatives of the king in the Parlement were collectively known as *'les gens du Roi'*: 'the king's men'.

[50]In French, 'subsistance'. See p.75, n12.

[51]In French, 'quartier d'hiver'. Seventeenth-century French troops were traditionally in winter quarters from the end of October to the end of March. In the absence of barracks they were lodged in those provinces and towns which had not bought exemption from the king, and on those inhabitants who were

'halts'[52]-taxes and loans, and paying the *paulette* and confirmation-tax[53], are re-taxed as 'the wealthy' *[aisés]*.

What security there is left in the sovereign companies is undermined this day by the creation of new offices, which are a perpetual burden on the State; for when they are established, the populace must pay for their upkeep and costs.

Be so good as to reflect a little, Madam, on this public wretchedness when you withdraw into your heart. This evening, in the solitude of your oratory, consider what grief, bitterness and consternation all the office-holders of the realm may be feeling at seeing all their property confiscated today, without their having committed any crime; add to that thought, Madam, the disastrous state of the provinces, where the hope of peace, the honour of winning battles, the glory of conquering provinces, cannot nourish those who have no bread, and who cannot count myrtles, palms, and laurels[54] among the ordinary fruits of the earth.
[*Mémoires*, op. cit., pp.210-11]

iii) *13th May 1648. The sovereign courts unite*

This thunderclap, which awoke everyone to the possibilities of defiance, was accompanied by one of the torrents of mockery and hilarity that not infrequently punctuated the Fronde.

* * * * * * * *

The cardinal [Mazarin], warned of this proposition [of union], sent for the deputies of all the sovereign companies to tell them that the Queen was totally opposed to decrees of union. Whereupon these gentlemen having answered that they were not contrary to the king's service, he replied that it was enough that the matter was displeasing to the Queen; and that if the King did not want people to wear tassels on their collar, tassels would have to be dispensed with, because it was not so much the thing prohibited as the prohibition which constituted the crime. That did not prevent these deputies from proceeding straight to report to their colleagues on what had happened and beginning this report with a joke, exaggeratedly deriding the cardinal for his comparison of the tassels, which they greatly ridiculed and about which numerous burlesque works of all kinds were composed in prose and verse. They also mocked him a great deal because instead of saying 'decree of union', he had said 'decree of onion' *['oignon']* on account of the difficulty that he had in speaking good French.
[Duchesse de Nemours, *Mémoires*, op. cit., p.614]

---

not sufficiently influential to protest successfully. The expression 'quartier d'hiver' also applied to a supplement to the *taille*, used to pay for billeting troops.

[52]In French, 'étapes': regulation stopping-places at which supplies were collected for distribution to troops on the march. The word was also employed with reference to the supplies in themselves, or to a tax levied to pay for them.

[53]The *droit de confirmation* was paid by office-holders to the king on his accession to the throne.

[54]i.e. traditional symbols of victory.

iv) *26th August 1648. Paris up in arms over Broussel's arrest*

The most reliable account of the arrest of Broussel is probably that of Mme de Motteville, who discussed the action with the man ordered to carry it out, the Comte de Comminges, lieutenant of Anne d'Autriche's guards. But Mme de Motteville is uninformative on the question of who precisely started the riots that led to scenes in Paris reminiscent of the Religious Wars at the end of the previous century. The relevant portion of her narrative is therefore followed here by a testimony which is more explicit than most on this particular point. It stems from another witness who took care to be well-informed: Nicolas-François Baudot, seigneur du Buisson et d'Ambenay. Dubuisson-Aubenay, as he is known to modern historians, was attached to the household of a secretary of state and was appointed royal historiographer in 1646. The detailed journal, quoted below, which he kept of events during the Fronde, until his death in 1652, was conceivably the framework for a full-length history book on the period.

According to Mme de Motteville, Comminges took his carriage and five men to the home of Broussel in the narrow Port-Saint-Landry street not far from Notre-Dame. Broussel tried to play for time by claiming that he had taken a laxative. An old servant-woman began shouting to the neighbours for help and swearing at Comminges.

* * * * * * * *

At the noise made by this woman, the populace *['peuple']* gathered in this small street: the first to come running brought others, and in a moment it was full of rabble *['canaille']*. When they saw this carriage full of weapons and men, they all began to shout that their liberator was being taken away. Some wanted to cut the horses' reins and spoke of smashing the carriage; but the guardsmen and a little page of Comminges protected it bravely and opposed their designs, threatening to kill anyone who tried. Comminges, who heard the noise from the populace and in the house, and who saw the disorder that would arise if he delayed any longer in carrying out his project, thought that he had better hurry; and taking forceful hold of Broussel, he threatened to kill him if he did not walk. He tore him from his home and the embraces of his family, and threw him willy-nilly into the carriage, his guards going ahead in order to clear the populace who were threatening, and wanting to attack, him. As a result of the noise, chains were hung across streets, and at the first detour, Comminges had to come to a halt. So that to escape he had frequently to turn the carriage round, and every few minutes he had to fight a sort of battle against the populace whose numbers swelled as he made his way along. By dint of keeping going he finally arrived opposite the residence of the First President [of the Parlement] on the quay, where his carriage overturned and smashed. It would have been the end of him, if he had not found at this same spot the soldiers of the Guards regiment who were still in line[55] and had orders to assist him. He had sprung from his overturned carriage; and seeing himself surrounded by enemies who wanted to

---

[55]A heavy guard of honour had been stationed in the vicinity of Notre-Dame for the service of celebration which immediately preceded, and masked preparations for, the arrest of Broussel. See above, p.17.

tear him apart, having only three or four of his guards, who were not capable of saving him from this danger, he shouted: 'To arms, comrades! Help!' The soldiers, always faithful to the king at all times during this regency, surrounded him and gave him all possible assistance. The populace surrounded him as well, with very different intentions; and there took place a battle limited to hands and insults, but no less perilous to the State than the greatest ones ever waged with fire and sword. Comminges was in this position for quite some time, until one of his guards brought him another carriage taken after threats from some female passers-by, whose coachman, despite their resistance, was forced to serve on this occasion. Comminges took it and abandoned on the spot his own, which the populace, out of rage and spite, smashed to smithereens. The carriage which he had commandeered broke again in the Rue Saint-Honoré, and these accidents served to notify the whole of Paris of what was going on, and to move to pity an infinite number of people who proceeded to stir up revolt.

[*Mémoires*, op. cit., pp.190-91]

Dubuisson-Aubenay, after outlining more dryly the incidents colourfully enumerated by Mme de Motteville, focuses attention on the mob and on those empowered to quieten them.

* * * * * * * *

Meanwhile, the populace was roused; the boatmen started up in the [Place de] Grève[56] on the one side, and the craftsmen in the vicinity of the Palais [de Justice] and the Pont Saint-Michel, then in the Halles [Markets] quarter; a large band carrying swords, pikes, pistols, and lifted paving-stones, charged down as far as the Rue Saint-Honoré, smashing the windows of houses, and breaking down the doors, nevertheless shouting 'Long live the king, freedom for the prisoner'.

Marshals de la Meilleraye and de l'Hôpital, assisted by the Grand Provost of the Hôtel[57] and more than fifty cavalrymen, went about the streets pushing this mob[58] away from the Halles and towards the Palais [de Justice], in order to re-open the shops which were all closed and to reassure the populace *['peuple']*, who continually demanded the prisoner Mr de Broussel. Squadrons from the regiments of Swiss and French guards were deployed around the Palais-Royal, the end of the Pont-Neuf, the Ecole Saint-Germain, the Place Dauphine, and the Palais [de Justice]. Several highly scatterbrained craftsmen, having fired on the men accompanying the aforementioned marshals, were shot dead.

[*Journal des Guerres Civiles (1648—1652)*, ed. G. Saige, Paris, Champion, 1883—85, 2 vols., Vol. I, p.51]

---

[56]This square adjoined the Seine, and boats could moor there.

[57]The Grand Prévôt de l'Hôtel (not to be confused with the Prévôt des Marchands) was responsible for matters of discipline, security, and subsistence in the royal entourage.

[58]The French word here is *'populace'*, which has a pejorative connotation that *'peuple'* does not.

v) *January 1649. A narrow escape in blockaded Paris*

Disorientated and frustrated by the brusque removal of celebrities for whom it had
strong feelings of affinity or antipathy, the Paris mob reacted to the exodus of the
royal entourage on 6th January 1649 with a violence equal to that displayed at the
time of the Barricades. Mme de Motteville, in another of her vivid 'snapshots',
explains how she personally came to be on the receiving end.

* * * * * * * *

The persons who were attached to the King, and who had remained in Paris, were the
only ones to be pitied; because the populace continually threatened to pillage them,
and we dared not show ourselves without endangering our lives. My sister and I
wanted to flee from Paris. We took with us one of our women friends who was
staying with me, a person of good birth and merit. We did what we could to get out
by the Saint-Honoré Gate, with the intention of availing ourselves of the assistance of
some persons awaiting us outside the city gate; but the poor who were by the
Capuchin monastery, seeing that we wanted to get out, thronged around us, and
forced us to retreat into the church belonging to these good fathers, whither they
followed us, murmuring. In the end they forced us to leave in order to try and find
help in the vicinity of the guardhouse, where we hoped to encounter a few reasonable
people; but the Parisian soldiers, hostile to anything seeming to want to go to Saint-
Germain, having frightened us with their threats, we retraced our steps in the direction
of the Hôtel de Vendôme. The porter of this house, far from receiving us, closed the
door on us, and precisely at a time when some rogues had torn up paving-stones to
serve as weapons with which to make martyrs of us after the fashion of Saint
Stephen[59]. Mlle de Villeneuve, this friend staying with me, seeing one of these
sidekicks approach her with a stone in his hand to throw at her head, told him in a
firm and calm tone that he was wrong to want to kill her, since she had never done
him any harm; she spoke to him with so much presence of mind and reasonableness,
that this scoundrel, despite his natural brutality, halted. He threw the stone elsewhere
and left her, but to head for my sister and myself who had kept running from the
Hôtel de Vendôme to take refuge in [the church of] Saint-Roch. We got there, thank
God, despite the insults and threats of this rabble thirsting for prey and pillage. As
soon as I got there, I went down on my knees before the main altar, where high mass
was being celebrated. These dragons who had followed us had so little respect for the
service that a woman, more horrible in my eyes than a Fury, came and tore my
mask[60] from my face, saying that I was a 'mazarine' and should be struck down and
torn to pieces. As I am not naturally valiant, I was very frightened. I wanted in this
turmoil to go to the house of the *curé* who was my confessor and seek help from him;
but my sister, who had more courage and better judgement than myself, seeing me
pursued by two rogues who, as soon as I neared the door, shouted at me: 'Your
money...!', rescued me from their clutches and stopped me going out of the church,
because everything was to be feared from their barbarity. The populace kept on
crowding into the church, which resounded with yells, from which I could only pick

---

[59]The first Christian martyr, stoned to death.

[60]Masks were worn by seventeenth-century Frenchwomen to protect their complexions against the
elements.

out that we had to be put to death. The noise attracted the *curé*, who spoke to them and had trouble in silencing them. For my part, pretending that I wanted to make confession, I begged him to send someone to get me help promptly. He did so immediately; and the Marquis de Beuvron my neighbour, with the officers from the area where the guardhouse was located at the time, and other people who heard tell of the danger I was in, came to get us out of it; and making all this rabble draw back, they would not leave us until they had escorted us back to our home, where we arrived feeling so ill that we had to go to bed.
[*Mémoires*, op. cit., pp.235-36]

vi) 13th January 1649. The storming of the Bastille

This incident, like the flight of the royal family before it, links the Fronde with the Revolution of 1789, but after the fashion of a burlesque dress rehearsal for a major tragedy.

* * * * * * *

This comedy (for there was not a single drop of blood shed on either side) ended up causing so much confusion to the said Sieur du Tremblay [governor of the Bastille[61]] that he was a long time absent from the royal court and the city: indeed, the nine or ten volleys of cannon-fire which had been directed at the drawbridge and the two towers at the side were barely noticeable and the damage could have been repaired for next to nothing[62]. In a word, this siege was all the more splendid and famous in that the ladies saw it from their carriages which filled the whole of the Rue Saint-Antoine as on carnival days, and remained there quite safely throughout the proceedings because, it was said in public, agreement had been reached with this brave captain not to fire on the bourgeois but only over the heads of the attackers: which [stipulation] he religiously observed.
[Jean Vallier, *Journal*, op. cit., Vol. I, pp.162-63]

vii)   February — March 1649. The bloodless rout of Turenne

The necessity to grasp the opportunity afforded by the Rueil peace-conferences to end the turmoil in the capital took on a fresh dimension of urgency when it became known that hitherto loyal Turenne, influenced by his brother Bouillon, was on the point of leading to the assistance of the rebel Parlement and generals an army of German mercenaries stationed on the banks of the Rhine. But before Turenne could get the army moving, it started to disappear. Mazarin had had the German officers informed of their commander's real plans and forestalled these by sending a Protestant banker supporter with a massive handout to persuade the men to desert to the governor of Brisach, Jean-Louis d'Erlach, a 'safe' German general in the employ of France. Turenne's embarrassment over this novel form of victory, so illustrative of

---

[61]Du Tremblay was also the brother of the famous Capuchin monk Father Joseph, who had acted in the previous reign as 'Eminence Grise' to cardinal Richelieu.

[62]The French has 'for less than a *pistole*'. A *pistole* was a Spanish coin in circulation in France.

Mazarin's contention that 'The possessor of finances has right and authority on his side'[63], is manifest in the style of his own account of what happened.

* * * * * * * *

When the Court [Anne d'Autriche and her ministers] knew that he [Turenne[64]] was going to cross the Rhine, they came right out into the open, which they had not done previously, having given no orders to Mr de Turenne, but simply sent word that they would be happy for the army to march to France after peace was made in Germany[65], the Court, I say, sent express orders to all the officers not to acknowledge Mr de Turenne [as commander], despatched three hundred thousand *écus*[66] to the Rhineland, plus a promise to provide four or five lots of pay owing to the soldiers, which, together with enticement from M[r] d'Erlac, swayed six German regiments into going by night to join him at Brisach. That caused great disorder in the rest of the army: three infantry regiments doing likewise and positioning themselves near Philippsburg, there remained with M[r] de Turenne nearly half the army, and very wavering at that, except for five or six regiments. He, seeing that he could no longer march as planned and unwilling also to rejoin the Court [...], ordered some of his general officers left at his side to take the rest of the troops to join M[r] d'Erlac. Thus, with fifteen to twenty of his friends, he withdrew to Holland.

[*Mémoires du Maréchal de Turenne*, ed. P. Marichal, Paris, Société de l'Histoire de France, 1909—14, 2 vols., Vol. I, pp.133-34]

viii)   *9th July 1649. Louis XIV is thrashed by proxy*

Paris had grown too used to unrest to settle down quickly once the Peace of Rueil was finally verified in Parlement on 1st April 1649. The continued absence of the king and his mother from the scene favoured the commission of some spectacular acts of public insolence which, though certainly not confined to the high-born, were a speciality of Frondeur aristocrats desirous of blazoning their freedom from the taint of reconciliation with Mazarin. One such act, as related by the Marquis de Montglat, has a sinister ring, occurring as it did only a few months after the decapitation of the King of England.

* * * * * * * *

---

[63]*Lettres*, op. cit., Vol. III, p.692.

[64]Turenne writes of himself in the third person.

[65]According to Mazarin's *Lettres* [op. cit., Vol. III, p.306], Turenne had been ordered not to pass across the Rhine until after peace in Germany because the restitution of fortresses there was to be made by him.

[66]The *écu* was a coin, the silver version of which, minted in 1641, had a value equivalent to three *livres*.

... one day some footmen of the King having been beaten up by those of the Duc de Brissac[67], Matas and Fontrailles[68] told them that they must respect the [royal] liveries that they were wearing; but the others replied, in a mocking tone, that kings were no longer fashionable, and that that was alright for times gone by. In Paris people talked publicly of nothing but a republic and liberty, citing the example of England; and it was said that the monarchy was too old, and that it was time it ended.
[*Mémoires*, op. cit., p.217]

ix) *2nd October 1649. Mazarin grovels to Condé*

When it came to insolence, Condé was a past master in the art. The declaration below, which Anne d'Autriche had to require Mazarin formally to make to the prince, granted the latter staggering rights of interference in government affairs, not to mention the prime minister's private affairs, and puts into perspective his arrest three months later.

* * * * * * * *

... Her said Majesty has deemed it appropriate that I promise, as I do on her part and by her order:

That appointments will not be made to any general or individual governorships, to Crown offices, to major offices in the King's household and in the war sector, nor to ambassadorships; that no one will be exiled from court and no resolution on any important state affair will be taken without prior consultation of M[r] le Prince [Condé], and that, when my said lord the Prince puts forward persons whom he believes capable of the said offices, Her Majesty will give them special consideration;

That on occasions when benefices fall vacant, Her said Majesty will give consideration to the friends and adherents of my said lord the Prince, when he recommends them;

Since a good relationship between M[r] le Prince and myself can be very useful to the service of the King [...], I promise to maintain perfect union with him, and I also promise him unreservedly my friendship and to serve him in all state concerns and his own private ones in the face of any opposition.

And, as an initial sign of my pledge, I promise to my said lord the Prince not to marry off my nephew, nor any of my nieces who are here, without having previously

---

[67]Louis de Cossé, Duc de Brissac, was related through his wife to Retz.

[68]Charles de Bourdeille, Comte de Matha, and Louis d'Astarac, Vicomte de Fontrailles, can only have been speaking tongue in cheek since both were impenitent conspirators from the days of Richelieu. In other memorialists' versions of the story, the drunken trio of nobles personally rained blows on their victims, saying, according to Mme de Motteville [*Mémoires*, op. cit., p.283], 'Take that to your master, to the Queen and to Cardinal Mazarin'. Retz describes Brissac, Matha, and Fontrailles as 'cruelly debauched' [*Mémoires*, op. cit., p.161].

agreed the matter with him; in witness whereof I have signed the present [declaration], at Paris, on 2nd October 1649.
[Mazarin, *Lettres*, op. cit., Vol. III, pp.411-12]

x) *18th January 1650. Condé goes quietly*

The Princes' arrest was better planned than that of Broussel in that it was timed to take place on a dark winter's evening and under cover of a regulation meeting of the royal council in the Palais-Royal to discuss peace with Spain. Contemporaries were sensitive in retrospect to the ironies and near-misses of the situation, culminating in the overturning of the carriage bearing the prisoners to Vincennes. The Princes had been advised never to be in attendance simultaneously upon the king or his mother, and the wily old Duc de Longueville had pretexted gout to evade any royal summons; but he was enticed by an invitation to be present at the oath-taking of a client-aristocrat in line for promotion. Condé fell for the tale that a witness who knew all about the Frondeurs' designs upon his person was about to be apprehended, and thus unwittingly made the arrangements for his own arrest. Then Gaston d'Orléans lost his nerve at the last minute and had to be re-primed. On the very day scheduled for the *coup*, Anne d'Autriche, feigning illness in order to be able to close her doors to the rank and file of courtiers, received a chance visit of condolence from the dowager Princesse de Condé, mother of Condé and Conti, and mother-in-law of Longueville. Condé himself, according to some memorialists, came within an inch or two of discovering the plot against his liberty when he unexpectedly accosted Anne's secretary, the future minister for foreign affairs Hugues de Lionne, in the process of writing out final details of the arrest. Though the Princes did not offer any resistance when apprised of their fate, the worries of those responsible for their capture were not at an end, as the unlucky Comte de Comminges relates.

* * * * * * * *

When it was time for the council meeting, the Queen told M. le Prince [Condé] and all these gentlemen [the members of the council] to go into the council gallery where she would follow them in a moment, but instead of following them she shut herself in her oratory with the King, and told M. de Guitaud[69] to carry out his appointed task. He entered the gallery, closing all the doors behind him. He went up to M. le Prince whom he saw by the hearth and who forestalled him by paying him the compliment of asking whether he could do anything for him. He [Guitaut] said that he had been ordered by the King to arrest him, to which he [Condé] replied, putting his hand on his [Guitaut's] shoulder: 'Guitaud, please let us not indulge in worthless mockery'. M. de Guitaud replied: 'Monsieur, Your Highness may well judge from my manner that I am speaking the truth, not mocking, and I have the same order for monsieur your brother and for M. de Longueville'. M. le prince de Conti, seeing that the conversation was somewhat animated, [said]: 'What is it, brother?' — 'It is nothing', he replied, 'Guitaud has an order to arrest us, you, me, and M. de Longueville. But I hope it will be nothing, and that Her Majesty will allow me to justify myself'.

---

[69]François, Comte de Guitaut, was captain of Anne's bodyguard and uncle of Gaston-Jean-Baptiste de Comminges, a lieutenant in the same bodyguard.

While he was speaking, M. de Guitaud made the same declaration to M. le prince de Conti and to M. de Longueville. M. le Prince asked M. de Guitaud to find out from the Queen if she would grant him the honour of an audience, which he did, but the Queen told him to carry out his appointed task [...].

I [Comminges] went to the gallery door to carry out my appointed task as soon as I was notified by M. de Guitaud who, having observed that M. le Prince was looking at the doors and windows and even glancing at his sword, knocked with his baton, which was the signal that we had arranged. At that moment I opened the door, and followed by nine guards and the sieur de Saint-Elam[70] whom I left at the entrance, I imparted to these gentlemen the order that I had to escort them.

At first they seemed taken aback, on seeing that I was leading them down a small staircase, dim and unlit, but they promptly regained their composure when I assured them that their lives were safe as long as I had the honour to have them in my custody [...].

We walked along the garden path, very slowly, on account of the indisposition of M. de Longueville, who was supported by two guards. It was here that M. le Prince made propositions to M. de Guitaud to free him, but having realised his modest and respectful loyalty from his silence, he stopped talking in this strain. We arrived at the gate which was opened to see if the appointed things were ready. I found there neither carriage, nor royal guardsmen, nor even the officers who, unforewarned of the importance of the affair, had not arrived punctually at the meeting-place, but luckily my carriage was at hand[71], harnessed with six good horses [...].

I left the Palais-Royal, then, [...] and went as fast as I could to the Porte [Gate] Richelieu which I found closed and which had to be forced open. Two hundred paces further on M. de Miossans and M. de la Sale[72], followed by nine men-at-arms and a page, joined me. We proceeded on our way over the worst and most unsuitable roads for carriages to be found anywhere [...].

... my carriage overturned and I found myself on the wrong side. His Highness [Condé], who was at the front, threw himself out of the carriage. I shouted simultaneously to the guards to keep an eye on him, which they did very faithfully. M. de Miossans having given him his hand to help him, received an appeal to save him, which was refused, whatever the rewards proposed. I got him into the carriage again and we continued on our way to Vincennes.

[Philippe Tamizey de Larroque, 'Le Comte de Cominges et sa relation inédite de l'arrestation des princes en 1650', *Revue des Questions Historiques*, (1st October 1871), pp. 597-600].

---

[70]An *exempt* of Anne's guards, i.e. an officer who would normally take command in the absence of captain and lieutenants.

[71]The precaution may well have been due to Comminges' recollection of the problems that he had had with carriages when arresting Broussel. See above, pp.93-4.

[72]The Comte de Miossans (or Miossens) was then a lieutenant of the king's men-at-arms, and the Marquis de la Salle was a sub-lieutenant.

xi) *April 1650. The king makes himself useful*

If Parisians seemed satisfied that the incarcerated Condé had got his just deserts, it was a different story in the provinces which received his fleeing relatives and officers, and rallied to their calls for assistance. In dislodging Condéens from the strongholds in which they were entrenched, Mazarin brought to bear a weapon which none of them could command: the presence of the king. Its efficacy, already proved in Normandy in February 1650, was demonstrated again in Burgundy in April, at the (so-called) siege of Seurre. The sobriety of the Marquis de Montglat's narrative enhances the triumph of the eleven-year-old Louis, impatient for a taste of warfare at close quarters.

* * * * * * * *

The Duc de Vendôme[73], on arrival at Dijon, attacked the château and took it in a few days; and Saint-Jean-de-Losne and Verdun-sur-Saône surrendered when first summoned to do so. There remained only Seurre[74], a well-fortified fortress into which the Comte de Tavannes, lieutenant of the prince's [Condé's] men-at-arms, and Le Passage, a man very attached to Marshal Turenne, had hurled themselves, resolved to put up a good defence. Since this town was important, the Queen did not want to leave it any longer in their hands [...] and the Duc de Vendôme laid siege to it on 21st March; and, in order to facilitate the siege, cardinal Mazarin advanced as far as Saint-Jean-de-Losne and went to visit the camp, where the king arrived several days later; and while he [Louis] was going around it [...], the soldiers inside Seurre, hearing the [royalist] infantry's shouts of joy on seeing the king, began likewise to shout 'Long live the king', throwing their hats in the air; so that their officers could no longer control them, and were in danger of being arrested by them and handed over to His Majesty. This consideration, along with the one that reinforcements could not be got to them, forced them to enter into a treaty on the day when the trenches were to be made, which was 9th April.
[*Mémoires*, op. cit., p.229]

xii)　　*1st June 1650. A watery day at Bordeaux*

Over in Guyenne, another youngster — Condé's six-year-old son Henri-Jules, duc d'Enghien — was also busy learning under the maternal eye how to become a prince charming and play on public sympathy. Groomed for their parts by Pierre Lenet and associates, the boy and his mother more than lived up to their instructors' expectations on the June day when they petitioned the Bordeaux Parlement for protection.

* * * * * * * *

On 1st June, the princess [Condé's wife] left her lodging around 10 a.m., followed by the same mass of the people and the nobility, and led the young duke her son to the

---

[73]Vendôme commanded the royal army in the region.
[74]Seurre, on the river Saône, was also known as Bellegarde, though it reverted to its original name of Seurre in modern times.

parlement, the great hall of which resounded with the same acclamations as on the previous day[75]. I [Lenet] had the honour of being near their persons; the princess appealed to the judges as they went into the Grand'Chambre; she burst into tears in representing to them the wretched state of her whole oppressed household, and asked them for a refuge against the violence of cardinal Mazarin. The young duke, whom Vialas[76] was carrying in his arms, threw himself on the neck of the parlementarians as they passed, and, embracing them, asked them with tears in his eyes to free his father; but in such a tender way that most of these gentlemen were weeping as bitterly as he and his mother, and all gave them good hopes of the success of their petition. This spectacle increased in everyone's heart the affection that they showed for the Condé household, and their aversion for all those intent on destroying it.

The parlement took a long time to assemble, but finally did so [...]. However, since other difficulties were cropping up[77], the Enquêtes members pressed for a plenary assembly, which was accorded straightaway. The princess, carried away by grief and impatience, took her son by the hand, and entered impulsively into the Grand'Chambre with him; she was bathed in tears; and wishing to throw herself on her knees, she was prevented by those who ran to her, and said to them: 'I come, Messieurs, to demand justice of the King, through your persons, against the violence of cardinal Mazarin, and to put my person and that of my son in your hands: I hope that you will be a father to him; that which he has the honour of being to His Majesty, and the badges of office that you wear, put you under that obligation. He is the only one of the royal household to be at liberty; he is only seven[78]; his father is in chains. You all know, Messieurs, the great services that he [Condé] has rendered to the State, the affection which he has shown you on different occasions, and that which my late father-in-law had for you: let yourselves be softened by pity for the most wretched household in the world, and the most unjustly persecuted'.

Her sighs and tears interrupted her speech; the young duke knelt down on one knee, and said to them: 'Messieurs, be a father to me; cardinal Mazarin has taken away mine'. They all rushed to raise him up, and the majority were moved to tears by this sight. President d'Affis[79] requested them to withdraw, and told them that the court acknowledged their justified grief and was going to deliberate on their petition.
[Lenet, *Mémoires*, MP, 3me Sér., Vol. II, pp.280-81]

---

[75]When the princess had made a triumphal entry into Bordeaux.

[76]Vialas was the child's *'écuyer'* or groom.

[77]The princess had been obliged to dispel a rumour that she had had an agent of Mazarin arrested and relieved of royal letters that he was bearing to the Bordeaux Parlement.

[78]Not quite seven. He was born on 29th July 1643.

[79]Acting head of the Bordeaux Parlement.

xiii)   *October 1650. Preoccupations of the prime minister*

Just as Mazarin was preparing to add Champagne to the list of more or less subdued provinces that the royal party had left in its wake earlier in 1650, Anne d'Autriche's health and morale gave way. The close and anxious watch that he kept on the progress of her maladies, which could only raise the hopes of foreign and domestic enemies waiting to move in for the kill, is observable in details from a confidential letter to Le Tellier, written from Amboise on 28th October 1650.

* * * * * * *

The Queen slept better last night than on the previous ones, but she is still feverish. Mr Seguin believes that it is only a fever from a cold, which will go as the cold abates. But Mr Vautier[80] judges its origin to lie in the putrefaction and decomposition of humours[81]. Her bowels opened last night, and she evacuated a quantity of waters and bile. She is very impatient to get to Fontainebleau, but she is in no state to leave tomorrow. As soon as the doctors give her permission, I am sure that she will not waste a moment's time [in leaving]. Despite that, I bet my life that there will be a number of people in Paris who will say and broadcast that the illness is feigned. Yet it is certain that her trouble has come on, or at least increased, only because she has often wanted to travel in one day, with difficulty, the distance that she could have covered, in comfort, in two days. I will also say to His Royal Highness [Gaston] — for his information only, if you please — that I notice a great sadness in Her Majesty. I was talking about it yesterday with Mademoiselle[82], who has also noticed it, and this sadness extends to not even wanting people to try and divert and amuse her. Her Majesty is very weak, but that is not a bad sign; it could not be otherwise since she does not sleep well and is reduced to soups, after being accustomed to eat a lot.
[*Lettres*, op. cit., Vol. III, pp.906-7]

xiv)   *February 1651. The stuff of which memories are made*

Anne had relatively little time to recover her health and spirits before his opponents drove Mazarin from her side on 6th February 1651 and confined her within her own palace walls. That the repeated humiliation which she suffered on this occasion left an indelible mark is noted with a certain satisfaction by the Duchesse de Montpensier, whose father Gaston d'Orléans had assumed the degrading function of royal jailer.

* * * * * * *

---

[80]Seguin and Vautier were royal physicians.

[81]According to ancient medical lore, the 'humours' were the four principal liquids (blood, phlegm, bile, and atrabile) which made up the body and determined physical characteristics and temperament.

[82]Mlle de Montpensier, 'La Grande Mademoiselle' as contemporaries called her, was Gaston's daughter by his first wife.

Every evening Monsieur [Gaston] sent Des Ouches, his retainer[83], to bid the queen goodnight, with orders to see the king, in order to prove wrong those who said that they [Anne and Louis] wanted to depart. Judge how agreeable this compliment was to the queen! Des Ouches was taken to the king's apartment and saw him in his bed; sometimes he came back twice and even woke him by drawing aside his bed-curtain. The queen has remembered it very well; in truth, such things are scarcely forgotten. [Mlle. de Montpensier, *Mémoires*, ed. A. Chéruel, Paris, Charpentier, 1857—59, 4 vols., Vol. I, pp.300-1]

xv)   *7th September 1651. The sovereign remedy for the queen regent's ills*

Mazarin was still in exile when Louis XIV rode to Parlement at 9 a.m. on 7th September 1651 for the proclamation of his majority. But Anne was present to relish a ceremony which promised liberation from the whims of Gaston and Condé, and put unique powers in the hands of a grateful son capable of using them to make good the loss of royal authority sustained during his minority. The stop-press publication of the proceedings scrupulously collected, along with other pieces of documentary history, by Mme de Motteville[84], steers clear of comments on the many diverse sentiments which must have agitated the participants, but it does not altogether empty of emotion the solemn moment when the mother relinquished power to the son.

* * * * * * *

Silence fell, and the King spoke in this way:

'MESSIEURS,

I have come to my parlement to tell you that, according to the law of my State, I wish to take over the government of it myself[85]; and I hope that, through God's goodness, I shall govern with piety and justice. My chancellor will tell you more specifically my intentions.'

In accordance with His Majesty's command, the chancellor, who had received it standing, returned to his seat and pronounced a harangue in which he elaborated very eloquently as usual on what the King had said, adding very judicious reflections on the past and present. After which the Queen, making a slight bow from her seat, addressed this speech to the King:

'MONSIEUR,

This is the ninth year that, through the last wish of the late king, my very honoured lord, I have taken care of your education and the government of your

---

[83]Des Ouches was captain of Gaston's Swiss guards.

[84]The 'sovereign remedy' phrase is also hers.

[85]The age at which the kings of France achieved their legal majority had been fixed, since 1374, at the beginning of their fourteenth year. Louis XIV, born on 5th September 1638, was a year ahead of the traditional schedule.

State: God having, in His goodness, blessed my work, and preserved your person which is so dear and precious to me, and to all your subjects. Now that the law of the realm summons you to govern this monarchy, I hand over to you with great satisfaction the power which had been given to me to govern it, and I hope that God will graciously assist you with His spirit of strength and prudence in order to make your reign happy.'

His Majesty replied:

'Madame, I thank you for the care that you have been pleased to take of my education and of the administratîon of my realm. I pray you to continue to give me your good advice, and I desire that, after myself, you shall be the head of my council'.

Then the Queen rose from her place, and went to hail him as King; but His Majesty, descending from his *lit de justice*[86], came to her, and putting his arms round her, kissed her; then each of them returned to their place.
[Mme de Motteville, *Mémoires*, op. cit., pp.421-22]

xvi)   *9th September 1651. Condé's mind is made up*

The Royal Majority ceremony was overshadowed by the absence of Condé who had pointedly journeyed to Normandy the morning before to consult his brother-in-law Longueville, leaving his brother Conti to present a letter of excuse to Louis XIV at the precise moment when the king was mounting his horse to go to Parlement on the 7th. Louis, tit for tat, had given the letter, unread, to a retainer. Two days later Condé's chief aides went to confer with him at Chantilly, and in the words of participant Pierre Lenet: 'war was decided there'. The inconsistencies of Condé's behaviour and the self-destructive course of action on which he embarked posed an enigma which was resolved at the time by blaming his entourage, especially his sister, for prodding him into open hostilities designed to serve their own separate ends (see above, p.45). A representative view of the situation is that of Guy Joli.

* * * * * * * *

It is certain that the prince [Condé] found it quite difficult to make this resolution [to withdraw to Bordeaux], which he could well see might have regrettable consequences for himself. Besides, he was loath to leave his fine house at Chantilly, and to part from Mme de Châtillon, with whom he was very much in love[87]. But Mme de Longueville, M. le duc de La Rochefoucauld, and a multitude of officers and men of war who hung around him continually, pestering for opportunities to better their fortunes, determined him in the end to take up arms [...]. Mme de Longueville had in addition a personal and secret interest in desiring a breakdown of negotiations

---

[86]The term was used in the mid-seventeenth century to denote both the action whereby the king went to Parlement to ensure registration of royal legislation, and the canopied and cushioned throne on which he seated himself for this purpose.

[87]Condé had shown himself grief-stricken over the death, at the combat of Charenton in February 1649, of the husband of the Duchesse de Châtillon, Isabelle-Angélique de Montmorency-Bouteville.

because at the time it was very important for her to be at a distance from her husband, who was pressing her hard to return to his side. To avoid doing so with some decorum, she needed a reason as specious as that of following her brother in a cause in which everyone knew that she had as much or more of a share than anyone. Thus Mr le prince let himself be carried away almost willy-nilly by the entreaties and passions of those around him, whose interested opinions were not unknown to him, and obliged him to tell them that if they once caused him to take his sword out of the sheath, he would not perhaps put it back as soon as they wanted, or in accordance with their caprices.

[*Mémoires*, MP, 3me Sér., Vol. II, p.61]

xvii)   *29th December 1651. Parlement loses its head*

Armed rebellion on Condé's part looked like serving Mazarin's interests well. Fretting over reiterated royal declarations debarring him from re-entry into France and over the possibility of being repatriated in disgrace, the cardinal saw the chance to make a forceful comeback by offering to levy troops and bring them to Anne d'Autriche's assistance and requested orders from her to that effect. Ironically, the implementation of his proposals proved less beneficial to himself in the first instance than to Condé whose fortunes on the field of combat were declining when public attention fortuitously switched to preventing mazarinist incursions. The Paris Parlement, egged on by Gaston and all those fearful of Mazarin's revenge, spurted decrees against him, culminating in the near-hysterical injunctions of 29th December, which were contrary to all established civil or military judicial procedures.

* * * * * * *

The Court [Parlement], after having seen, in the presence of the *gens du Roi*, the declaration of His Majesty, verified on 6th September last, forbidding cardinal Mazarin, his relatives and foreign domestics from re-entering his realm or territory under his dominion, for whatever reason or occasion, on pain of the crime of *lèse-majesté*, and [forbidding] all governors and others to give him refuge or have dealings with him; and after M. le duc d'Orléans' statement that he has received sure notification[88] that the said cardinal Mazarin had arrived at Sedan, has decreed and ordered that its [Parlement's] deputies shall go immediately in search of the king as decreed on the 18th of this month; and, on the basis of the assurances of the said sieur[89] duc d'Orléans concerning the notification given to him of the entry of the said cardinal Mazarin into Sedan, [Parlement] has declared and declares the said cardinal Mazarin and his adherents to have incurred the penalties contained in the said declaration; commands the countryfolk to fall upon them, and the mayors and aldermen of the towns to stop them passing; orders that out of the library and movable goods of the said cardinal Mazarin, which shall be sold, and out of the revenues from his benefices and other goods belonging to him in France and to those

---

[88] The hearsay element was not lost on contemporary commentators. Gaston d'Orléans was not a man whose word was his bond.

[89] 'Sieur' is an honorific title used in seventeenth-century legal documents, and in letters where a superior refers to an inferior. Cf. section xxi below.

who assist him, a sum of up to one hundred and fifty thousand *livres* will be taken in preference to and despite all seizures of property [by creditors], and will be given to he or those who bring the said Cardinal to justice, dead or alive, or to their heirs[90]; and if the man who brings him to justice is found to be accused of a crime, the King will be very humbly begged to pardon him, provided that the crime is not that of *lèse-majesté*; the said Court also declares officers of the King and governors of fortresses who have assisted the Cardinal on his way and escorted him with their persons or their troops guilty of *lèse-majesté*, deprived of all offices and governorships, likewise of privileges of nobility, in conformity with the said declaration and decrees of the said Court. And the said sieur duc d'Orléans will be requested by the Court to employ the authority of the King and his own[91] to implement this declaration and decrees; and that the members of Parlement appointed and others will be sent to provinces and places as needful for the implementation of the present decree: notification of which will be given to the other Parlements.
[Vallier, *Journal*, op. cit., Vol. III, pp.99-100]

xviii)   *May 1652. Misery at grass-roots level*

The number of men of war on French soil in the opening months of 1652 rose markedly as Gaston set up an army under Beaufort, and Nemours brought one along for Condé, so that they could combine to oust the forces assembled by Mazarin. In June the Duc de Lorraine added his particular host for good measure. While the leaders and officers of the troops courted popularity by playing jolly good fellows with princes and ladies in the capital, the rank and file earned fear and detestation for occasioning endless subsistence taxes but continuing to live, violently, off the land. The plight of civilians dwelling along routes habitually used by the soldiery is exposed by a humble provincial, Clément Macheret, who kept a diary of events from 1628—58 in and around Langres, a locality on the much-trampled borders of Champagne, Burgundy, and Lorraine. The almost matter-of-fact catalogue of horrors in the entry for late May 1652 evokes the resigned or powerless observer who has seen it all before.

* * * * * * *

In this week, that is to say towards the end of May and the beginning of June, such great poverty has come about that the starving of this region have eaten even the rotting carcasses of horses: and at Mussy-l'Evêque there was even a big carriage-horse

---

[90]Jean Vallier, who quotes this decree in his *Journal*, comments that people could not understand how Parlement had arrogated the right to commandeer the revenues from benefices which the founders of the latter had destined for the upkeep of the poor, in order to pay a reward to the assassin of the benefice-holder, a prince of the Church. The justification for prejudicing the interests of legitimate creditors by taking the reward-money out of Mazarin's possessions was also queried. The sale and dispersal of the cardinal's library caused an outcry amongst learned men, especially since he had made known his intention to leave it to the public on his death.

[91]Omer Talon points out in his *Mémoires* (op. cit., pp.459-60] that, Louis XIV having come of age, Gaston was no longer lieutenant-general of the realm, and therefore had no authority other than that attaching to his royal birth.

belonging to Monseigneur the very reverend bishop-duke of Langres, peer of France, which [...] gave off such a stench that people could neither tolerate it nor bear to smell it, and it was taken outside the said town to be skinned quite close to the Seine. That job had no sooner been done than the populace rushed up so avidly that several were wounded on the hands by the knives of others while cutting up the flesh of the said horse, which flesh was entirely carried off in less than an hour [...].

A pauper carrying and suckling her little child was found dead in a meadow, her mouth still full of the grass which she had been eating like an animal, and her little child still alive in her arms.

The people of Lorraine and other neighbouring regions are reduced to such great extremities that they eat the grass in the meadows like animals, and especially those of the villages of Poully and Parnot en Bassigny eat it in the meadows, and are blackened and emaciated like skeletons and can no longer walk.

[Macheret, *Journal de ce qui s'est passé de mémorable à Lengres et aux environs depuis 1628 jusqu'en 1658*, ed. E. Bougard, Langres, 1880, 4 vols., Vol. III, pp.141-43]

xix)   *4th July 1652. The princes canvass for support at the Town Hall*

On his reappearance in Paris in April 1652, Condé had been twice reproached in public, by Président Le Bailleul in Parlement on the 12th and by Président Amelot in the Cour des Aides on the 23rd, for venturing to show himself in the sovereign courts with the blood of royalist troops on his hands. On the occasion of Bléneau, to which the presidents alluded (see above, p.51), blood had at least been shed by the prince in 'honourable' combat. Three months later it was a question of herding unarmed dignitaries, including priests, into a convenient pen where they could be raked with gunfire and scorched with flames.

The principal source of details about the Town Hall Massacre is Valentin Conrart, the first record-keeper of the French Academy (founded in 1635), who appears particularly knowledgeable about individuals' attempts to escape death by bullets or burning. On all essential points, Conrart is at one with Jean Vallier, an eye-witness who got away in the nick of time. Vallier was one of the notables elected to go to the meeting at the Town Hall, but left the building prematurely because of an indisposition and a premonition that catastrophe was impending.

* * * * * * *

Messieurs the Princes, seeing themselves utterly ruined by the loss which they had just sustained in the faubourg Saint-Antoine[92] if the city of Paris did not join their party by closely embracing their interests, resolved to take advantage of this assembly and to gain control of it at all costs. To this end they used their influence to ensure that, in all quarters, no one was elected who was not one of their partisans. They selected

---

[92]On 2nd July, see above, p.53.

the company of Trottier (a notorious Frondeur...93) to guard the Town Hall, commanded the majority of their troops to stand by in the [Place de] Grève94, and the officers to hold themselves in readiness to carry out what they would be ordered to do; and, so that they could better recognise those of their party, and slaughter all the rest, they gave them as a password: 'Long live Roger!', and as a sign, a bit of straw [...].

At the foot of the stone steps leading down [from the Town Hall] onto the Place [de Grève] was the said Trottier with twenty or thirty soldiers from his company holding some straw and presenting it to all those who made to enter, saying to them: 'No Mazarin!'; the meaning of which was that one must unite with the Princes against him [the cardinal], and they noted very carefully those who made any objection to taking some: so that two of my friends [...] and myself, entering the room, were very surprised to see straw on the hats of most of those whom we encountered.
[Vallier, *Journal*, op. cit., Vol. III, pp.315-17]

Vallier withdrew well before the tardy arrival of the princes, who did not themselves tarry long inside. Conrart continues the story.

... as soon as they [Gaston and Condé] appeared on the stone steps in the [Place de] Grève, they said to the populace: 'Those people don't want to do anything for us; they're even planning to drag things out and to put off coming to a decision for a week; they're mazarins, do what you like with them'. Hardly were these words pronounced than there were several musket-shots fired into the Town Hall windows, which astonished all the deputies [...].

In effect, they [the deputies] were highly surprised when suddenly the shots no longer came from below, as in the first instance, but in a straight line, from directly opposite: which made them think that all was lost for them, and that it was part of a conspiracy. It turned out that some of the soldiers in charge of this execution, having seen the populace shooting over-hastily, had gone up into the rooms of neighbouring houses whence they kept up a steady stream of fire from the front. Nevertheless it was not alleged that any one of the deputies was killed by the gunfire; because immediately they saw the musket-shots coming straight at them, some threw themselves on the ground, and others scattered in search of refuge in the areas of the Town Hall furthest away. The majority made confession to the clerics among them, who had tried in vain to calm this fury when they believed that it stemmed only from the populace. The terror was all the greater in that apart from the ceaseless musket- and gunfire, a quantity of wood was brought to all the Town Hall doors; they were rubbed with pitch, oil, and other combustible materials, and then set on fire: which

---

93Conrart describes Trottier as a merchant 'of seditious temperament', accustomed to negotiating in Spain, and adds that his lieutenant, an ironmonger named Pijart, was an equally 'great Frondeur'.
94Conrart puts the number of soldiers at eight hundred, of whom some were in disguise, 'and one secondhand clothes-dealer alone said that he had hired out two hundred pairs of clothes for that purpose'. Alongside the soldiers were 'rabble worked up by agitators expressly paid for the job', and boatmen and wharf-porters 'of which that quarter is full'. By the time that the princes emerged from the Town Hall, late on this sultry July afternoon, the crowd outside were suffering from the effects of the fifty or so large casks of wine which they had used to quench their thirst.

caused such stifling smoke and stench even in the apartments furthest away from the meeting-room, that no one knew where to turn [...].

Goulas, secretary to M^r d'Orléans, had accompanied him to the Town Hall and remained behind after the princes' departure. All the others, seeing themselves in this extreme danger, implored him to write to his master for help. He did so, and his note was rushed to the duc d'Orléans who, pressed by the bearer, said while scraping his teeth with his fingernails that he could not do anything and that they should go to his nephew Beaufort[95].
[Conrart, *Mémoires*, MP, 3me Sér., Vol. IV, pp.568, 569, 570, 571]

xx)   *17th September 1652. A royal bid to restore law and order*

Violence notoriously begets violence. In a remarkable letter judged by Denis Talon, son and successor in office of Omer Talon (who died in December 1652), to be 'capable of giving rise to greater carnage than that at the Town Hall'[96], Louis XIV gave his supporters in Paris not merely permission but a formal and comprehensive order to rise up and use force to restore royal authority.

* * * * * * * *

By order of the King.

His Majesty being well informed that the *bourgeois* and inhabitants of his good city of Paris persist in their good intentions for his service and for the common good of the said city, and that they are disposed to do their utmost to restore all things there to the state in which they should be, and to free themselves from their present oppression and set themselves at liberty under his dominion, His Majesty has permitted and permits the said inhabitants and each one individually, and, as far as is necessary, he very expressly commands and orders them to take up arms, assemble, occupy the places and [city-] gates[97] which they deem appropriate, combat those who try to oppose their plan, arrest the leaders and apprehend the factious by any means, and generally do everything that they see to be necessary and suitable to bring about

---

[95]Cf. Vallier: 'The presence of this highly popular prince [Beaufort] slowed down a little this great and fatal disorder which lasted no less than seven or eight hours, without His Royal Highness [Gaston] or M^r le Prince [Condé] putting themselves out to calm it, whatever entreaties were made to them by a number of distinguished persons and ladies of rank' [Vol. III, p.323].
    The role of Gaston and Condé, before and after as well as during the Fronde, makes it easier to understand the biting terms in which contemporaries referred to princes. 'What is a prince?', asks a *mazarinade* of 1649 in catechism-form, entitled *Catéchisme des Courtisans de la Cour de Mazarin*: 'A criminal whom one dare not punish' [*Choix de Mazarinades*, ed. Moreau, op. cit., Vol. II, p.7]. 'Scourges of the people and enemies of the monarchy' is how Président Molé described them in Parlement on 23rd November 1651, in Gaston's hearing [Talon, *Mémoires*, op. cit., p.450]. Gédéon Tallemant des Réaux, the 'gossip-columnist' of the century, defines them as 'animals who break out only too often' [*Historiettes*, ed. A. Adam, Paris, Bibliothèque de la Pléiade, 1960—61, 2 vols., Vol. I, p.23].
[96]Talon, *Mémoires*, op. cit., p.510.
[97]Other versions of this document have *'postes'* ('posts') instead of *'portes'* ('gates').

calm and total obedience to His Majesty, and ensure that the said city is governed in the old accustomed way and by its legitimate magistrates under the authority of His Majesty; he gives them complete power to do this by the present [declaration], which he has signed with his own hand, and to which he has appended the seal bearing his arms, wishing it to serve as an authorisation and a command to all those who take action, in whatever way, to carry it out.

Issued at Compiègne, on 17th September 1652. Signed: LOUIS, and lower down: LE TELLIER.
[*Registres de l'Hôtel de Ville de Paris pendant la Fronde*, op. cit., Vol. III, pp.292-93]

xxi)   *December 1652. Retz enjoys personal attention from his master*

It was fitting that Retz, the most dangerous of those whom Mazarin designated as 'pack-leaders', should have a warrant of arrest all to himself, complete with a handwritten addition in which the king reproduced the 'dead or alive' formula that had figured in the 29th December 1651 decree outlawing his godfather. As it happened, everything passed off without bloodshed, in the course of a duty call that his dissembling sovereign judiciously waited for Retz to pay at the Louvre on 19th December 1652.

* * * * * * *

By order of the King.

The sieur Pradelles, captain of an infantry company in His Majesty's regiment of French guards, is ordered to seize and arrest the sieur cardinal de Retz and take him to his [the king's] château of the Bastille[98] to be held there under good and safe guard until further orders; and if persons of whatever rank show signs of preventing the present order from being carried out, His Majesty likewise orders the sieur Pradelles to arrest and take them prisoner, and to employ force if necessary, so that the authority of His Majesty is preserved, and he commands all his officers and subjects to see to it that this is done, on pain of disobedience.

Issued in Paris on [day blank] December 1652.
LOUIS

I[99] have ordered Pradelle to carry out the present order on the person of cardinal de Retz, even to arrest him dead or alive in the eventuality of resistance on his part.
[*Oeuvres du Cardinal de Retz*, eds A. Feillet, J. Gourdault and R. Chantelauze, Paris, Hachette, 1870—96, 10 vols, Vol. VI, p.461]

---

[98]Retz was in fact taken to Vincennes.
[99]Whereas the first part is in Le Tellier's hand in the original, the second is in Louis' own handwriting.

xxii)   *February — March 1653. The return of the knave*

With Retz cut off, in theory, from the outside world, Mazarin felt safe to terminate his second exile, though he was a little diffident about Louis XIV underlining the safety factor by riding out of Paris to escort him back in the royal carriage.

The dramatic reversals in the cardinal's fortunes could not fail to impress onlookers, especially those who, like Jean Vallier, had difficulty in discarding their prejudices against him.

* * * * * * *

... on 3rd February, this outlaw, this disturber of the public peace and this obstacle to general peace [with Spain], on whose head had been put a price of fifty thousand *écus*, returned to this great city [Paris], not only without causing any upset or murmur, but as if triumphant and covered in glory, the King having deigned to advance three leagues to meet him, and most of the court fifteen or twenty [leagues] [...].

This self-interestedness which reigns so powerfully over the majority of men figured all too shamefully at a great feast given by the city of Paris to Mr le cardinal Mazarin on the 29th of the said month of March, in order to show His Eminence how obliged all its inhabitants were to him for re-establishing their *rentes*. For what flattery and what grovelling were not employed by the most notorious frondeurs to efface the memory of what had happened in the past and to render more propitious this divinity which they had so offended previously! Profusion and superfluousness were conspicuous, as if it had been a question of entertaining the King on his return from the conquest of a great province [...].
[Vallier, *Journal*, op. cit., Vol. IV, pp.171-72, 197-98]

xxiii)   *July 1653. In the shadow of the elms*

Bordeaux, well stirred by Condé's agents and subjected to a terrorist *régime* organised by the Ormée, had to be forced to bend the knee. As royalist armies under the Duc de Vendôme and the Duc de Candale closed in from the exterior, capturing one rebel-held stronghold after another in the neighbourhood of the city, royalist agents and sympathisers renewed their hitherto thwarted efforts to maintain a substantial resistance party within its walls, risking torture or death by order of the Prince de Conti or the uncompromising Ormiste allies of whom he strove to stay at the head. The Franciscan François Berthod, who had proved his worth in helping to prepare the terrain for Louis XIV's return to Paris in September 1652, was sent three months later to Bordeaux on a similar mission aimed at restoring royal authority. Betrayed to Conti from the start, he had a price put on his head, but managed to preserve his liberty and his liaisons with the government ministers and local helpers vital to the success of his enterprise, crowned, as he explains, by the youth of Bordeaux.

* * * * * * *

... in the end, the more acts of cruelty the princes' party committed, the more intent well-intentioned persons became on re-establishing royal authority and demanding peace. They got to the point of writing to M. de Boucaut[100], via his wife, to get Father Berthod[101] to come incognito to the suburbs of Bordeaux to confer with the leading townsfolk. He went to the rendezvous to confer with them on the means of recovering their freedom and putting the city back into the King's hands. He notified M. de Vendôme, who then left Bourg for Lormont[102] in order to be nearer Bordeaux in case he was required for purposes of negotiation.

During this time Mme. de Boucaut continued her intrigues with so much ardour[103] that she provided grounds for the Sieur Raymond, who was commanding at the Town Hall gate in the absence of the captain, to refuse entry therein to some Ormistes[104] and even to Duretête, who was one of their head men[105]. That caused a great uproar, and led Duretête and Villars[106] to complain to the Prince de Conti, who, to satisfy them, had Raymond ordered out of the city; but as he was being put on a boat to cross the river, some young men declared for the King, boarded boats, seized Raymond from the hands of the officer in charge of him, and returned him to his home. A large number of these young folk then went to request M[r] le Prince de Conti to free him and to order Villars not to walk about the streets with guards as he was accustomed to do; otherwise he and his guards would be killed. Their request was granted; and thereafter Villars rarely appeared in the streets, because he walked there alone.

In all encounters, these young folk beat the Ormistes, expelled the garrisons put in private houses, and manhandled the soldiers in the pay of M[r] le prince [Condé] [...]. After that they convoked a great assembly in the Hôtel de la Bourse where it was resolved that citizen representatives from every company should be sent to M[r] le prince de Conti to ask for the captains in the city to be changed, all soldiers to be removed, the Ormée forbidden from assembling, and peace to be negotiated without delay. This deliberation was a sequel to the resolution made at Father Berthod's conference with the townsfolk in the suburbs of Bordeaux a week to ten days

---

[100]Pierre de Boucaut, a royalist member of the Bordeaux Parlement obliged to leave the city.

[101]He writes of himself in the third person.

[102]Bourg, on the right bank of the river Dordogne, had fallen to royalist troops on 3rd July. Lormont, on the right bank of the Garonne, a kilometre away from Bordeaux, had been recaptured on 26th May.

[103]Berthod has warm praise for this lady activist, née Isabeau de Bouldron — one of a number collaborating with him — who did much to revive royalist opposition after the betrayal in March 1653 of a plot to drive the princely and Ormiste rebels out of the city.

[104]The incident in question took place on 12th July. The Ormistes had attempted to enter Bordeaux's Town Hall, where Conti was lodging at the time, without divesting themselves of their swords, whereupon they were stopped by members of the citizen militia, amongst whom were royalist sympathisers. Jean de Raymond, a *greffier* (clerk) in the Cour des Aides et Finances de Guyenne, was one such.

[105]Joseph Dureteste, a judicial official, was executed in 1654 and his head was spiked on a stake at the top of a tower overlooking the Ormistes' original meeting-place.

[106]Pierre de Villars, a Parlement lawyer, was another Ormée leader, pardoned in 1658.

previously. The Prince de Conti promised to reply to all these propositions the next day, which was 19th July [...].

On leaving the Prince de Conti's house, these young folk went all round the town shouting: 'Long live the King!' and 'peace!'; and in less than three or four hours their numbers had swelled to four or five thousand persons who forced the Ormistes also to shout 'Long live the King!' and 'peace!'; and some of them climbed up into the belltowers on which the Ormistes had for so long flown red flags, as a mark of their pro-Spanish inclination. They tore them down and put in their place white flags, as a sign of their submission to France and their obedience to the King.
[Berthod, *Mémoires*, MP, 2me Sér., Vol. X, p.616]

IV AFTERTHOUGHTS

i)   Conspiracy is quite often a foolish thing; but there is nothing like it for making people behave circumspectly afterwards, at least for a while.
[Retz, *Mémoires*, op. cit., p.25]

ii)   One cannot but agree that, however bad a ruler may be, revolt on the part of his subjects is always infinitely criminal. He who has given kings to men wished them to be respected as His lieutenants, reserving for Himself alone the right to examine their conduct. His will is that, whoever is born a subject, should obey unquestioningly; and this law, so express and so universal, is not made in favour of rulers only, but is salutary to the very subjects on whom it is imposed and who can never transgress it without exposing themselves to evils much more terrible than those from which they seek to protect themselves.
[Louis XIV, *Mémoires*, ed. J. Longnon, Paris, Tallandier, 1927, pp.254-55]

* * * * * * * *

APPENDIX

This section comprises the original French equivalents of the translated passages which appear on pp. 69-115. To facilitate perusal by non-specialist readers, the spelling of all but a few variable proper names has been modernised.

Notes on Dates of First Publication of Memoirs

With the outstanding exception of La Rochefoucauld, none of the memoir-writers quoted in this work broke into print prior to the early eighteenth century, and in certain cases (e.g. that of Lenet) publication was even then only partial by comparison with the fuller and more accurate versions established by scholars from the mid-nineteenth century onwards.

The order of appearance was as follows:

La Rochefoucauld	1662
Duchesse de Nemours	1709
Retz	1717
Joly	1718
Mme de Motteville	1723
Montglat	1727
Duchesse de Montpensier	1728
Lenet	1729
Talon	1732
Turenne	1735
Louis XIV	1806
Berthod	1826
Coligny-Saligny	1826
Conrart	1826
d'Ormesson	1860-61
Goulas	1879-82
Vallier	1902-18

* * * * * * * *

I i)   Ce qui cause l'assoupissement dans les états qui souffrent est la durée du mal, qui saisit l'imagination des hommes et qui leur fait croire qu'il ne f........rouvent jour à en sortir, ce qui ne manque jamais lorsqu'il est venu jusqu'à un certain point, ils sont si surpris, si aises et si emportés, qu'ils passent tout d'un coup à l'autre extrémité, et que bien loin de considérer les révolutions comme impossibles ils les croient faciles: et cette disposition toute seule est quelquefois capable de les faire. Nous avons éprouvé et senti toutes ces vérités dans notre dernière révolution. Qui eût dit trois mois devant la petite pointe des troubles, qu'il en eût pu naître dans un état où la maison royale était parfaitement unie, où la cour était esclave du ministre, où les provinces et la capitale lui étaient soumises, où les armées étaient victorieuses, où les compagnies paraissaient de tout point impuissantes: qui l'eût dit eût passé pour insensé [...]. Il paraît un peu de sentiment, une lueur, ou plutôt une étincelle de vie; et ce signe de vie dans les commencements presque imperceptibles, ne se donne point par Monsieur, il ne se donne point par M. le prince, il ne se donne point par les grands du royaume, il ne se donne point par les provinces; il se donne par le parlement qui, jusqu'à notre siècle, n'avait jamais commencé de révolution, et qui certainement aurait condamné par des arrêts sanglants celle qu'il faisait lui-même, si tout autre que lui l'eût commencée. Il gronda sur l'édit du tarif; et aussitôt qu'il eut seulement murmuré, tout le monde s'éveilla. L'on chercha en s'éveillant, comme à tâtons, les lois: on ne les trouva plus, l'on s'effara, l'on cria, on se les demanda; et dans cette agitation les questions que leurs explications firent naître, d'obscures qu'elles étaient et vénérables par leur obscurité, devinrent problématiques; et de là, à l'égard de la moitié du monde, odieuses. Le peuple entra dans le sanctuaire: il leva le voile qui doit toujours couvrir tout ce que l'on peut dire, tout ce que l'on peut croire du droit des peuples et de celui des rois, qui ne s'accordent jamais si bien ensemble que dans le silence.

I ii)   Mais il est arrivé dans la régence que la Reine a eu à récompenser tous ceux qui avaient été maltraités par M. le cardinal de Richelieu, et lesquels en cette qualité avaient eu quelque sorte de relation avec elle dans sa mauvaise fortune pendant la vie du Roi son mari; et outre elle n'a pas voulu mécontenter les autres, de crainte de faire jalousie. D'ailleurs l'esprit de la Reine naturellement est bon, bienfaisant et sans malice; et quoiqu'elle ne souffre pas facilement qu'injure lui soit faite, elle ne la fait pas facilement à autrui si elle n'y est obligée par quelque sorte d'outrage qui la porte à l'extrémité.

Ainsi la Reine s'est trouvée obligée de faire de grandes et immenses gratifications qui ont épuisé l'épargne, et lesquelles dès la première année de sa régence ont engagé les finances du Roi de douze millions d'emprunt et de reculement.

M. d'Emery, qui fut fait contrôleur général, et depuis surintendant, était infiniment facile à faire gratification à ceux qui pouvaient servir à sa fortune, ou desquels il craignait l'autorité, principalement du parlement, dont il appréhendait la colère et la justice: il avait méprisé toute sorte d'ordre de finances, tant en la recette que dans la dépense; car pour avoir des deniers comptants il avait baillé toutes les tailles en parti, et payait quinze pour cent d'intérêt à ceux qui lui avançaient les deniers. Il faisait le même sur les fermes, et ainsi il mangeait par avance en l'année 1648 les années 1650 et 1651, et avait porté les choses si avant, qu'ayant engagé les finances du Roi de plus de cent millions envers les partisans et gens d'affaires, il ne faisait plus subsister l'Etat que des retranchements qu'il faisait sur les officiers et sur les rentes. Les compagnies souveraines avaient souffert un quartier de retranchement de leurs gages; les présidiaux n'en recevaient aucune chose; les trésoriers de France, les élus, les grenetiers et tous les officiers comptables, n'en touchaient rien du tout, car ce qui leur était laissé de fonds était épuisé en droits nouveaux et imaginaires, en taxes et en hérédité; et de tous ces retranchements et taxes qui se faisaient au conseil, M. d'Emery en traitait avec des partisans, qui en prenaient le recouvrement; et moyennant icelui ils avançaient leurs deniers, à la charge de grosses remises. D'ailleurs les gens de guerre n'étaient point payés; les gardes françaises et suisses étaient en arrière de douze montres, les Suisses prêts à quitter.

Ce procédé était le sujet d'une plainte publique; non seulement le peuple de la campagne, le plat pays était maltraité, mais même les personnes de condition médiocre: les artisans seuls, et les gens de journée, subsistaient dans les villages; car n'ayant aucuns meubles qui pussent être saisis, ils vivaient de l'argent qu'ils recevaient de leur travail. Dans Paris, la plupart du luxe était fondé sur ces gros intérêts que le Roi payait; les marchands avaient la plupart abandonné leur trafic actuel pour mettre leur argent dans cette espèce de négociation infâme.

Ce qui restait de gens dans quelque sorte d'abri étaient les officiers des compagnies souveraines dans Paris et dans toutes les autres provinces du royaume, lesquels subsistaient des trois quartiers de leurs gages, lesquels M. d'Emery leur ayant voulu ôter par l'établissement du droit annuel, et s'imaginant le pouvoir faire en indemnisant le parlement de Paris, lequel seul il appréhendait, il fut trompé dans son compte; car les maîtres des requêtes et les officiers des autres compagnies souveraines s'étant rassemblés et reconnu leurs forces, et ayant attiré avec eux le parlement de Paris, ils ont abandonné en apparence leurs intérêts pour travailler à ceux du public, et dans les considérations publiques ils y ont trouvé ce qu'ils désiraient.

I iii)   Après la mort du Roi, la Reine devenue régente n'avait aucune expérience dans les affaires, non plus que ses nouveaux ministres; et comme elle était bonne et bienfaisante, elle accordait tout ce qu'on lui demandait, n'en connaissant pas les conséquences; en sorte qu'elle épuisa en peu de temps tout l'argent qui était à l'épargne. Le cardinal Mazarin étant demeuré seul maître du cabinet trouva fort à redire à ces grandes libéralités, et ayant pour contrôleur général des finances d'Emery, il lui en confia la direction tout entière, au préjudice du président Le Bailleul, surintendant, qui ne servait que d'ombre. D'Emery chercha tous les moyens possibles de trouver de l'argent pour soutenir la guerre, et pour satisfaire l'avarice du cardinal, qui était insatiable. Comme il était dur et impitoyable, il ne se souciait pas, pour complaire à son bienfaiteur, de ruiner tout le monde. Il commença par la maison du Roi, qu'il ne paya plus, même ceux qui fournissaient les tables, qui étaient tous les jours prêtes à renverser. Il raya toutes les pensions, et retrancha les rentes de l'hôtel de ville et celles des provinces; fit imposer des taxes sur ceux qui tenaient les domaines, et sur les aisés; mit les tailles en parti, y établissant la solidité: tellement que les partisans se faisaient payer avec une telle rigueur, qu'on prenait les meubles et les bestiaux des laboureurs, qui étaient contraints de tout quitter et laisser les terres en friche. Cette misère des paysans et l'opulence des gens d'affaires, auxquels on donnait de si gros intérêts de leurs avances qu'ils devenaient riches en moins de rien, faisait murmurer tout le monde: si bien que le parlement voulut faire des remontrances, qui furent mal reçues[...]. Quoique le parlement prît son prétexte pour le bien public, son intérêt particulier le faisait principalement agir, parce que d'Emery avait ôté les gages de tous les officiers des cours souveraines, et leur refusait le renouvellement de la paulette, qui était finie.

I iv)   ... Sa Majesté, du consentement des traitants qui l'ont assistée jusqu'ici, et avec leur entière satisfaction parce qu'ils appréhendaient pis, a reculé leurs assignations et leur remboursement et assuré un fonds certain pour la continuation de la guerre tout autant de temps que l'opiniâtreté des Espagnols nous forcera de la faire. On avait mangé toute l'année courante et les deux suivantes, et on a trouvé moyen de les remanger une seconde fois, Sa Majesté rentrant dans tous ses revenus et ne donnant à ceux à qui elle doit que l'intérêt de leur argent à six pour cent. Ainsi le revenu de Sa Majesté passant plus de soixante millions, on en aura conservé plus de cinquante-quatre de net, qui suffiront, étant bien ménagés, pour toutes les dépenses de la guerre sans être obligés de prendre une année sur l'autre; les six autres millions, ou environ, seront pour les intérêts de cent millions et plus que le Roi doit. J'oubliais de vous faire remarquer un autre avantage bien considérable en ceci: c'est que, par la résolution que le Roi a prise de retrancher les quinze pour cent qu'il donnait d'intérêt, il a gagné en un instant cinquante millions, pour lesquels les traitants avaient de bonnes assignations aussi bien que pour le principal de leur dette.

II A i)   Le jeudi 21 février, le Roi vint au parlement de fort bonne heure, et si matin que M. le chancelier y arriva avant que messieurs les présidents eussent pris leurs robes rouges; de sorte qu'après son arrivée étant allés les uns après les autres prendre leurs robes rouges et leurs manteaux, lorsqu'ils retournèrent en leurs places M. le chancelier ne se leva pas au devant d'eux, dont ils furent irrités[...].

Pour cet effet, M. le chancelier ayant pris jour au mercredi troisième juillet, deux ou trois difficultés se présentèrent, 1° savoir en quel habit seraient messieurs les maîtres des requêtes qui viendraient avec lui, si en robes ordinaires ou en robes de soie; 2° si M. le chancelier, prenant les opinions de messieurs les présidents, ne se découvrirait pas; 3° et si quand messieurs les présidents entreraient pour prendre leurs places, il ne se lèverait pas devant eux[...].

Le vendredi 5 juillet, M. le chancelier retourna au parlement. Question s'émut si l'on devait envoyer deux de messieurs au devant de lui, aucuns soutenant que cela ne se devait faire que la première fois qu'il prend place, et qu'en l'an 1584, quand M. le chancelier y était venu, qu'il avait été arrêté de députer vers lui *pour cette fois*, lesquels termes étaient restrictifs et limitatifs; qu'au procès de M. le maréchal de Biron, auquel M. le chancelier de Bellièvre avait assisté sept ou huit séances continues, le registre ne portait pas que l'on y eût envoyé. Les autres au contraire soutenaient que cette civilité était due à sa personne et à sa qualité; que toutes fois et quantes qu'il y venait avec le Roi cet honneur lui était rendu, et partant qu'il ne lui pouvait être dénié. Et de fait le dernier avis a prévalu.

II A ii)   Les compagnies souveraines se renferment dans les règles de leurs formalités, quand l'espérance d'accroître leur autorité, ou la crainte de la voir entièrement abattue, ne leur fait pas franchir les bornes qu'elles leur prescrivent; mais quand par l'un ou par l'autre de ces principes elles ont commencé à quitter leur chemin ordinaire, elles se portent facilement à de grandes extrémités, parce que ceux qui ont le plus de prudence ne prévalent pas pour l'ordinaire en nombre, et qu'ils sont considérés comme suspects quand ils veulent s'opposer aux délibérations trop hardies, qui, dégénérant pour la plupart en une espèce d'attentat contre l'autorité du souverain, portent ceux qui en ont été les auteurs à tout entreprendre, croyant que c'est l'unique moyen d'éviter les châtiments dont ils sont menacés.

II A iii)   Articles des propositions faites par les députés des compagnies assemblés en la salle Saint-Louis, suivant l'arrêt du 13 mai 1648.

Que les intendants de justice, et toutes autres commissions extraordinaires, non vérifiées aux cours souveraines, seront révoqués dès à présent.

Les traités des tailles, taillons, subsistances et autres, seront dès à présent révoqués, et lesdites tailles imposées, assises, levées en la forme ancienne et comme auparavant, lesdits traités à la diminution du quart au profit du peuple [...].

Qu'il sera établi une chambre de justice, composée des officiers des quatre cours souveraines, et par icelles nommés pour connaître et juger des abus et malversations commis en l'administration et maniement des affaires du Roi, et exactions sur ses sujets [...].

Ne seront faites aucunes impositions et taxes qu'en vertu d'édits et déclarations bien et dûment vérifiés aux cours souveraines, auxquelles la connaissance en appartient, et l'exécution desdits édits et déclarations sera réservée auxdites cours [...].

Qu'il ne sera à l'avenir fait aucune création d'office, tant de judicature que de finances, que par édits vérifiés aux cours souveraines, avec liberté entière de suffrages[...] et que l'établissement de ces compagnies souveraines ne pourra être changé ni altéré, soit par augmentation d'offices de chambre, établissement de semestre, ou par démembrement du ressort des compagnies, pour en créer et établir de nouvelles [...].

Que les officiers des quatre cours souveraines de Paris, payeurs, greffiers, et autres officiers du corps d'icelles, seront payés par chacun an des gages à eux attribués et augmentation d'iceux, sans aucun retranchement [...].

Que les arrêts donnés aux cours souveraines ne pourront être cassés, révoqués ni sursis, sinon par les voies de droit permises par les ordonnances [...].

Qu'aucuns des sujets du Roi, de quelque qualité et condition qu'ils soient, ne pourront être détenus prisonniers passé vingt-quatre heures sans être interrogés suivant les ordonnances, et rendus à leurs juges naturels [...] et que ceux qui sont de présent détenus sans forme ni figure de procès seront mis en liberté, remis en l'exercice de leurs charges et possession de leurs biens; et ne seront tenus les officiers de déférer à aucunes lettres de cachet portant défenses de faire la fonction de leurs charges ou ordre de s'absenter, ains que leurs procès leur seront faits par les voies ordinaires.

II A iv)   ... l'indignation éclatant contre la Grand'Chambre, que l'on disait avoir donné cet arrêt pour conserver cette bibliothèque au cardinal Mazarin, la confusion des voix et la contention a été fort grande jusqu'à dix heures que M. Le Bailleul avec les autres présidents se sont levés, ce qui a donné lieu aux Enquêtes de dire fort haut que, en l'absence de ceux qui se retireraient, il serait délibéré; mais nonobstant ce, les présidents s'étant avancés, les Enquêtes se sont opposées à leur passage et l'ont empêché plus d'un demi quart d'heure, jusqu'à ce que M. Sevin, s'étant mis en état de faire violence et levé la main sur quelqu'un de Messieurs pour le frapper, il a reçu quelques coups sous sa robe et s'est trouvé environné des Enquêtes, lesquels ont à cet effet franchi les barreaux de tous côtés: en sorte que la confusion a été grande, et M. Sevin est devenu pâle, blême et si interdit qu'il n'est possible de l'exprimer; sur quoi les présidents étant forcés de reprendre leurs places, pour éviter à une plus grande confusion dans un temps auquel l'union est si nécessaire, M. Vedeau a proposé de nommer des commissaires pour la vente de la bibliothèque avec ceux lesquels ont été déjà nommés, aviser ce soir lequel est le plus expédient de vendre la bibliothèque en gros ou en détail, et, suivant cela, passer outre à la vente d'icelle: ce qui a été agréé de toute la compagnie.

II B i)   ... il s'est rencontré que tout ce que nous avons de fidèles serviteurs dans notre conseil, et en dehors, nous ont représenté en même temps qu'une plus longue patience rendrait bientôt le mal sans remède, et que l'unique moyen d'en garantir notre Etat, aussi bien que notre personne, était de faire arrêter nosdits cousins, qui, tenant tous les jours des conseils de famille pour l'établissement de cette puissance qu'ils voulaient opposer à la nôtre, n'avaient pas honte de compter entre les moyens d'y parvenir, outre les grandes charges et les gouvernements de province qui sont à eux ou dans leur dépendance, qu'ils étaient déjà maîtres de toutes les grandes rivières du royaume par les diverses places qu'ils ont entre leurs mains ou qu'ils croyaient avoir à leur dévotion sur les rivières de Seine, de Meuse, de Saône, du Rhône, de Loire, de Garonne et de Dordogne.

II B ii)   Il résolut d'assembler pour ce sujet ses amis, sous un prétexte qui ne fit rien connaître de son intention [...]. Il crut n'en pouvoir prendre un plus spécieux que celui de l'enterrement de son père, dont la cérémonie se devait faire à Verteuil, l'une de ses maisons. Il convia pour cet effet toute la noblesse des provinces voisines, et manda à tout ce qui pouvait porter les armes dans ses terres de s'y trouver: de sorte qu'en très peu de temps il assembla plus de deux mille chevaux et huit cents hommes de pied [...].

... le duc de la Rochefoucauld fit assembler toute la noblesse qui était chez lui pour les funérailles de son père, et leur dit qu'ayant évité d'être arrêté prisonnier à Paris avec Monsieur le Prince, il se trouverait peu de sûreté dans ses terres, qui étaient environnées de gens de guerre qu'on avait affecté de disposer tout autour, sous prétexte du quartier d'hiver, mais en effet pour pouvoir le surprendre dans sa maison; qu'on lui offrait une retraite assurée dans une place voisine, et qu'il demandait à ses véritables amis de l'y vouloir accompagner et laissait la liberté aux autres de faire ce qu'ils voudraient. Plusieurs parurent embarrassés de cette proposition, et prirent divers prétextes pour se retirer [...] mais il y eut sept cents gentilshommes qui lui promirent de le suivre. Avec ce nombre de cavalerie et l'infanterie qu'il avait tirée de ses terres, il prit le chemin de Saumur [...].

II B iii) Qui ne craint point la mort ne craint point les menaces.
    J'ai le coeur au-dessus des plus fières disgrâces;
    Et l'on peut me réduire à vivre sans bonheur,
    Mais non pas me résoudre à vivre sans honneur.
                    (*Le Cid*, II, 1)

    Il y va de ma gloire, il faut que je me venge;
    Et de quoi que nous flatte un désir amoureux,
    Toute excuse est honteuse aux esprits généreux.
                    (Ibid., III, 3)

    Le sort qui de l'honneur nous ouvre la barrière
    Offre à notre constance une illustre matière,
    Il épuise sa force à former un malheur

Pour mieux se mesurer avec notre valeur;
Et comme il voit en nous des âmes peu communes,
Hors de l'ordre commun il nous fait des fortunes.

(*Horace*, II, 3)

... ne crois pas que le peuple stupide
Soit le maître absolu d'un renom bien solide[...].
C'est aux rois, c'est aux grands, c'est aux esprits bien faits,
A voir la vertu pleine en ses moindres effets;
C'est d'eux seuls qu'on reçoit la véritable gloire:
Eux seuls des vrais héros assurent la mémoire.

(Ibid., V, 3)

Plus le péril est grand, plus doux en est le fruit;
La vertu nous y jette, et la gloire le suit.

(*Cinna,* I, 2)

Qu'une âme généreuse a de peine à faillir!

(Ibid., III, 3)

II B iv)   M. le duc de Beaufort y arrivait [...], avec une forte résolution de s'unir à tant d'illustres paladins qui en avaient entrepris la défense, les uns par un pur objet de compassion et de justice (disaient-ils), et les autres par la haine qu'ils portaient au cardinal Mazarin et à la violence (pour ne pas dire tyrannie) du conseil d'en haut; mais qui ne savait point que la seule considération de leurs intérêts particuliers les y avait appelés, ou les y avait retenus?

II B v)   Demandes des Princes et Seigneurs qui ont pris les armes avec le Parlement et Peuple de Paris.

Monsieur le Prince de Conti demande d'avoir entrée et place dans le Conseil du Roi; une Place forte dans son gouvernement de Champagne; le retour de Madame de Chevreuse; qu'on fasse Duc et Pair le Marquis de Noirmoustier; qu'on lui donne 42,000 livres; qu'on accorde le tabouret à la femme du Prince de Marsillac; qu'on paie audit Prince 18,000 livres par an qu'on avait accoutumé de lever pour des Fusiliers en Poitou, quoique lesdits Fusiliers ne subsistent pas; qu'on donne la généralité des Galères au Duc de Retz [...].

Monsieur le Duc de Longueville demande une charge de la Couronne, un Gouvernement de considération dans la Normandie et la survivance de tous ses Gouvernements et Charges à celui de ses enfants qui le survivra; qu'on lui paie en assignations sur la Province tous les deniers qui lui sont dus pour pensions et avances; qu'on fasse Duc et Pair Monsieur de Matignon, et qu'on donne la survivance de sa Charge à son fils; qu'on fasse aussi Duc et Pair le Marquis de Beuvron et qu'on donne la survivance de ses charges à son fils [...].

Monsieur le Duc de Beaufort demande le Gouvernement de Bretagne pour Monsieur de Vendôme, son père; son dédommagement des maisons et châteaux qui lui ont été rasés en Bretagne du temps du feu Roi; le paiement de tous les arrérages de ses pensions [...].

Monsieur le Duc d'Elbeuf demande Montreuil; le paiement de tout ce qui est dû à Madame sa femme; cent mille francs pour le Comte de Rieux, son second fils; et récompense des services du Comte de Lillebonne, son cadet.

Monsieur le Duc de Bouillon demande Sedan ou une prompte récompense de ce qu'il vaut; qu'on ôte le Gouvernement d'Auvergne au Duc de Chaune et qu'on le lui donne; qu'on reconnaisse pour princes de

France lui et tous ceux de sa maison; qu'on rende le commandement de l'armée d'Allemagne à Monsieur le Maréchal de Turenne; qu'on donne audit Maréchal le Gouvernement de la haute et basse Alsace; qu'on lui donne encore en propre les domaines de Thone et d'Haguenau, et tous les autres que le Roi possède en Alsace; et qu'on lui donne le Gouvernement de Philisbourg.

Monsieur le Maréchal de la Motte demande la récompense du Gouvernement de Bellegarde et ses états et revenus depuis six ans; cent mille livres de la rançon du Marquis de Pouar; cinq cent mille livres pour la non jouissance pendant quatre ans du Duché de Cardone qu'il prétend lui appartenir; cent mille livres d'un don que le feu Roi lui fit et dont il n'a pu rien toucher; toutes ses pensions, états, et appointements pendant sa prison; et qu'on lui redonne son régiment de Cavalerie.

Monsieur le Duc de la Trimouille demande le Comté de Roussillon en propre à cause des droits de sa trisaïeule; demande Amboise, Montrichard et Bléré qu'il dit lui appartenir, comme au seul héritier de la Maison d'Amboise; le Comté de Guines comme étant de l'ancien domaine de la Maison de la Trimouille; lettres de distraction du Comté de Laval, du présidial de Château Gontier; et que le contrat de vente qu'il fit avec feu Monsieur le Cardinal de Richelieu de la Baronnie de l'Ile Bouchard soit rompu [...].

II C i)   La Reine, qui n'avait pas gratifié le parlement de bon coeur, disait, en parlant de cette affaire, qu'elle croyait bien qu'il se repentirait de ce qu'il avait fait, et qu'elle n'était pas fâchée d'avoir été contrainte de révoquer la grâce qu'elle lui avait accordée malgré elle, le traitant plus favorablement qu'il ne méritait. Comme le sang de Charles-Quint lui donnait de la hauteur, elle ne croyait pas qu'aucune créature pût ou dût oser se défendre contre la volonté du Roi; de sorte que dans toutes les affaires du parlement, dont elle n'entendait point l'ordre ni la chicane, elle voulait toujours le terrasser, et que tout ce qui était ordonné dans son conseil s'exécutât dans cette compagnie. Mais comme ils sentaient en eux les premières impulsions de la révolte, ils se défendaient méthodiquement, et se servaient en habiles gens des hauteurs de la Reine et des bassesses de celui qui la conseillait, pour le faire tomber dans des fautes qu'il avait après bien de la peine à réparer. Cela était cause que cette princesse a souvent paru plus colère qu'elle ne l'était, et plus sévère que douce, quoiqu'en effet dans les matières qui étaient de sa connaissance elle fût la plus raisonnable et la plus modérée de toutes les femmes.

* * * * * * * *

La reine avait plus que personne que j'aie jamais vue, de cette sorte d'esprit qui lui était nécessaire, pour ne pas paraître sotte à ceux qui ne la connaissaient pas. Elle avait plus d'aigreur que de hauteur, plus de hauteur que de grandeur, plus de manière que de fond, plus d'inapplication à l'argent que de libéralité, plus de libéralité que d'intérêt, plus d'intérêt que de désintéressement, plus d'attachement que de passion, plus de dureté que de fierté, plus de mémoire des injures que des bienfaits, plus d'intention de piété que de piété, plus d'opiniâtreté que de fermeté, et plus d'incapacité que de tout ce que dessus.

II C ii)   Le cardinal Mazarin avait autant de lumières qu'un homme qui avait été artisan de sa propre grandeur en pouvait avoir. Il avait une grande capacité, et surtout une industrie et une finesse merveilleuse pour conduire et amuser les hommes par mille douteuses et trompeuses espérances. Il ne faisait du mal que par nécessité à ceux qui lui déplaisaient. Pour l'ordinaire, il se contentait de s'en plaindre, et ses plaintes produisaient toujours des éclaircissements qui lui redonnaient aisément l'amitié de ceux qui lui manquaient de fidélité, ou qui prétendaient se pouvoir plaindre de lui. Il avait le don de plaire, et il était impossible de ne se pas laisser charmer par ses douceurs; mais cette même douceur était cause, quand elle n'était pas accompagnée des bienfaits qu'il faisait espérer, que ces hommes, lassés d'attendre, tombaient ensuite dans le dégoût et le chagrin. Jusque-là, les plaintes des particuliers n'avaient pas fait une grande impression sur les esprits: elles étaient plutôt fondées sur l'aversion de sa faveur que sur la haine de sa personne. Le respect que le rayon de la puissance royale, qui l'environnait glorieusement, devait graver dans les coeurs des sujets du Roi arrêtait ce que la malice humaine cherchait à blâmer en lui: et la tranquillité de la cour, jointe aux heureux succès de la guerre, lui avait donné jusqu'alors plus de réputation que le moindre des courtisans ne lui pouvait donner de honte; mais peu à peu on allait découvrant en lui plusieurs défauts, dont les uns se pouvaient attribuer à tous les favoris, et les autres étaient plus essentiels. On disait qu'il ignorait nos coutumes, et qu'il ne s'appliquait pas assez soigneusement à les faire observer; qu'il ne se souciait pas, comme il l'aurait dû faire, de gouverner l'Etat par les lois anciennement établies, et qu'il ne protégeait pas la justice selon qu'il y était obligé par sa qualité de premier ministre, et manquait aux soins qu'il devait au bien public. Ces péchés d'omission, quoique grands, ne pouvaient avec justice le déshonorer, parce qu'il pouvait alors avoir de bonnes intentions qui peut-être, étant connues, l'auraient dû justifier dans le public. On peut dire néanmoins que, du tempérament dont il était, on ne l'accusait pas trop à tort; car son caractère était de négliger trop à faire du bien. Il semblait n'estimer aucune vertu ni haïr aucun vice. Il paraissait n'en avoir pas un: il passait pour un homme habitué à l'usage des vertus chrétiennes, et ne témoignait point en désirer la pratique. Il ne faisait nulle profession de piété, et ne donnait par aucune de ses actions des marques du contraire: si ce n'est qu'il lui échappait quelquefois des railleries qui étaient opposées au respect qu'un chrétien doit avoir pour tout ce qui touche la religion. Malgré son avarice, il n'avait pas encore paru avare; et, dans son administration, les finances ont été plus dissipées par les partisans qu'en aucun autre siècle. Il a de même [...] accordé des dignités de l'Eglise à beaucoup de personnes qui les ont voulu prétendre par des motifs profanes, et n'a pas toujours nommé aux évêchés des hommes qui pussent honorer son choix par leur vertu et leur piété. La religion a été trop abandonnée par lui, et il a toujours eu trop d'indifférence pour ce sacré dépôt que Dieu lui avait commis. Il était naturellement défiant, et un de ses plus grands soins était d'étudier les hommes pour les connaître, pour se garantir de leurs attaques et des intrigues qui se formaient contre lui. Il faisait profession de ne rien craindre, et de mépriser même les avis qu'on lui donnait à l'égard de sa personne, quoiqu'en effet sa plus grande application eût pour objet principal sa conservation particulière.

* * * * * * * *

Il n'y a récompense qu'on ne puisse promettre à ceux qui serviraient pour les faire arrêter, afin d'en faire un châtiment exemplaire, me confirmant toujours de plus en plus que, sans cela, nous serons incessamment à recommencer. Vous devez croire que, quand je vous en écris si souvent, il faut que ce soit la force de la raison qui m'y oblige, n'étant pas trop porté de mon naturel à la sévérité.

Pour bien servir la Reine il faut être bien alerte pour être informé de tout ce qui se passe et profiter des conjonctures; car si une fois le chapelet commence à se défiler et que la Reine s'en prévaille, tout changera à souhait pour Sa Majesté; mais il faut agir et avoir, par diverses voies inconnues, des négociations partout.

Il faut pourtant que M. Colbert dissimule, faisant semblant d'être assuré de leur bonne volonté, car le temps pourra accommoder beaucoup de choses.

Je m'assure que la Reine aura fort bien reçu Mme de Longueville et aura tâché de la satisfaire, autant qu'Elle aura pu; car, dans la disposition où sont présentement les affaires et les esprits, il faut bien traiter et cajoler tout le monde, étant fort possible que les intérêts et les passions soient capables de diviser les meilleurs amis et les parents les plus proches, et je vois qu'avec un peu d'adresse, la conduite de M. le Prince donnera lieu à faire diminuer à vue d'oeil le nombre de ses amis et aliéner la plus grande partie de ceux qui, par parenté, étaient liés avec lui.

II C iii) Gaston ne sait quel parti prendre,
     Tant il a peur de se méprendre.
     Madame la Fronde et la Cour
     Attirent son coeur tour à tour;
     Aujourd'hui l'une le possède,
     Une heure après l'autre l'obsède:
     Il est entre deux suspendu,
     Et, n'étant gagné ni perdu,

Il dit à l'une: "Allez au peautre",
Puis il en dit autant à l'autre;
A l'une il dit: "Je suis à vous",
A l'autre il dit: "Unissons-nous."
On lui fait harangue: il écoute,
Il conteste, il balance, il doute,
Il voit le mal, il voit le bien,
Mais enfin il ne résout rien [...].
Comment se démêlera-t-il
D'un labyrinthe si subtil,
Et que faudra-t-il qu'il réponde?
Sera-t-il Cour, sera-t-il Fronde?
Je n'en sais rien, foi de Normand,
Et, si je disais autrement,
Mon audace serait extrême,
Car il ne le sait pas lui-même.

* * * * * * *

Enfin Monsieur signa son traité (mais d'une manière qui vous marquera mieux son génie que tout ce que je vous ai dit). Caumartin l'avait dans sa poche avec une écritoire de l'autre côté, il l'attrapa entre deux portes, il lui mit une plume entre les doigts et il signa (à ce que mademoiselle de Chevreuse disait en ce temps-là), comme il aurait signé la cédule du sabbat, s'il avait eu peur d'y être surpris par son bon ange.

II C iv) Je ne reprends jamais la plume que ma première pensée ne soit de dire pis que pendre de M. le Prince de Condé, duquel, à la vérité, je n'en saurais jamais assez dire. Je l'ai observé soigneusement durant treize ans que j'ai été attaché à lui; mais je dis devant Dieu, en la présence duquel j'écris, et dans un livre fait pour l'honorer [...] que je n'ai jamais connu une âme si terrestre, si vicieuse, ni un coeur si ingrat que celui de M. le Prince, ni si traître, ni si malin. Car dès qu'il a obligation à un homme, la première chose qu'il fait est de chercher en lui quelque reproche par lequel il puisse en quelque façon se sauver de la reconnaissance à laquelle il est obligé [...]. M. de La Rochefoucauld m'a dit cent fois qu'il n'avait jamais vu homme qui eût plus d'aversion à faire plaisir que M. le Prince, et que les choses même qui ne lui coûtaient rien, il enrageait de les donner, vu qu'en les donnant il aurait fait plaisir [...]. Le bougre donc, avéré, fieffé, n'a que deux bonnes qualités, à savoir de l'esprit et du coeur. De l'un il s'en sert fort mal, et de l'autre il s'en est voulu servir pour ôter la couronne de dessus la tête du Roi; je sais ce qu'il m'en a dit plusieurs fois, et sur quoi il fondait ses pernicieux desseins; mais ce sont des choses que je voudrais oublier, bien loin de les écrire.

Dans les choses de conséquence ils s'attachaient à fâcher les gens, et dans la vie ordinaire ils étaient si impraticables qu'on n'y pouvait pas tenir. Ils avaient des airs si moqueurs, et disaient des choses si offensantes, que personne ne les pouvait souffrir. Dans les visites qu'on leur rendait, ils faisaient paraître un ennui si dédaigneux, et ils témoignaient si ouvertement qu'on les importunait, qu'il n'était pas malaisé de juger qu'ils faisaient tout ce qu'ils pouvaient pour se défaire de la compagnie. De quelque qualité qu'on fût, on attendait des temps infinis dans l'antichambre de M. le prince; et fort souvent, après avoir bien attendu, il renvoyait tout le monde, sans que personne eût pu le voir. Quand on leur déplaisait, ils poussaient les gens à la dernière extrémité, et ils n'étaient capables d'aucune reconnaissance pour les services qu'on leur avait rendus.

II C v)   Quant au coadjuteur, quoiqu'il parût et si empressé et si zélé pour grossir le parti du parlement, et quoiqu'il en fût entêté, il n'avait jamais eu aucun sujet de se plaindre de la cour: au contraire, il devait à la Reine sa coadjutorerie de Paris. Mais il avait une ambition sans bornes, et à quelque prix que ce fût il voulait être cardinal, comme l'avaient été deux évêques de Paris de son nom. Un homme de bon sens, d'un coeur droit et d'une conduite régulière, aurait dû croire que la voie la plus sûre, la plus courte, la plus honnête et la plus juste pour parvenir à ses desseins auprès du prince, était sa fidélité; il en aurait fait ses principaux moyens, il n'aurait cherché à établir sa grandeur et sa gloire que dans ses devoirs seuls; et enfin ses devoirs et sa fidélité sur prince lui auraient tenu lieu de toutes choses. Mais comme le coadjuteur ne pouvait trouver que dans les aventures extraordinaires de quoi remplir ses idées vastes, et satisfaire toute l'étendue de son imagination, il crut au contraire qu'il trouverait beaucoup mieux son compte dans les partis et dans les troubles. Outre qu'ils flattaient bien davantage son inclination, il en avait tant pour toutes les choses extraordinaires, qu'il en aurait préféré une de cette nature qui aurait été médiocre ou mauvaise, à une qui aurait été bonne et solide, s'il n'avait pu y parvenir que par des voies ordinaires. Son esprit, quoique pénétrant et d'une étendue assez vaste, était cependant sujet à de si grandes traverses, qu'il se piquait généralement de tout ce qui ne lui pouvait convenir, jusqu'à se piquer de galanterie, quoique assez mal fait, et de valeur quoiqu'il fût prêtre.

––––––––––––

... je ne trouvai pas que la prison lui eût donné plus de sens. Il est toutefois vrai qu'elle lui avait donné plus de réputation. Il l'avait soutenue avec fermeté, et en était sorti avec courage; ce lui était même un mérite que de n'avoir pas quitté les bords de Loire, dans un temps où il est vrai qu'il fallait et de l'adresse et de la fermeté pour les tenir. Il n'est pas difficile de faire valoir dans le commencement d'une guerre civile, celui de tous ceux qui sont mal à la cour. C'en est un grand que de n'y être pas bien. Comme il y avait déjà quelque temps qu'il m'avait fait assurer par Montrésor, qu'il serait très-aise de prendre liaison avec moi, et que je prévoyais bien l'usage auquel je le pourrais mettre, j'avais jeté par intervalle et sans affectation dans le peuple des bruits avantageux pour lui [...]. Montrésor, qui l'informait avec exactitude des obligations qu'il m'avait, avait mis toutes les dispositions nécessaires pour une grande union entre nous. Vous croyez aisément qu'elle ne lui était pas désavantageuse dans l'état où j'étais dans le parti; et elle m'était comme nécessaire, parce que ma profession pouvant m'embarrasser en mille rencontres, j'avais besoin d'un homme que je pusse dans les conjonctures mettre devant moi [...]. Il me fallait un fantôme, mais il ne me fallait qu'un fantôme; et par bonheur pour moi, il se trouva que ce fantôme fut petit-fils d'Henri-le-Grand; qu'il parla comme on parle aux halles, ce qui n'est pas ordinaire aux enfants d'Henri-le-Grand, et qu'il eut de grands cheveux bien longs et bien blonds. Vous ne pouvez vous imaginer le poids de cette circonstance; vous ne pouvez concevoir l'effet qu'ils firent dans le peuple.

Nous sortîmes ensemble de chez Prudhomme, pour aller voir M. le prince de Conti. Nous nous mîmes en même portière. Nous nous arrêtâmes dans la rue Saint-Denis et dans la rue Saint-Martin. Je nommai, je montrai et je louai M. de Beaufort. Le feu se prit en moins d'un instant. Tous les hommes crièrent: vive Beaufort! toutes les femmes le baisèrent: et nous eûmes sans exagération, à cause de la foule, peine de passer jusqu'à l'Hôtel de Ville.

II C vi) ... conseiller de la grand'chambre, personnage d'une ancienne probité, de médiocre suffisance, et qui avait vieilli dans la haine des favoris. Ce bon homme, inspiré par ses propres sentiments et par les persuasions de Longueil et d'autres qui avaient pris créance dans son esprit, ouvrait les avis les plus vigoureux, qui étaient suivis de la cabale des Frondeurs: de sorte que son nom faisait bruit dans les assemblées des chambres, et il s'était rendu chef de ce parti dans le Parlement, d'autant plus accrédité que son âge et sa pauvreté le mettaient hors des atteintes de l'envie. Or, comme le peuple, qui ne bougeait du Palais, était informé qu'il s'intéressait puissamment pour son soulagement, il le prit en affection, et lui donna ce beau titre de son père.

III i)   L'on ajoutait que ce n'était pas prudence de nous attaquer et nous obliger de montrer la désobéissance aux autres compagnies dans le temps présent, nous qui servions à faire obéir les autres, et que nous connaissions trop le fin des affaires et des ministres des finances pour nous obliger à les révéler, comme nous ferions assurément.

III ii)   Vous êtes, Sire, notre souverain seigneur; la puissance de Votre Majesté vient d'en haut, laquelle ne doit compte de ses actions, après Dieu, qu'à sa conscience; mais il importe à sa gloire que nous soyons des hommes libres, et non pas des esclaves; la grandeur de son Etat et la dignité de sa couronne se mesurent par la qualité de ceux qui lui obéissent [...].

Il y a, Sire, dix ans que la campagne est ruinée, les paysans réduits à coucher sur la paille, leurs meubles vendus pour le paiement des impositions, auxquelles ils ne peuvent satisfaire; et que pour entretenir le luxe de Paris des millions d'âmes innocentes sont obligées de vivre de pain, de son et d'avoine, et n'espérer autre protection que celle de leur impuissance. Ces malheureux ne possèdent aucuns biens en propriété que leurs âmes, parce qu'elles n'ont pu être vendues à l'encan; les habitants des villes, après avoir payé la subsistance et le quartier d'hiver, les étapes et les emprunts, acquitté le droit royal et de confirmation, sont encore imposés aux aisés.

Ce qui reste de sûreté dans les compagnies souveraines reçoit atteinte dans cette journée par la création de nouveaux offices, qui sont une charge perpétuelle à l'Etat; car lorsqu'ils sont établis il faut que le peuple les nourrisse et les défraie.

Faites, Madame, s'il vous plaît, quelque sorte de réflexion sur cette misère publique dans la retraite de votre coeur! Ce soir, dans la solitude de votre oratoire, considérez quelle peut être la douleur, l'amertume et la consternation de tous les officiers du royaume, qui peuvent voir aujourd'hui confisquer tout leur bien sans avoir commis aucun crime; ajoutez à cette pensée, Madame, la calamité des provinces, dans lesquelles l'espérance de la paix, l'honneur des batailles gagnées, la gloire des provinces conquises, ne peut nourrir ceux qui n'ont point de pain, lesquels ne peuvent compter les myrtes, les palmes et les lauriers entre les fruits ordinaires de la terre.

III iii)   Le cardinal, ayant été averti de cette proposition, envoya quérir les députés de toutes les compagnies souveraines, pour leur déclarer qu'absolument la Reine ne voulait point de ces arrêts d'union. Sur quoi ces messieurs ayant répondu qu'ils n'étaient point contre le service du Roi, il leur répliqua que c'était assez que la Reine ne l'eût pas agréable: et que si le Roi ne voulait pas qu'on portât des glands à son collet, il n'en faudrait point porter, parce que ce n'était pas tant la chose défendue que la défense qui en faisait le crime. Cela n'empêcha pas que ces députés, en le quittant, n'allassent faire le rapport à leurs chambres de ce qui s'était passé, et qu'ils ne commençassent ce rapport par une plaisanterie, en faisant des dérisions extraordinaires du cardinal sur sa comparaison des glands, laquelle ils tournèrent dans un très grand ridicule, et dont on composa pour lors force ouvrages burlesques de toutes sortes d'espèces, en vers et en prose. Ils se moquèrent encore beaucoup de lui sur ce qu'au lieu de dire l'arrêt d'union, il avait dit l'arrêt d'oignon, par la difficulté qu'il avait à parler bon français.

III iv)   Au bruit de cette femme, le peuple s'assembla dans cette petite rue: les premiers qui accoururent en amenèrent d'autres, et en un moment elle fut pleine de canaille. Comme ils virent ce carrosse plein d'armes et d'hommes, ils se mirent tous à crier qu'on voulait emmener leur libérateur. Il y en eut qui voulurent couper les rênes des chevaux, et qui parlèrent de rompre le carrosse: mais les gardes et un petit page de Comminges le défendirent vaillamment, et s'opposèrent à leur dessein, menaçant de tuer ceux qui voudraient l'entreprendre. Comminges, qui entendit la rumeur du peuple et de la maison, et qui vit le désordre qui pouvait arriver s'il tardait davantage à exécuter son dessein, crut qu'il fallait se hâter; et prenant Broussel par force, le menaça de le tuer s'il ne marchait. Il l'arracha de sa maison et des embrassements de sa famille, et le jeta dans son carrosse malgré qu'il en eût, ses gardes allant devant pour écarter le peuple qui le menaçait et le voulait attaquer. Sur ce bruit, les chaînes se tendent dans les rues, et au premier détour Comminges se trouva arrêté: si bien que pour s'échapper il fallut souvent faire tourner le carrosse, et donner à tout moment une espèce de bataille contre le peuple, dont la troupe grossissait à mesure qu'il avançait dans son chemin. A force d'aller, il arriva enfin vis-à-vis du logis du premier président sur le quai, où son carrosse versa et se rompit. Il était perdu, si dans ce même endroit il n'eût trouvé les soldats du régiment des Gardes qui étaient encore en haie, et qui avaient ordre de lui prêter main forte. Il s'était élancé hors de son carrosse versé; et se voyant environné d'ennemis qui le voulaient déchirer, n'ayant que trois ou quatre de ses gardes qui n'étaient pas capables de le sauver de ce péril, il s'écria: *Aux armes, compagnons! à mon secours!* Les soldats, toujours fidèles au Roi dans tous les temps de cette régence, l'environnèrent, et lui donnèrent toute l'assistance qu'il leur fut possible. Le peuple l'environnait aussi avec des intentions bien contraires; et là se forma un combat de main et d'injures seulement, qui n'était pas moins périlleux à l'Etat que les plus grands qui se sont jamais donnés avec le fer et le feu. Comminges demeura dans cet état assez longtemps, jusqu'à ce qu'un de ses gardes lui eût amené un autre carrosse qu'il prit à des passants, dont par menaces il avait fait sortir quelques femmes, et dont le cocher, malgré leur résistance, fut contraint de servir en cette occasion. Comminges le prit, et laissa le sien sur la place, que le peuple, de rage et de dépit, rompit en mille morceaux. Celui qui le menait par force se rompit tout de nouveau à la rue Saint-Honoré; et ces accidents servirent à faire savoir cette action à toute la ville de Paris, et à émouvoir la compassion d'une infinité de gens qui fomentèrent ensuite la sédition.

Cependant le peuple s'émut; les bateliers commencèrent en la Grève d'un côté et les artisans vers le Palais et Pont Saint-Michel, puis du côté des Halles; une grosse bande avec épées, épieux, pistolets et pavés levés allaient à la charge jusqu'en la rue Saint-Honoré, cassant les vitres des maisons et rompant les portes, criant néanmoins 'Vive le Roi, liberté au prisonnier'.

Les maréchaux de la Meilleraye et de l'Hopital, assistés du grand prévôt de l'Hôtel et de plus de cinquante cavaliers, furent par les rues repousser cette populace des Halles et vers le Palais, pour faire rouvrir les boutiques, qui étaient toutes fermées et rassurer le peuple, qui toujours demandait le prisonnier, M. de Broussel. On fit tenir des escadres des régiments des gardes suisses et françaises vers le Palais-Royal, le bout du Pont-Neuf, à l'école Saint-Germain et place Dauphine et Palais. Quelques artisans des plus étourdis, ayant tiré sur les gens accompagnant les susdits maréchaux, ont été tués de coups de pistolet.

III v)   Les personnes qui étaient attachées au Roi, et qui étaient restées à Paris, étaient les seules qui fussent à plaindre; car le peuple les menaçait continuellement de les piller, et nous n'osions nous montrer sans danger de nos vies. Ma soeur et moi voulûmes nous sauver de Paris. Nous menâmes avec nous une de nos amies qui demeurait avec moi, personne de naissance et de mérite. Nous fîmes ce que nous pûmes pour sortir par la porte Saint-Honoré, avec intention de nous servir de l'assistance de quelques personnes qui nous attendaient hors la porte de la ville; mais les pauvres qui se trouvèrent auprès des Capucins, voyant que nous voulions sortir, se mirent par troupes autour de nous, et nous forcèrent de nous retirer dans l'église de ces bons pères, où ils nous suivirent avec rumeur. Ils nous obligèrent enfin d'en sortir pour tâcher de trouver du secours vers le corps de garde, où nous espérâmes rencontrer quelques gens raisonnables; mais les soldats parisiens, animés contre tout ce qui paraissait vouloir aller à Saint-Germain, nous ayant fait peur par les menaces, nous retournâmes sur nos pas pour aller vers l'hôtel de Vendôme. Le suisse de cette maison, bien loin de nous recevoir, nous ferma la porte, et justement dans un temps où des coquins avaient dépavé la rue pour en tirer des armes, afin de nous martyriser à la manière de saint Etienne. Mademoiselle de Villeneuve, cette amie qui demeurait avec moi, voyant un de ces satellites venir à elle avec un grès dans la main pour lui jeter sur la tête, lui dit d'un ton ferme et tranquille qu'il avait tort de la vouloir tuer, puisqu'elle ne lui avait jamais fait de mal: elle lui parla avec tant d'esprit et de raison, que ce maraud, malgré sa naturelle brutalité, s'arrêta. Il jeta la pierre ailleurs, et s'éloigna d'elle; mais ce fut pour venir à ma soeur et à moi, qui depuis l'hôtel de Vendôme avions toujours couru pour nous sauver dans Saint-Roch. Nous y arrivâmes, grâce à Dieu, malgré les injures et les menaces de cette canaille animée à la proie et au pillage. Aussitôt que j'y fus, je me mis à genoux devant le grand autel, où se célébrait une grand'messe. Ces dragons qui nous avaient suivies respectèrent si peu le service divin, qu'une femme, à mes yeux plus horrible qu'une furie, me vint arracher mon masque de dessus le visage, en disant que j'étais une mazarine, et qu'il me fallait assommer et déchirer par morceaux. Comme naturellement je ne suis pas vaillante, je sentis une très grande peur. Je voulus dans ce trouble m'en aller chez le curé qui était mon confesseur, pour lui demander du secours; mais ma soeur, qui eut plus de courage et de jugement que moi, me voyant poursuivie par deux filous qui, aussitôt que j'approchai de la porte, me crièrent: *La bourse!* ' me retira de leurs mains et m'empêcha de sortir de l'église, car tout était à craindre de leur barbarie. Le peuple s'assemblait de plus en plus dans l'église où il entrait en foule, et qui retentissait de hurlements où je n'entendais autre chose, sinon qu'il nous fallait tuer. Le curé vint à ce bruit qui leur parla, et eut de la peine à leur imposer silence. Pour moi, faisant semblant de me vouloir confesser, je le priai d'envoyer quelqu'un me quérir promptement du secours. Il le fit aussitôt; et le marquis de Beuvron mon voisin, avec les officiers du quartier qui se trouvèrent alors au corps de garde, et d'autres gens qui entendirent parler du péril où j'étais, vinrent nous en tirer; et, faisant écarter toute cette canaille, ne nous voulurent point quitter qu'ils ne nous eussent remenées en notre logis, où nous arrivâmes si malades qu'il nous fallut mettre au lit.

III vi)   Cette comédie (car il n'y eut pas une seule goutte de sang répandue de part ni d'autre) se termina si fort à la confusion dudit sieur du Tremblay [...], qu'il fut longtemps sans paraître ni à la cour, ni dans la ville: en effet, à peine pouvait-on remarquer les neuf ou dix volées de canon qui avaient été tirées contre le pont-levis et contre les deux tours qui sont à côté, et en eût-on réparé les ruines pour moins d'une pistole. En un mot, ce siège fut d'autant plus beau et fameux, que toutes les dames le virent de leurs carrosses, dont toute la rue Saint-Antoine était aussi couverte qu'aux jours du carnaval, et y furent, autant de temps qu'il dura, en toute sûreté, parce que, disait-on publiquement, l'on était demeuré d'accord avec ce brave capitaine qu'il ne tirerait point sur le bourgeois, mais seulement par-dessus la tête de ceux qui l'attaqueraient: ce qu'il observa religieusement.

III vii)   Comme la Cour sut qu'il allait passer le Rhin, elle se découvrit tout à fait ce qu'elle n'avait pas fait jusqu'à ce temps-là, n'ayant envoyé nuls ordres à M. de Turenne, mais seulement fait dire qu'elle serait bien aise que la paix étant faite en Allemagne, que l'armée marchât en France; la Cour, dis-je, envoya des ordres exprès à tous les officiers de ne plus reconnaître M. de Turenne, fit tenir trois cent mille écus sur le Rhin et promesse du paiement de quatre ou cinq montres dues, ce qui, avec la sollicitation de M. d'Erlac, ébranla six régiments allemands, qui allèrent toute la nuit le joindre à Brisac. Cela fit un grand désordre dans le reste de l'armée: trois régiments d'infanterie faisant la même chose, et se mettant sous Philipsbourg, il y resta, avec M. de Turenne, près de la moitié de l'armée, et encore tout ébranlée, excepté cinq ou six régiments. Lui voyant qu'il ne pouvait plus marcher sur le dessein qu'il s'était proposé, ne voulant pas aussi aller trouver la Cour [...], donna ordre à quelques officiers généraux demeurés auprès de lui d'emmener le reste des troupes joindre M. d'Erlac. Ainsi, avec quinze ou vingt de ses amis, il se retira en Hollande [...].

III viii)   ... un jour des valets de pied du Roi ayant été battus par ceux du duc de Brissac, Matas et Fontrailles leur dirent qu'ils devaient respecter les couleurs qu'ils portaient; mais les autres répondirent, avec un ton de moquerie, que les rois n'étaient plus à la mode, et que cela était bon du temps passé. On ne parlait publiquement dans Paris que de république et de liberté, en alléguant l'exemple de l'Angleterre; et on disait que la monarchie était trop vieille, et qu'il était temps qu'elle finît.

III ix)   ... sadite Majesté a trouvé bon que je promette comme je fais, de sa part et par son ordre:

Qu'il ne sera pourvu à aucuns gouvernements généraux ou particuliers, aux charges de la Couronne, aux charges principales de la maison du Roi et de la guerre, ni aux ambassades, qu'on n'éloignera personne de la Cour et qu'on ne prendra point de résolution sur aucune affaire important à l'Etat sans avoir au préalable l'avis de Monsieur le Prince, et que, lorsque mondit sieur le Prince proposera des personnes qu'il croira capables des dites charges, sa Majesté y fera particulière considération;

Que dans l'occurrence de la vacance des bénéfices, sadite Majesté considérera les amis et serviteurs de mondit sieur le Prince, lorsqu'il les recommandera.

Comme la bonne correspondance d'entre Monsieur le Prince et moi peut être très utile au service du Roi [...], je promets d'entretenir une parfaite intelligence avec lui, et en outre je lui promets entièrement mon amitié et de le servir dans tous les intérêts de l'Etat et les siens particuliers envers tous et contre tous.

Et, pour commencer à lui en donner des marques, je promets à mondit sieur le Prince, de ne marier mon neveu, ni aucunes de mes nièces, qui sont ici, sans l'avoir au préalable arrêté avec lui. En foi de quoi j'ai signé la présente, à Paris le deux octobre 1649.

III x)   L'heure du conseil étant venue, la Reine dit à M. le Prince et à tous ces messieurs qu'ils passassent dans la galerie du conseil, et qu'elle les allait suivre un moment après, mais au lieu de les suivre elle s'enferma dans son oratoire avec le Roi, et dit à M. de Guitaud de faire sa charge. Il entra dans la galerie, ayant fermé sur lui toutes les portes. Voyant M. le prince auprès de la cheminée, il s'approcha de lui qui le prévint par un compliment qu'il lui fit en lui demandant s'il désirait quelque chose de son service. Il lui dit qu'il avait ordre du Roi de l'arrêter, à quoi il répondit en lui mettant la main sur l'épaule: 'Guitaud, la raillerie ne vaut rien, cessons-la, je te prie.' M. de Guitaud lui répondit: 'Monsieur, Votre Altesse peut bien connaître à mon air que ce n'est pas raillerie, c'est tout de bon que je parle, et j'ai le même ordre pour monsieur votre frère et pour M. de Longueville.' M. le prince de Conti voyant quelque émotion dans cette conversation: 'Qu'y a-t-il, monsieur mon frère?' - 'Ce n'est rien, lui répondit-il, c'est que Guitaud a ordre de nous arrêter, vous et moi et M. de Longueville. Mais j'espère que ce ne sera rien, et que Sa Majesté me recevra à justification.'

Pendant ce discours M. de Guitaud, parlant à M. le prince de Conti et à M. de Longueville, leur déclara la même chose. M. le Prince pria M. de Guitaud de savoir de la Reine si elle voulait lui faire l'honneur de l'ouïr, ce qu'il fit, mais la Reine lui dit de faire sa charge [...].

... je m'en allai à la porte de la galerie pour faire ma charge, sitôt que je fus averti par M. de Guitaud qui, ayant observé que M. le Prince regardait les portes et les fenêtres, et même qu'il jetait les yeux sur son épée, frappa de son bâton, qui était le signal que vous avions pris. Dans ce moment j'ouvris la porte, et suivi de neuf gardes et du sieur de Saint-Elam que je laissai à l'entrée, je dis à ces messieurs l'ordre que j'avais de les conduire.

D'abord ils parurent étonnés, voyant que je les faisais passer par un petit degré assez obscur et sans lumière, mais ils se remirent promptement par l'assurance que je leur donnai que leur vie était en sûreté, tant que j'aurais l'honneur de les avoir entre mes mains [...].

Nous marchâmes le long de l'allée du jardin, fort lentement, à cause de l'indisposition de M. de Longueville, que deux gardes soutenaient. Ce fut dans ce lieu que M. le Prince fit quelques avances à M. de Guitaud sur le sujet de sa liberté, mais ayant trouvé en lui une fidélité modeste et respectueuse par son silence, il cessa ce discours. Nous arrivâmes à la porte que je fis ouvrir pour voir si les choses destinées étaient prêtes. Je n'y trouvai ni carrosse, ni gardes du Roi, ni même les officiers, qui n'ayant pas été avertis de l'importance de l'affaire, ne s'étaient pas rendus ponctuellement à l'assignation, mais de bonne fortune mon carrosse s'y trouva attelé de six bons chevaux [...].

Je partis donc du Palais Royal[...] et allai le plus vite que je pus jusqu'à la porte Richelieu que je trouvai fermée, et qu'il fallut faire ouvrir par force. A deux cents pas de là, messieurs de Miossans et de la Sale, suivis de neuf gens d'armes et d'un page, me joignirent. Nous continuâmes notre marche par les plus mauvais chemins et les plus incommodes pour les carrosses qui soient en lieu du monde [...].

... mon carrosse versa, et je me trouvai du mauvais côté. Son Altesse qui était au devant se jeta hors du carrosse. Je criai en même temps aux gardes de l'observer, ce qu'ils firent fort fidèlement. M. de Miossans lui ayant donné la main pour l'aider, fut sollicité de le vouloir sauver, ce qu'il lui refusa quelques avantages qu'il lui proposât. Je le fis remonter en carrosse et nous continuâmes notre chemin jusqu'au bois de Vincennes.

III xi) Le duc de Vendôme après son arrivée à Dijon attaqua le château, et le prit en peu de jours; et Saint-Jean-de-Losne et Verdun-sur-Saône se rendirent à la première sommation. Il ne restait plus que Seurre, place bien fortifiée, dans laquelle s'étaient jetés le comte de Tavannes, lieutenant des gendarmes du prince, et Le Passage, homme fort attaché au maréchal de Turenne, dans la résolution de se bien défendre. Comme cette ville était importante, la Reine ne la voulut pas laisser plus longtemps entre leurs mains [...], et le duc de Vendôme l'investit le 21 de mars; et, pour faciliter le siège, le cardinal Mazarin s'avança jusqu'à Saint-Jean-de-Losne, et se fut promener au camp, où le Roi arriva quelques jours après; et faisant le tour de la place [...], les soldats qui étaient dans Seurre, entendant les cris de joie que faisait l'infanterie de l'armée en voyant le Roi, se mirent aussi à crier *vive le Roi!* en jetant leurs chapeaux en l'air; en sorte que leurs officiers n'en étaient plus les maîtres, et se trouvèrent en péril d'être arrêtés, et livrés par eux à Sa Majesté. Cette considération, avec celle qu'ils ne pouvaient être secourus, les obligèrent d'entrer en traité le jour que la tranchée devait être ouverte, qui était le 9 d'avril.

III xii) Le premier jour de juin, la princesse sortit de son logis sur les dix heures du matin, suivie de la même foule de peuple et de noblesse, et mena le jeune duc son fils au parlement, dont la grand'salle retentissait des mêmes acclamations qu'on y avait faites la veille. J'avais l'honneur d'être près de leurs personnes; la princesse sollicitait les juges à mesure qu'ils sortaient dans la grande chambre; elle fondait en larmes en leur représentant le malheureux état de toute sa maison opprimée, et leur demandait un refuge contre la violence du cardinal Mazarin. Le jeune duc, que Vialas portait sur ses bras, se jetait au cou des conseillers quand ils passaient, et, les embrassant, leur demandait, les larmes aux yeux, la liberté de monsieur son père; mais d'une manière si tendre, que la plupart de ces messieurs pleuraient aussi amèrement que lui et que madame sa mère, et leur donnaient tous bonne espérance du succès de leur requête. Ce spectacle augmentait dans le coeur de tout le monde l'affection qu'il témoignait pour la maison de Condé, et l'aversion pour tous ceux qui la voulaient détruire.

Le parlement tarda beaucoup à s'assembler, mais enfin il le fit [...]. Cependant, comme il se formait d'autres difficultés, les enquêtes pressèrent l'assemblée des chambres, et l'obtinrent incontinent. La princesse, outrée de douleur et d'impatience, prit monsieur son fils par la main, et entra de son mouvement avec lui dans la grand'chambre. Elle était tout en pleurs; et voulant se jeter à genoux, elle en fut empêchée par ceux qui coururent à elle, et leur dit: 'Je viens, Messieurs, demander justice au Roi, en vos personnes, contre la violence du cardinal Mazarin, et remettre ma personne et celle de mon fils entre vos mains: j'espère que vous lui servirez de père; ce qu'il a l'honneur d'être à Sa Majesté, et les caractères que vous portez, vous y obligent. Il est le seul de la maison royale qui soit en liberté; il n'est âgé que de sept ans; monsieur son père est dans les fers. Vous savez tous, Messieurs, les grands services qu'il a rendus à l'Etat, l'amitié qu'il vous a témoignée aux occasions, celle qu'avait pour vous feu monsieur mon beau-père: laissez-vous toucher à la compassion pour la plus malheureuse maison qui soit au monde, et la plus injustement persécutée'.

Ses soupirs et ses larmes interrompirent son discours; le jeune duc mit un genou à terre, et leur dit: 'Servez-moi de père, Messieurs, le cardinal Mazarin m'a ôté le mien'. Ils se jetèrent tous à lui pour le relever, et la plupart furent attendris à cette vue jusqu'à en pleurer. Le président d'Affis les pria de se retirer, et leur dit que la cour reconnaissait leur juste douleur, et qu'elle allait délibérer sur leur requête.

III xiii) La Reine a mieux reposé cette nuit que les précédentes; mais elle est toujours en fièvre. M. Seguin croit que ce n'est qu'une fièvre de rhume qui s'en ira à mesure que le rhume diminuera. Mais M. Vautier juge qu'elle est véritablement dans la pourriture et corruption des humeurs. Son ventre s'est ouvert cette nuit, et elle a mis dehors quantité d'eaux et de bile. Elle a grande impatience d'arriver à Fontainebleau; mais elle n'est pas en état de partir demain. Aussitôt que les médecins en donneront la permission, je crois bien qu'elle n'y perdra pas un moment de temps. Avec cela je gagerais ma vie qu'il y aura quantité de gens à Paris qui diront et publieront que c'est une maladie feinte. Cependant il est certain que son mal ne vient, ou pour le moins ne s'est augmenté, que pour avoir souvent voulu faire avec peine, en un jour, le chemin qu'elle aurait pu faire en deux avec commodité. Je diray aussi à S.A.R., pour n'être, s'il vous plaît, su que d'elle, que je remarque une grande tristesse en Sa Majesté. J'en parlais hier avec Mademoiselle, qui s'en est aussi aperçue, et cette tristesse va à ne pas même vouloir qu'on tâche de la divertir et de la réjouir. Sa Majesté est fort faible, mais ce n'est pas un mauvais signe, ne pouvant être autrement, puisqu'elle ne dort pas bien et qu'elle est réduite aux bouillons, ayant accoutumé de beaucoup manger.

III xiv) Monsieur envoyait tous les soirs Des Ouches, qui était à lui, donner le bonsoir à la reine, et avait ordre de voir le roi, afin de détromper les gens qui disaient qu'ils s'en voulaient aller. Jugez comme ce compliment était agréable à la reine! L'on menait Des Ouches chez le roi, qui le voyait dans son lit; quelquefois il revenait deux fois, et même le réveillait en tirant son rideau. La reine s'en est fort bien souvenue; à dire le vrai, ce sont de ces choses qui ne s'oublient guère.

III xv)   ... le silence fut fait, et le Roi parla en cette sorte:

'MESSIEURS,

Je suis venu en mon parlement pour vous dire que, suivant la loi de mon Etat, j'en veux prendre moi-même le gouvernement; et j'espère de la bonté de Dieu que ce sera avec piété et justice. Mon chancelier vous dira plus particulièrement mes intentions.'

Suivant lequel commandement de Sa Majesté, le chancelier, qui l'avait reçu debout, s'étant remis en son siège, fit une harangue en laquelle il s'étendit à son ordinaire fort éloquemment sur ce qu'avait dit le Roi, y ajoutant des réflexions très judicieuses sur le passé et sur le présent. Après quoi la Reine, s'inclinant un peu de son siège, fit ce discours au Roi:

'MONSIEUR,

Voici la neuvième année que, par la volonté dernière du défunt Roi mon très honoré seigneur, j'ai pris le soin de votre éducation et du gouvernement de votre Etat: Dieu ayant, par sa bonté, donné bénédiction à mon travail, et conservé votre personne qui m'est si chère et précieuse, et à tous vos sujets. A présent que la loi du royaume vous appelle au gouvernement de cette monarchie, je vous remets avec grande satisfaction la puissance qui m'avait été donnée pour la gouverner, et j'espère que Dieu vous fera la grâce de vous assister de son esprit de force et de prudence pour rendre votre règne heureux.'

Sa Majesté lui répondit:

'Madame, je vous remercie du soin qu'il vous a plu prendre de mon éducation et de l'administration de mon royaume. Je vous prie de continuer à me donner vos bons avis, et je désire qu'après moi vous soyez le chef de mon conseil.'

La Reine se leva ensuite de sa place, et s'approcha du Roi pour le saluer; mais Sa Majesté, descendant de son lit de justice, vint à elle, et, l'embrassant, la baisa; puis chacun d'eux s'en retourna à sa séance.

III xvi) Il est certain que le prince eut assez de peine à prendre cette résolution, dont il voyait bien que les suites pourraient être fâcheuses pour lui. D'ailleurs il avait de la répugnance à quitter sa belle maison de Chantilly, et à s'éloigner de madame de Châtillon, dont il était fort amoureux. Mais Madame de Longueville, M. le duc de La Rochefoucauld, et une infinité d'officiers et de gens de guerre dont il était continuellement obsédé, qui ne demandaient que les occasions d'une meilleure fortune, le déterminèrent enfin à prendre le métier de la guerre [...]. Madame de Longueville avait de plus un intérêt particulier et secret de souhaiter une rupture, parce qu'alors il lui importait beaucoup d'être éloignée de monsieur son mari, qui la pressait fort de retourner avec lui. Pour s'en dispenser avec quelque bienséance, elle avait besoin d'une raison aussi spécieuse que celle de suivre monsieur son frère dans une querelle où tout le monde savait qu'elle avait autant et plus de part que personne.

Ainsi M. le prince se laissa emporter presque malgré lui aux sollicitations et aux passions de ceux qui l'environnaient, dont les vues intéressées ne lui étaient pas inconnues; et l'obligèrent de leur déclarer que si une fois ils lui faisaient mettre l'épée hors du fourreau, il ne la remettrait peut-être pas sitôt qu'ils voudraient, ni selon leurs caprices.

III xvii) La Cour, après avoir vu, en présence des gens du Roi, la déclaration de Sa Majesté, vérifiée le 6ᵉ septembre dernier, portant défense au cardinal Mazarin, ses parents et domestiques étrangers de rentrer dans son royaume ni aux terres de son obéissance, pour quelque cause et occasion que ce fût, à peine de crime de lèse-majesté, et à tous gouverneurs et autres de lui donner retraite et avoir commerce avec lui; et après que M. le duc d'Orléans a dit avoir avis certain que ledit cardinal Mazarin était arrivé à Sedan, a arrêté et ordonné que les députés d'icelle partiront incessamment pour aller trouver le Roi à l'effet de l'arrêt du 18ᵉ de ce mois; et, sur les assurances dudit sieur duc d'Orléans des avis à lui donnés de l'entrée dudit cardinal Mazarin dans Sedan, a déclaré et déclare ledit cardinal Mazarin et ses adhérents avoir encouru les peines portées par ladite déclaration; enjoint aux communes de leur courir sus, et aux maires et échevins des villes de s'opposer à leur passage; ordonne que, sur la bibliothèque et meubles dudit cardinal Mazarin, qui seront vendus, et sur les revenus de ses bénéfices et autres biens qui se trouveront lui appartenir en France et à ceux qui l'assistent, il sera pris par préférence, et nonobstant toutes saisies, jusqu'à la somme de cent cinquante mille livres, qui sera donnée à celui ou ceux qui représenteront ledit Cardinal à justice, mort ou vif, ou à leurs héritiers; et si celui qui le représentera se trouve prévenu de crime, sera le Roi très humblement supplié de lui octroyer pardon, pourvu que ce ne soit point crime de lèse-majesté; déclare aussi ladite Cour les officiers du Roi et les gouverneurs de places qui auront favorisé le passage dudit Cardinal et l'auront escorté de leurs personnes ou de leurs troupes criminels de lèse-majesté, déchus de toutes charges et gouvernements, même des privilèges de noblesse, conformément à ladite déclaration et arrêts de ladite Cour. Et sera ledit sieur duc d'Orléans prié par la Cour d'employer l'autorité du Roi et la sienne pour l'exécution d'icelle déclaration et arrêts; et que les conseillers commis et autres seront envoyés aux provinces et lieux que besoin sera pour l'exécution du présent arrêt: duquel sera donné avis aux autres Parlements.

III xviii) En cette semaine c'est à dire sur la fin de mai et au commencement du mois de juin est arrivée une pauvreté si grande que les affamés de ce pays ont mangé jusqu'aux charognes des chevaux: et même à Mussy l'Evêque il y avait un gros cheval de carrosse appartenant à mgr. le Reverendissime évêque duc de Lengres, pair de France, qui [...] rendait une telle puanteur qu'on ne le pouvait ni souffrir ni sentir et fut conduit hors de ladite ville pour être écorché assez proche de la Seine, lequel ne fut pas plutôt dévêtu, que le peuple y accourut avec une telle avidité que plusieurs furent blessés aux mains des couteaux des autres en coupant la chair dudit cheval, laquelle chair fut entièrement enlevée en moins d'une heure [...].

Une pauvre portant et allaitant son petit enfant a été trouvée morte en une prairie, ayant encore la bouche pleine d'herbe et en mangeant comme une bête, et son petit enfant encore vivant entre ses bras.

Les peuples de Lorraine et autres pays circonvoisins sont réduits à une si grande extrémité qu'ils mangent dans les prairies l'herbe comme des bêtes, et particulièrement ceux des villages de Poully et Parnot en Bassigny la mangent dans les prés et sont noirs et maigres comme des squelettes et ne peuvent plus cheminer.

III xix) MM. les Princes, se voyant entièrement ruinés par la perte qu'ils venaient de faire dans le faubourg Saint-Antoine si la ville de Paris n'entrait dans leur parti par une étroite union à leurs intérêts, résolurent de se prévaloir de cette assemblée et de s'en rendre les maîtres, à quelque prix que ce fût. A cet effet, ils employèrent tout leur crédit afin que, dans tous les quartiers, aucun ne fût élu qui ne fût à leur dévotion. Ils firent choix de la compagnie de Trottier (insigne frondeur...) pour la garde de l'Hôtel de ville, ordonnèrent à la plupart de leurs troupes de se trouver dans la Grève, et aux officiers de se tenir tout prêts pour exécuter ce qui leur serait commandé; et, afin de mieux reconnaître ceux de leur parti et faire main basse sur tous les autres, ils leur donnèrent pour mot de guerre: 'Vive Roger!' et pour signal un brin de paille [...].

Au pied du perron qui sort dans la place, était ledit Trottier avec vingt ou trente soldats de sa compagnie, qui tenaient de la paille et en présentaient à tous ceux qui voulaient y entrer, en leur disant: 'Point de Mazarin!'; et cela s'expliquait qu'il fallait s'unir avec les Princes contre lui, remarquant fort exactement ceux qui faisaient difficulté d'en prendre; de sorte que deux de mes amis [...], et moi, entrant dans la salle, nous fûmes fort surpris de voir de la paille aux chapeaux de la plus grande partie de ceux que nous y rencontrâmes.

[...] dès qu'ils parurent sur le perron qui est dans la Grève, ils dirent à la populace: 'Ces gens-là ne veulent rien faire pour nous; ils ont même dessein de tirer les choses en longueur et de tarder huit jours à se résoudre: ce sont des mazarins, faites-en ce que vous voudrez'. A peine ces paroles furent-elles prononcées, que plusieurs coups de mousquet furent tirés dans les fenêtres de l'Hôtel de Ville, ce qui étonna tous les députés [...].

En effet, ils furent fort surpris que tout d'un coup les coups ne venaient plus de bas en haut, comme au commencement, mais en droite ligne, et de vis-à-vis d'eux: ce qui leur fit croire qu'ils étaient perdus et qu'il y avait une conspiration faite pour cela. Il se trouva que plusieurs des soldats qui avaient eu la conduite de cette exécution, ayant vu le peuple tirer avec précipitation, étaient montés dans les chambres des maisons voisines d'où ils tiraient régulièrement et de front. Néanmoins il ne s'est pas dit que pas un des députés en ait été tué; car, à l'instant qu'ils virent venir les mousquetades à leur hauteur, les uns se couchèrent tout à plat, les autres s'écartèrent, cherchant les lieux les plus reculés de l'Hôtel de Ville pour se sauver. La plupart se confessèrent aux curés qui étaient parmi eux, lesquels avaient essayé en vain d'apaiser cette fureur lorsqu'ils croyaient qu'elle ne procédait que de la populace. La terreur était d'autant plus grande qu'outre les coups de mousquet et de fusil qui se tiraient sans cesse, on apporta quantité de bois à toutes les portes de l'Hôtel de Ville; on les frotta de poix, d'huile et d'autres matières combustibles, et ensuite on y mit le feu: ce qui faisait une fumée et une puanteur dont on était tellement étouffé jusque dans les appartements les plus éloignés de la grand'salle, que tout le monde ne savait que devenir [...].

Goulas, secrétaire des commandements de M. d'Orléans, et qui l'avait suivi en venant à l'Hôtel de Ville, y était demeuré après que les princes en furent partis. Tous les autres se voyant en cet extrême péril, le conjurèrent d'écrire à son maître qu'il leur envoyât du secours. Il le fit, et son billet fut porté en diligence au duc d'Orléans, lequel, étant pressé par celui qui le portait, dit en grattant ses dents avec ses ongles qu'il n'y pouvait que faire, et qu'on allât à son neveu de Beaufort.

III xx)   De par le roi.

Sa Majesté étant bien informée de la continuation des bonnes intentions des bourgeois et habitants de sa bonne ville de Paris pour son service et pour le bien commun de ladite ville, et des dispositions dans lesquelles ils sont de s'employer de tout leur pouvoir pour y remettre toutes les choses en l'état auquel il se doit, et pour se tirer de l'oppression où ils sont présentement et se remettre en liberté sous son obéissance, Sa Majesté a permis et permet auxdits habitants et à chacun d'eux en particulier, et, en tant que de besoin, elle leur enjoint et ordonne très expressément de prendre les armes, s'assembler, occuper les lieux et portes qu'ils jugeront à propos, combattre ceux qui se voudront opposer à leur dessein, arrêter les chefs et saisir les factieux par toutes voies, et généralement tout ce qu'ils verront nécessaire et convenable pour établir le repos et l'entière obéissance envers Sa Majesté, et pour faire que ladite ville soit gouvernée par l'ordre ancien et accoutumé et par ses magistrats légitimes, sous l'autorité de Sa Majesté: laquelle leur donne tout pouvoir de ce faire par la présente, qu'elle a signée de sa main et y fait apposer le cachet de ses armes, voulant qu'elle serve de décharge et de commandement à tous ceux qui agiront, en quelque manière que ce soit, pour l'exécution d'icelle. Donné à Compiègne, le 17e jour de septembre 1652. Signé *LOUIS*; et plus bas: *LE TELLIER*.

III xxi) DE PAR LE ROI,

Il est ordonné au sieur Pradelles, capitaine d'une compagnie d'infanterie au régiment des Gardes françaises de Sa Majesté, de saisir et arrêter le sieur cardinal de Retz, et le conduire en son château de la Bastille pour y être tenu sous bonne et sûre garde jusqu'à ce qu'il en soit autrement ordonné; et au cas que des personnes de quelque condition qu'elles fussent se missent en devoir d'empêcher l'exécution du présent ordre, Sadite Majesté ordonne pareillement audit sieur Pradelles de les arrêter et constituer prisonnières, et d'y employer la force si besoin est, en sorte que l'autorité en demeure à Sa Majesté, laquelle enjoint à tous ses officiers et sujets d'y tenir la main sur peine de désobéissance. Fait à Paris le .... de décembre 1652.

LOUIS.

J'ai commandé à Pradelles l'exécution du présent ordre en la personne du cardinal de Retz, même de l'arrêter mort ou vif en cas de résistance de sa part.

III xxii) ...le 3e février, ce proscrit, ce perturbateur du repos public et cet obstacle à la paix générale, dont la tête avait été mise à cinquante mille écus, rentra dans cette grande ville, non seulement sans bruit et sans murmure, mais comme en triomphe et tout couvert de gloire, le Roi n'ayant point dédaigné d'aller trois lieues au-devant de S.E., et la plus grande partie de la cour quinze ou vingt [...].

Cet intérêt particulier qui règne si puissamment parmi la plupart des hommes ne parut que trop honteusement dans un grand festin qui fut fait par la ville de Paris à M. le cardinal Mazarin, le 29e dudit mois de mars, afin de témoigner à S.E. combien tous ses habitants lui étaient obligés du rétablissement de leurs rentes. Car quelles flatteries et quelles bassesses ne furent point mises en usage par les plus insignes frondeurs pour effacer le souvenir des choses passées et se rendre plus propice cette divinité, qu'ils avaient naguère tant outragée! La profusion et la superfluité s'y firent remarquer, comme s'il eût été question de régaler le Roi au retour de la conquête d'une grande province [...].

III xxiii)   [...] enfin plus le parti des princes faisait de cruautés, plus les bien intentionnés s'échauffaient pour le rétablissement de l'autorité royale et pour demander la paix. On en vint jusqu'au point d'écrire à M. de Boucaut, par le moyen de sa femme, de faire avancer le père Berthod aux faubourgs de Bordeaux *incognito*, pour conférer avec des principaux bourgeois. Ce père fut au rendez-vous conférer avec eux sur les moyens de recouvrer leur liberté, et de remettre la ville entre les mains du Roi. Il en fit le récit à M. de Vendôme, qui pour lors quitta Bourg pour venir à Lormont, afin d'être plus proche de Bordeaux au cas que l'on voulût traiter avec lui.

Pendant ce temps-là madame de Boucaut continue ses brigues avec tant d'ardeur, qu'elle donna sujet au sieur Raymond, qui commandait à la porte de l'hôtel de ville en l'absence du capitaine, d'en refuser l'entrée à quelques ormistes, et même à Duretête, qui en était un des principaux chefs. Cela causa grande rumeur, et donna lieu à Duretête et à Villars d'en faire leurs plaintes au prince de Conti, qui, pour les satisfaire, fit faire commandement à Raymond de sortir de la ville; mais comme on l'embarquait pour passer la rivière, des jeunes gens se déclarèrent pour le Roi, montèrent sur des bateaux, enlevèrent Raymond des mains de l'exempt qui le conduisait, et le ramenèrent en sa maison. De là, cette jeunesse en grand nombre fut demander sa liberté à M. le prince de Conti, et le prier de commander à Villars de ne marcher plus dans les rues avec des gardes, comme il avait accoutumé; autrement qu'on ferait main basse sur lui et sur ses gens. Ce qui leur fut accordé; et depuis ce jour-là Villars ne parut plus guère dans les rues, parce qu'il y marchait seul.

Dans toutes les rencontres cette jeunesse battait les ormistes, chassait les garnisons qu'on avait mises dans les maisons particulières, maltraitait les soldats payés par M. le prince [...]. Après cela ils convoquèrent une grande assemblée dans l'hôtel de la Bourse, où il fut résolu qu'on députerait des bourgeois de chaque corps à M. le prince de Conti, pour lui demander qu'on changeât les capitaines de la ville, qu'on fît sortir tous les gens de guerre, qu'il fût défendu à l'Ormée de s'assembler, et qu'on travaillât incessamment à la paix. Cette délibération était une suite de la résolution prise, en la conférence du père Berthod avec les bourgeois aux faubourgs de Bordeaux, huit ou dix jours auparavant. A toutes ces propositions le prince de Conti promit de répondre le lendemain, qui était le 19 de juillet [...].

Au sortir de chez M. le prince de Conti, cette jeunesse alla par toute la ville, criant *vive le Roi!* et *la paix!* et en moins de trois ou quatre heures leur troupe se trouva grosse de quatre ou cinq mille personnes, qui obligeaient par force les ormistes de crier aussi *vive le Roi!* et *la paix!* et une partie d'eux montèrent aux clochers, sur lesquels les ormistes avaient arboré depuis si longtemps des pavillons rouges, qui était la marque de leur inclination pour l'Espagne. Ils les arrachèrent, et mirent à la place des drapeaux blancs, qui témoignaient leur soumission pour la France et leur obéissance au Roi.

IV i)   Il y a assez souvent de la folie à conjurer; mais il n'y a rien de pareil pour faire les gens sages dans la suite, au moins pour quelque temps.

IV ii)   Il faut assurément demeurer d'accord que, pour mauvais que puisse être un prince, la révolte de ses sujets est toujours infiniment criminelle. Celui qui a donné des rois aux hommes a voulu qu'on les respectât comme ses lieutenants, se réservant à lui seul le droit d'examiner leur conduite. Sa volonté est que, quiconque est né sujet, obéisse sans discernement; et cette loi, si expresse et si universelle, n'est pas faite en faveur des princes seuls, mais est salutaire aux peuples mêmes auxquels elle est imposée, et qui ne la peuvent jamais violer sans s'exposer à des maux beaucoup plus terribles que ceux dont ils prétendent se garantir.

GLOSSARY

Terms already explained in the body of the text or in footnotes have not, as a rule, been repeated in this Glossary.

Aides: a type of customs duty levied on diverse commodities, principally drink.

Arrêt: the written expression of a final decision reached by the king acting through his Council or his sovereign courts.

Assemblée du clergé: an assembly of elected representatives from the provincial and Parisian clergy which met every five years, normally in the capital, to discuss clerical affairs in general, and how big a subsidy they could afford to pay the king in particular.

Chambre de justice: a showpiece tribunal periodically set up by the king with the avowed objective of enquiring into corruption in financial affairs, but with the ulterior motive of siphoning money from the intimidated tax-collectors in the form of bribes or fines.

Chancelier: head of all the law courts in the realm and president of most royal councils, he acted as spokesman for the king on state occ.eal to royal missives and legislative documents. The post was held for life, though the king could circumvent the problem of an incompetent or 'difficult' chancellor by appointing a Garde des Sceaux (Keeper of the Seals) and transferring sealing duties to him.

Comptables: office-holders occupied with accounting to the Chambres des Comptes for the receipt and expenditure of royal revenues passing through their hands.

Conseil (du Roi): a singular term denoting a plurality of councils theoretically dealing with separate sectors of government and administration but overlapping in practice. The names and number of these councils fluctuated in the course of the seventeenth century, but at the top there was always a supreme council (the 'Conseil d'en Haut' at the time of the Fronde) at which major affairs were discussed by varying proportions of ministers and/or secretaries of state; experts in technical fields such as finances or warfare; and possessors of the title of 'conseiller d'état' ('councillor of state'), the latter often drawn from the upper magistracy.

Contrôleur-Général des finances: second-in-command, officially, to the Surintendant des finances.

Cours souveraines: legal tribunals whose 'sovereignty' consisted in the fact that no appeal could be lodged against their verdicts.

Domaine royal: the immovable properties owned by the king (land, palaces, etc.), plus all those rights accruing to him in his capacity as sovereign.

Elu: for tax-collecting purposes, a distinction was made in seventeenth-century France between 'pays d'états' and 'pays d'élections'.   The former were provinces which retained the nominal right to vote the amount of *taille* payable by each of them to the king and to hold assemblies of local dignitaries (Etats Provinciaux) to that end. 'Pays d'élections' was a term applied to provinces containing administrative sections (élections) in which royal office-holders called 'élus' (= 'elected', because originally they were so) had responsibility for overseeing the equitable repartition of the *taille* and for pronouncing judgement in the event of disputes.

Etats généraux: an assembly convoked, often unwillingly, by the king to advise him on ways of overcoming perceived obstacles to the efficient conduct of state affairs. The assembly comprised locally elected but largely élite members of the three political compartments into which French opinion had long divided the population — Clergy, Nobility, and the rest, lumped under the heading of Tiers Etat (= 'Third Estate').

Fermiers: men who entered into contracts with the king entitling them to collect specified royal revenues in return for advancing him part of an agreed sum and paying the rest in instalments. Contracts were called 'traités' or 'partis', whence the names of *traitants* and *partisans* additionally used to denote, and very often to denigrate, tax-collectors.

Financiers: a flexible expression covering all those — finance office-holders as well as bankers and businessmen — involved in keeping the monarchy financially afloat; but also frequently synonymous with *fermiers*.

Gouverneur: the person appointed to command of a province, or to that of a town or fortress within a province. Provincial governorships were traditionally confided to members of the royal family or the high aristocracy who, prior to the personal reign of Louis XIV, were apt to be economical with their loyalty to the sovereign.

Grenetiers: front-line judges in cases of contention arising over the *gabelle*, the tax on salt, a commodity which was stored in royal warehouses called 'greniers à sel'.

Hôtel de Ville: the headquarters of municipal officials in Paris, and in other large French towns, and, by extension, municipal authorities and institutions.

Intendants: *maîtres des requêtes*, for the most part, commissioned by the king to oversee the implementation of his orders in the provinces, with special reference to the proper functioning of judicial and financial mechanisms, and the maintenance of troops and of public order.

Maîtres des requêtes: an influential body of magistrates, found in all the important places: on the Conseil du Roi, reporting on matters within their competence; at the Chancellor's side, presenting him with royal acts to seal; presiding over the Grand Conseil court; sitting in the Paris Parlement; conducting their own separate tribunal, the 'Requêtes de l'Hôtel'; and touring the provinces in the capacity of *intendants*.

Montre: a review of troops, and also the pay given to soldiers on such an occasion.

Officier: an individual discharging the (regularly overlapping) judicial, administrative, or financial responsibilities attached to a post conferred upon him, usually in return for a sum of money, by royal warrant.

Parlement: a term habitually employed in the singular to refer to the Parlement of Paris which served as a model for the provincial *parlements* subsequently created at intervals from the fourteenth century onwards.

Partisan: see **Fermier**.

Paulette: so called after Charles Paulet, who devised and originally administered this scheme whereby an office-holder could designate his successor on condition that he made an annual payment to the king of one-sixtieth of the value of the office.

Receveurs: full title 'receveurs-généraux des finances', receivers of tax-money collected from the *taille*.

Rentes: a form of investment in which private individuals parted with capital in exchange for entitlement to quarterly payments of interest 'guaranteed' to come out of particular sources of royal revenue. Since the sources in question were highly likely to be drained, in advance, for other purposes, interest-payments correspondingly dwindled or petered out. Fund-less monarchs resorted to establishing fresh *rentes* in the hope of paying off arrears, and did not stop short of coercion when prospective purchasers hung back.

Secrétaire d'Etat: the four secretaries of state drafted and countersigned documents arising from decisions taken in the royal council. In addition, each secretary had responsibility for a number of French provinces and for a particular sector, such as War, Foreign Affairs, and the King's Household.

Semestre: a system designed to increase the number of venal posts by having two groups of office-holders each exercising the same function for half the year.

Surintendant des finances: principal director of financial administration, a post abolished after the downfall of its current holder, Nicholas Fouquet, in 1661.

Survivance, droit de: the right to take over an office vacated by the death of the existing holder.

Taille: the chief tax levied since Medieval times to pay for the upkeep of armies. The higher échelons of society, including office-holders and town-dwellers, were ingenious in obtaining exemption from the *taille*, so that the brunt of it fell upon the peasantry.

Traitant: see **Fermier**.

Vénalité des offices: trafficking in public office, a much decried but much exploited means of creating extra crown revenue. Though the king could legally repossess any post sold by reimbursing the purchaser, the latter regarded his acquisition as a piece of personal property of which he could dispose at will.

FURTHER READING

D. Bitton, *The French Nobility in Crisis 1560—1640*, Stanford University Press, California, 1969.

R. Bonney, *Political Change in France under Richelieu and Mazarin, 1624—1661*, Oxford University Press, 1978.

R. Bonney, *The King's Debts*, Oxford: Clarendon Press, 1981.

H. Carrier, *La Presse de la Fronde (1648—53). Les Mazarinades*, Geneva: Droz, 1989, 1991, 2 Vols.

A. Chéruel, *Histoire de France pendant la minorité de Louis XIV*, Paris: Hachette, 1879—1880, 4 Vols.

J. Dent, *Crisis in France. Crown, Financiers and Society in Seventeenth-Century France*, Newton Abbot: David and Charles, 1973.

P.R. Doolin, *The Fronde*, Cambridge, 1935.

P. Goubert, *Mazarin*, Paris: Fayard, 1990.

A. Jouanna, *Le Devoir de Révolte*, Paris: Fayard, 1989.

P. Knachel, *England and the Fronde*, Ithaca, New York, 1967.

E. Kossman, *La Fronde*, Leyden, 1954.

A. Lloyd Moote, *The Revolt of the Judges*, Princeton University Press, New Jersey, 1971.

H. Méthivier, *Le Siècle de Louis XIII*, Paris: Presses Universitaires de France, 1967.

R. Mettam, *Power and Faction in Louis XIV's France*, Oxford: Blackwell, 1988.

R. Mousnier, *La Vénalité des Offices sous Henri IV et Louis XIII*, Rouen, 1945.

R. Mousnier, *Les Institutions de la France sous la Monarchie Absolue*, Paris: Presses Universitaires de France, 1974, 1980, 2 Vols. Translated as *The Institutions of France under the Absolute Monarchy*, University of Chicago Press, 1979, 1984.

R. Mousnier, *Paris, Capitale au Temps de Richelieu et de Mazarin*, Paris: Pedone, 1988.

J.H. Shennan, *The Parlement of Paris*, London, 1968.

S.A. Westrich, *The Ormée of Bordeaux*, Baltimore and London: Johns Hopkins University Press, 1972.

INDEX